DYNAMICS OF AMERICAN POLITICAL PARTIES

In *Dynamics of American Political Parties*, Mark D. Brewer and Jeffrey M. Stonecash examine the process of gradual change that inexorably shapes and reshapes American politics. Parties and the politicians that comprise them seek control of government to implement their visions of proper public policy. To gain control, parties need to win elections. Winning elections requires assembling an electoral coalition that is larger than that crafted by the opposition. Parties are always looking for opportunities to build such winning coalitions, and opportunities are always there, but they are rarely, if ever, without risk. Uncertainty rules and intraparty conflict rages as different factions and groups within the parties debate the proper course(s) of action and battle it out for control of the party. Parties can never be sure how their strategic maneuvers will play out, and even when it appears that a certain strategy has been successful, party leaders are unclear about how long the apparent success will last. Change unfolds slowly, in fits and starts.

Mark D. Brewer is Associate Professor of Political Science at the University of Maine. His research focuses on partisanship and electoral behavior at the mass and elite levels, the linkages between public opinion and public policy, and the interactions that exist between religion and politics in the United States. Brewer is the author of *Relevant No More? The Catholic/Protestant Divide in American Politics* (2003) and *Party Images in the American Electorate* (2009), and he is coauthor of *Diverging Parties: Realignment, Social Change, and Party Polarization* (2003); *Split: Class and Cultural Divides in American Politics* (2007); and *Parties and Elections in America*, fifth edition (2008). He has published articles in *Political Research Quarterly*, *Political Behavior*, *Legislative Studies Quarterly*, and *Journal for the Scientific Study of Religion*.

Jeffrey M. Stonecash is Maxwell Professor in the Department of Political Science, The Maxwell School of Citizenship and Public Affairs, Syracuse University. He researches political parties, changes in their electoral bases, and how these changes affect political polarization and public policy debates. His recent books are *Class and Party in American Politics* (2000), *Diverging Parties* (2003), *Parties Matter* (2005), *Split: Class and Cultural Divides in American Politics* (2007), *Political Polling*, second edition (2008), and *Reassessing the Incumbency Effect* (2008). He has done polling and consulting for political candidates since 1985.

Dynamics of American Political Parties

Mark D. Brewer
University of Maine

Jeffrey M. Stonecash
Syracuse University

CAMBRIDGE
UNIVERSITY PRESS

CAMBRIDGE UNIVERSITY PRESS
Cambridge, New York, Melbourne, Madrid, Cape Town, Singapore, São Paulo, Delhi

Cambridge University Press
32 Avenue of the Americas, New York, NY 10013-2473, USA

www.cambridge.org
Information on this title: www.cambridge.org/9780521708876

First published 2009

Printed in the United States of America

A catalog record for this publication is available from the British Library.

Library of Congress Cataloging in Publication data

Brewer, Mark D.
Dynamics of American political parties / Mark D. Brewer, Jeffrey M. Stonecash.
     p.   cm.
Includes bibliographical references and index.
ISBN 978-0-521-88230-9 (hardback) – ISBN 978-0-521-70887-6 (pbk.)
1. Political parties – United States – History.   2. United States – Politics and
government – 1865–1933.   3. United States – Politics and government – 20th century.
4. United States – Politics and government – 2001–   I. Stonecash, Jeffrey M.   II. Title.
JK2261.B79   2009
324.273–dc22   2009019276

ISBN   978-0-521-88230-9 hardback
ISBN   978-0-521-70887-6 paperback

From Mark Brewer: To Megan and Jack

From Jeff Stonecash: To Lindsay, Cassie, and Maggie

Contents

Figures and Tables

FIGURES

TABLES

Preface

Political parties are an essential and often puzzling element of American politics. They consist of individuals with varying degrees of attachment to a party trying to gain representation of their concerns. Officeholders and prospective officeholders hope to attract enough voters with diverse concerns so they may control government. Although this interaction seems simple, parties are often puzzling. They pursue policies and constituents in ways that often leave us wondering: Why are they trying to advocate for specific groups and win their votes? Why are they supporting a position that we might think does not make sense? Why are they pursuing a particular strategy in a particular election cycle? Then about the time we figure out these various interactions, something changes, leaving us puzzled again.

At various points in our careers, each of us has experienced such puzzlement. We also share the experience of reading James Sundquist's *The Dynamics of the American Party System* and finding the book enormously helpful in providing a broad overview of parties and their constituencies and why both changed over time. Sundquist wrote the book in the 1970s, a time of enormous change in American political parties.[1] Each party was seeking and incorporating new constituencies and changing its bases of support. He finished that book at a time when it was very difficult to see where that change was headed. It is now clearer. We humbly submit this book as an update and expansion of his work and hope we can contribute to understanding the last several decades of change. Indeed, at its most fundamental level, this book is about change and the attempt to make sense of it.

---

[1] Sundquist did offer a slightly revised edition in 1983.

There are numerous excellent texts about political parties that explain the intricacies of party rules and organization, candidate selection, campaign finance, and how specific election rules vary across the states.[2] This book has a different focus. The goal is to understand how change occurs and how change has brought us to the point where the parties differ significantly in whom they attract and what policies they support. The process of change is lengthy and often confusing while occurring. It is driven by political actors who believe in some policies but also want to build a majority so that they can enact their policies. The following provides an example of change that was driven by political hopes and that was gradual, erratic, but persistent and ultimately successful.

In the late 1950s and early 1960s, conservatives in America were frustrated. They felt that government was becoming too big and too intrusive. They saw the state as providing too many benefits to individuals that undermined individual initiative, which they saw as the bedrock of a growing economy. Liberals appeared to be dominating American politics, and conservatives felt underrepresented with their concerns neglected.

They channeled this frustration into the Republican Party, seeking to get the party to nominate someone who would forcefully make the conservative case. They eventually worked to nominate Barry Goldwater as their presidential candidate in 1964. He was then soundly beaten by Lyndon Johnson. The defeat carried many Democrats into Congress, and they enacted a flood of liberal legislation.

Conservatives were discouraged but persisted. In 1968, the party accepted Richard Nixon as their presidential nominee. He gave voice to some conservative views, backing law-and-order positions, but he was not consistently conservative. Then conservatives suffered a severe setback in 1973 when Nixon was forced to resign because of scandal. The party lost numerous seats in Congress in 1974, and conservatives had to rededicate themselves to finding someone to give voice to conservative views.

Finally, in 1980 the GOP nominated Ronald Reagan, the former conservative governor of California, as its candidate. Helped along by bad economic conditions, Reagan defeated the incumbent Democratic president

---

[2] John F. Bibby and Brian F. Schaffner, *Politics, Parties, and Election in America*, sixth edition (Boston: Thomson/Wadworth, 2008); Marjorie Randon Hershey, *Party Politics in America*, thirteenth edition (New York: Pearson/Longman, 2009); Marc J. Hetherington and William J. Keefe, *Parties, Politics, and Public Policy in America*, tenth edition (Washington, DC: CQ Press, 2007); L. Sandy Maisel and Mark D. Brewer, *Parties and Election in America*, fifth edition (Lanham, MD: Rowman & Littlefield, 2008).

Jimmy Carter. Reagan then proceeded to finally give a clear voice to conservative concerns. He opposed many government programs. He sought and won large tax cuts. He expressed support for numerous conservative social principles, such as the idea that welfare was undermining personal responsibility, a constitutional amendment banning abortion, and the return of prayer to public schools. It was the beginning of greater impact for conservative ideas.

It was a long struggle for conservatives to gain a strong voice through the Republican Party. Conservatives had been trying to reestablish the credibility and relevance of their views since the 1930s. The Republican Party, long based in the less conservative Northeast, had been uneasy about pursuing voters by focusing on conservative social issues. Gradually, the party began to gain seats in the more conservative South, and more party members saw the possibilities of expanding their base into the South. As they won seats in the South, they added members who were conservative on fiscal and social issues and steadily lost Northeast Republicans. The party changed its electoral base and composition, and the views of conservatives became more prominent. The struggle of some groups to work through a party eventually gave conservative views greater prominence in American politics. Representation was achieved, and a political party was changed.

Conservatives' effort to take over the Republican Party is just one example of the dynamic between representation and parties, of the change that ultimately defines American politics. This type of dynamic is the focus of this book.

In the course of completing this project, we each incurred a number of debts that need to be acknowledged here. Brewer wishes to thank his colleagues in the Department of Political Science at the University of Maine for the wonderful intellectual environment that they create, and also Nancy Lewis, Head Reference Librarian at Fogler Library, for her assistance in tracking down historical data. Lauren Laroche did an excellent job entering historical election data. Brewer promises his children, Megan and Jack, more playtime now that this project is completed, and thanks his wife, Tammy, for picking up the slack at home and for her strong support throughout this process. Stonecash wishes to again express his appreciation for the supportive environment within the Maxwell School at Syracuse University. Brewer and Stonecash both thank Ed Parsons and the staff at Cambridge University Press for all of their advice and assistance with this project.

1 Democracy, Representation, and Parties

The premise and hope of democracy is that voters matter. In a representative democracy, we want politicians to be sensitive to the concerns of voters and accountable to voters when they do or do not take action. The process of gaining representation for voters, with all their differing needs and ideas, is not simple. Voters have a multitude of differing and conflicting opinions, interests, and needs. Some want government to intervene and help solve social problems. Others strongly oppose government intrusion because they think government will do harm. There are virtually endless numbers of such conflicts that exist within any free society.

Somehow those differing needs and concerns have to achieve representation. There has to be some organized and sustained effort to raise issues, make arguments for or against public policies, and keep attention on those issues. *Political parties* are crucial actors in this process.[1] They seek to bring together different electoral groups to create a majority that can win elections and control government. Sometimes a social or demographic group may initiate a focus on an issue, and party politicians see the potential to win the votes of that group. Other times, party politicians see a problem emerging and formulate a set of policies to respond with the hope of winning the votes of those affected. However the interaction

---

[1] For a recent defense of parties in a democracy, see Russell Muirhead, "A Defense of Party Spirit," *Perspectives on Politics* 4 (2006), 713–27. For the classic statement of the necessity of parties in a democracy, see E. E. Schattschneider, *Party Government* (New York: Holt, Rinehart, and Winston, 1942). For recent research demonstrating that voters do have meaningful issue positions and that these positions strongly affect individuals' electoral behavior, see Stephen Ansolabehere, Jonathan Rodden, and James M. Snyder, Jr., "The Strength of Issues: Using Multiple Measures to Gauge Preference Stability, Ideological Constraint, and Issue Voting," *American Political Science Review* 102 (May 2008), 215–32.

begins, the goal of a party is to represent concerns, build a coalition, win votes and create a majority. That dynamic creates representation for interests in society. The party then uses whatever unity it can create among party officeholders to get policy proposals enacted into law. The aspiration of a party is to attract voters, construct a coalition big enough to win control of government and then enact public policy as it sees fit. Interests that might struggle to be recognized and heard acting alone are formed into a coalition that gets representation. In turn, public sentiments get translated into specific policy proposals.

The dynamics of interaction between parties then comes into play and further helps representation. Ideas proposed by one party are critiqued by the other because the electorate needs to hear critical evaluations. A proposed tax cut is said to help everyone, but the opposing party works hard to point out that it helps some (of the presenting party) more than others (of the dissenting party). As one party gains power and enacts new policies, it is critiqued and held accountable by the other party that seeks to challenge the enacted policies and regain power for itself. Debate and disagreement between the parties (all too often referred to by the media as *bickering*) are central to the vigorous public dialogue that a healthy representative democracy requires. Although the public often expresses its dismay at these exchanges, they are a valuable part of the process of public review of proposals. These exchanges create party images – perceptions about which concerns and groups each party favors – within the electorate, a development that allows voters to register their preferences more easily and more effectively at the ballot box.[2] All in all, the aspirations for the role parties can play in a democracy are significant.

ISSUE CONTINUITIES AND CHANGE

The simple model of parties just described is often presented as if there are enduring broad and fundamental differences in society for the parties to represent. Yet it also assumes that somehow parties recognize and incorporate changes in society into party concerns. Parties do both of these. Some concerns have existed and endured over time, but remarkable social changes have occurred, pushing new concerns to the surface. Parties have responded, represented new issues, new constituents and

---

[2] Richard J. Trilling, *Party Image and Electoral Behavior* (New York: John Wiley and Sons, 1976). See also Mark D. Brewer, *Party Images in the American Electorate* (New York: Routledge, 2009).

areas, and changed their electoral bases, while also representing enduring interests.

The broad historical continuity has involved the economy and the role
of government in trying to affect it. *Capitalism* – the faith in and reliance
on free markets and their outcomes – produces some businesses and individuals that succeed and some who do not. Social and economic changes
reduce the fortunes of some and boost those of others. Those who struggle to succeed economically and doubt the fairness of outcomes seek representation to help them. Those who are succeeding are more likely to
believe in how the American economy and society are evolving. They
stress the importance of encouraging individual efforts and the dangers
of government trying to intrude and protect individuals and firms that
are not succeeding.

While economic issues have always been with us, there have been fluctuations over time in the relative prominence of economic issues. Poverty
and wealth have always been with us, as have conflicts between labor and
management. But issues of prosperity and inequality wax and wane over
time. Prosperity and inequality grew throughout the 1920s and were followed by the Great Depression of the 1930s, making economic issues central to American politics. After World War II, incomes grew and inequality declined, somewhat diminishing the focus on economic issues. Then
during the 1970s inequality began a steady increase, once again bringing the conflict of the haves and the have-nots into the spotlight. The
broad issue of satisfaction with economic and social conditions has provided a basis for enduring partisan division in the United States.[3] As John
Gerring put it in his examination of almost 170 years of partisanship in
America:

> It might be said that through all periods of American history one party
> has adhered to the interests of business and the advance of a capitalist
> economy, whereas the other has often been more critical of this advance.
> One has been more concerned with preserving social order and liberty,
> the other has emphasized equality.[4]

For much of American history there have been two major parties to
represent these broad differences. Democrats have largely represented
those less well off or those who struggle to prosper in a capitalistic

---

[3] Keith T. Poole and Howard Rosenthal, *Congress: A Political-Economic History of Roll Call
Voting* (New York: Oxford University Press, 1997).
[4] John Gerring, *Party Ideologies in America, 1828–1996* (New York: Cambridge University
Press, 1998), 20.

society. Who comprises the party's base has changed enormously over time, but the Democratic Party's concern for the have-nots has persisted. Republicans, on the other hand, have largely defended free markets and represented those who have fared relatively well. There have been overlaps, times when these differences were more muted, and times when other issues emerged that added to and complicated the mix – issues surrounding race and religion have been particularly important – but broad economic differences have continued to provide a basis for enduring differences in party concerns. After all, as Key pointed out, "Politics generally comes down, over the long run, to a conflict between those who have and those who have less." Partisan conflict in the United States has always reflected this cleavage to some degree.[5]

However, there have also been remarkable changes that parties have had to react to, either by resisting action or by responding to change with new policies in an effort to maintain or attract constituents. New issues constantly emerge with the potential to disrupt party electoral bases. Slavery lingered on the back burner for a long time in American politics, but eventually became an issue that could not be ignored. Industrialization emerged and displaced farm life, pulling people to cities and creating new relationships and tensions between workers and owners of businesses. Huge numbers of immigrants, many with a Catholic heritage, entered a Protestant nation and created issues of whether a different religion would be accepted and how immigrants would be treated. The Great Depression and its massive poverty and unemployment challenged the then-dominant idea that the federal government should play a limited role in the economy in particular and in American society in general. The cold war provoked the issue of how big the defense establishment should be and how high taxes should be to fund it. Racial inequality emerged as an explosive issue that was hard to avoid. The federal government took on a greater role in the 1960s, providing programs and benefits and regulating private activities in ways not done before. Conservatives in turn felt bound to critique this growth in the role of government. Over time, the population has moved from rural to urban and now to suburban areas, creating shifts in concentrations of wealth and opportunity. Disputes about what is moral and immoral have existed since the earliest days of the American experience but have become more divisive from time to time throughout history. Issues concerning social values and behavior – prayer in schools, the role of religion in society, abortion,

---

[5] V. O. Key, Jr., *Southern Politics in State and Nation* (New York: Knopf, 1949).

illegitimate births, and homosexuality – were largely absent until the 1970s and have become highly visible in subsequent years. Issues rise and fall in prominence. However, these social and economic changes do not automatically or by necessity produce political change. Rather, they produce an opportunity for political change, an opportunity that parties must capitalize on for political change to occur.[6]

CHANGE AND PARTY RESPONSES

Political parties are the primary mechanism for interpreting and responding to these changes. They interact with groups of citizens and organized interest groups to form responses to change. They seek to represent voters because they believe in their causes.[7] They also wish to get their candidates and officials elected and reelected.[8] Political parties want to build majorities. This way parties can acquire power and enact policies that they believe in and that respond to the constituencies they need to achieve and maintain power. Every politician and every party faces a balancing act of pursuing their convictions while trying to bring in new supporters who may be less enthusiastic about the concerns of the existing electoral base.

The process of responding to new groups and issues can make this balancing act particularly difficult. Political parties worry that reaching out to new groups can muddle their image and leave core supporters less enthusiastic. Incorporating new groups can add to an electoral base or create conflict and perhaps drive away parts of the existing base. When the Democrats took a strong stand on civil rights issues in the 1960s, there was concern that it would drive away conservative Southern whites. When the Republicans took a strong stand on social issues in the early 2000s, there was concern that it would drive away moderates.

The crucial imperative for a party is if they are in the minority. If so, they may be willing to take risks to expand their base to try to become the majority party. As immigrants poured into the nation in the late 1800s and early 1900s, their presence presented both parties with the challenge

---

[6] Jerome M. Clubb, William H. Flanigan, and Nancy H. Zingale, *Partisan Realignment: Voters, Parties, and Government in American History* (Beverly Hills, CA: Sage Publications, 1980); David Plotke, *Building a Democratic Political Order: Reshaping American Liberalism in the 1930s and 1940s* (New York: Cambridge University Press, 1996).

[7] Grant Reeher, *Narratives of Justice: Legislator's Beliefs about Distributive Justice* (Ann Arbor: University of Michigan Press, 1996).

[8] David Mayhew, *The Electoral Connection* (New Haven: Yale University Press, 1974).

of whether and how to respond to their concerns. Civil rights activism in the 1950s and 1960s prompted the issue of whether to respond with legislation and perhaps attract the blacks who might register to vote.The emergence in the late twentieth century of religious conservatives who were concerned about moral decline represented a constituency Republicans could appeal to and expand their electoral base. Each situation created opportunities and risks.

Presidential candidates have been particularly important in creating changes in party bases and alignments. Presidential candidates run within the context of the Electoral College. A presidential candidate must win a majority of the electoral votes. State electoral votes (based on the number of House and Senate seats) are awarded on winner-take-all basis, or the candidate with the most popular votes within a state wins all the electoral votes of that state, with few exceptions.[9] That means that it is often not sufficient for a candidate to win large majorities in some states and lose many others. The math of creating a majority of electoral votes in presidential elections is complicated, but it often drives a candidate to seek votes in at least a few states (and often more than a few) that the candidate and his or her party might not win without making an appeal that is at least somewhat different from the party's standard fare.

Over the last century there have been strings of years where presidential candidates have faced an electoral record of regular party losses, forcing them to consider how to expand the party's electoral appeal. As Table 1.1 indicates, from 1900 through 1928 Democrats lost six of eight presidential campaigns. They averaged 40.1 percent of the popular vote and 39.3 percent of the electoral college. Their base was in the South, but they knew they had to expand beyond that base to have a chance to win the presidency. The drive to attract more votes outside of the South – especially in urban areas – eventually changed the party's base.

From 1932 through 1964 Republican presidential candidates found themselves facing a string of defeats, losing seven of nine contests. By the end of this time period Republican presidential candidates knew they had to expand their base, and the South became their target of opportunity. They eventually succeeded, and that began a long process of changing the party's base. Then from 1968 through 2004 Democrats lost seven of ten presidential elections. That indicated to Bill Clinton in 1992 and Barack Obama in 2008 that they had to position themselves and their

---

[9] The two exceptions are Maine and Nebraska.

TABLE 1.1. Party success by years, 1900–2004

Years	Party and campaigns won	Democratic % of		Republican % of	
		Popular vote	Electoral college	Popular vote	Electoral college
1900–1928	R – 6/8	40.1	39.3	50.2	60.7
1932–1964	D – 7/9	52.6	66.0	45.8	34.0
1968–2004	R – 7/10	44.9	36.5	49.3	63.5

party to attract a larger constituency. Whether their victories will initiate more changes remains to be seen. Over the last century the recognition of repeated losses has set off efforts to alter the electoral appeal of a party in an effort to win the presidency.

These efforts by presidential candidates constitute the most visible expression of party concerns. The stances these candidates adopt are the ones voters are most likely to hear, thus they can play a significant role in redefining a party. These party images created by presidential candidates then affect congressional candidates and even state and local candidates. If a party is in the minority and a presidential candidate demonstrates that inroads can be made into a new electoral base, then candidates for lower-level offices will also pursue that base. Over time, those efforts may redefine the image of the party and prompt further change, causing the loss of some of the party's prior electoral base.

THE DEBATE ABOUT THE NATURE OF POLITICAL CHANGE

Although we know that political change occurs, the issue of how major changes occur in party bases and voter loyalties has been a matter of some difference of opinion. In the study of American electoral politics, there have been two primary ways of thinking about how the interaction of social change and parties leads to political change.[10] One interpretation presupposes that electoral loyalties and party systems are relatively stable and resistant to gradual change. Voters develop attachments to parties

[10] Each of these primary views of changes – or *realignment*, to use the accepted term – has a seemingly endless number of slightly different variations. However, at the end of the day, it seems to us that all of these explanations of change can be boiled down to one of the two primary schools of thought outlined here. For an intellectual history of the concept of realignment, see Theodore Rosenof, *Realignment: The Theory that Changed the Way We Think about American Politics* (Lanham, MD: Rowman & Littlefield, 2003).

and only change them if there is a social crisis that prompts substantial numbers to embrace another party and to stick with the new party for a long time.[11] This is called the *critical realignment perspective*.[12] The argument is essentially that political stability prevails until social or economic change and events swiftly overtake party leaders, they do not respond well, and voters move to support a new party, which they then stick with. The process results in dramatic and lasting change.

The quintessential example offered as an instance of critical realignment is the Great Depression and the large, rapid shift to the Democratic Party that occurred in the early 1930s. Republican President Herbert Hoover argued against government action and expressed his faith that private market adjustments would eventually solve the enormous increase in unemployment and other economic problems that developed from late 1929 onward. According to the critical realignment perspective, voters saw in Hoover's GOP a party that would not respond to a severely declining economy. In response, they quickly shifted their support to the Democratic Party, and many stayed there for decades. As Key describes, a critical realignment is both "sharp and durable."[13] Once voters form an attachment to a party, there is little change until another major event occurs. In this view, significant change in electoral loyalties to a party is only occasional but enduring.[14]

In contrast is a view of democracy that places much more emphasis on gradual social and economic change, on the strategies and actions

[11] It is also argued that in addition to conversion – voters previously identified with one party switching their allegiance to the other – episodes of critical realignment mobilize previously nonparticipatory citizens and those just reaching full political citizenship age to strongly identify with the new majority party. For a debate on whether conversion or mobilization is more important to the process of critical realignment, see Kristi Andersen, *The Creation of a Democratic Majority, 1928–1936* (Chicago: University of Chicago Press, 1979); James L. Sundquist, *Dynamics of the Party System: Alignment and Realignment of Political Parties in the United States*, revised edition (Washington, DC: Brookings Institution Press, 1983).

[12] The original statement of critical realignment originates in V. O. Key, Jr., "A Theory of Critical Elections," *Journal of Politics* 17 (1955), 3–18. For the classic amplification of Key's theory, see Walter Dean Burnham, *Critical Elections and the Mainsprings of American Politics*. For a critique of the critical realignment framework, see David R. Mayhew, *Electoral Realignments: A Critique of an American Genre* (New Haven, CT: Yale University Press, 2002).

[13] Key, "A Theory of Critical Elections," 4.

[14] Angus Campbell, Philip E. Converse, Warren E. Miller, and Donald E. Stokes, *The American Voter* (New York: John Wiley and Sons, 1960); Donald Green, Bradley Palmquist, and Eric Schickler, *Partisan Hearts and Minds: Political Parties and the Social Identities of Voters* (New Haven, CT: Yale University Press, 2002).

of party leaders in response to these changes, and on the ability and willingness of voters to respond to party actions. This approach is called *secular realignment*.[15] The presumption is that change comes from groups and partisan politicians seeking to alter an existing state of affairs. New social and economic conditions emerge, and various groups in society seek policy responses from parties, or parties and their officials and candidates for public office see a newly emerging constituency or a constituency attached to the opposing party that could be brought onboard to create a majority. These situations present party candidates with the possibility of responding to and acquiring new constituents. A nonresponse from one party can lead to efforts by the other party to respond and move constituents from one party to the other. Common examples given of secular realignment in American political history include the gradual movement of the urban working class in the North from the Republican Party to the Democratic Party in the 1910s through the 1930s, and the equally gradual shift of southern whites from the Democratic Party to the GOP beginning in earnest in the 1960s (although at least stirring in the late 1940s) and finally culminating in the 1990s.

The essence of secular realignment is slow and incremental change. As stated by Key, secular realignment operates "inexorably, and almost imperceptibly, election after election, to form new party alignments and to build new party groupings."[16] Party candidates are regularly assessing social and economic conditions and considering how they can best

---

[15] Key is also responsible for the original statement of secular realignment: see V. O. Key, Jr., "Secular Realignment and the Party System," *Journal of Politics* 21 (1959), 198–210. For works that utilize the secular realignment approach to explain political change, see Earl and Merle Black, *The Rise of Southern Republicans* (Cambridge, MA: Harvard University Press, 2002); Earl and Merle Black, *Divided America: The Ferocious Power Struggle in American Politics* (New York: Simon & Schuster, 2007); John R. Petrocik, *Party Coalitions: Realignments and the Decline of the New Deal Party System* (Chicago: University of Chicago Press, 1981); Kevin P. Phillips, *The Emerging Republican Majority* (New Rochelle, NY: Arlington House, 1969); Richard M. Scammon and Ben J. Wattenberg, *The Real Majority* (New York: Conrad-McCann, 1970); Byron E. Shafer and Richard Johnston, *The End of Southern Exceptionalism: Class, Race, and Partisan Change in the Postwar South* (Cambridge, MA: Harvard University Press, 2006); Jeffrey M. Stonecash, Mark D. Brewer, and Mack D. Mariani, *Diverging Parties: Social Change, Realignment, and Party Polarization* (Boulder, CO: Westview Press, 2003); Alan Ware, *The Democratic Party Heads North, 1877–1962* (New York: Cambridge University Press, 2006). In addition, the prominent theory of issue evolution outlined by Carmines and Stimson bears at least a moderate resemblance to the concept of secular realignment as well – Edward G. Carmines and James A. Stimson, *Issue Evolution: Race and the Transformation of American Politics* (Princeton, NJ: Princeton University Press, 1989).

[16] Key, "Secular Realignment and the Party System," 198–9.

respond. When party positions change, voters (at least some of them) are presumed to be able to sort out these evolving positions. They engage in a crude, and perhaps inaccurate, "running tally"[17] of party positions. They have existing loyalties that they can change, and some do, shifting the electoral bases of the parties.[18]

However, the acquisition of new constituents is not without its costs. As a party adopts new positions and attracts new voters to its coalition, it can also alienate existing constituencies. For example, as the Democratic Party acquired more black constituents in the 1960s and 1970s, many white voters moved to the Republican Party. As the Republican Party acquired more social conservatives who opposed abortion and gay rights, its image and eventually the makeup of its coalition changed as many Republicans who were fiscally conservative but more moderate or libertarian on social issues gradually abandoned the party. In each instance, the parties' coalitions changed but in a slow, gradual manner.

The main difference between secular realignment and critical realignment is that under the theory of secular realignment, parties and their politicians are not seen as largely locked into preestablished positions as social and economic change unfolds. Parties and their officeholders and candidates are engaged in an ongoing search for constituencies. This search is especially intense for the so-called "out" party because it desperately wants to return to power. Some party candidates are constrained in espousing changing party positions knowing that their existing base may be uneasy with a different policy emphasis of the party. Newer party candidates may strongly believe in a changed emphasis and that the change will generate more supporters, particularly more supporters who are stronger believers in the party's positions.

---

[17] Morris P. Fiorina, *Retrospective Voting in American National Elections* (New Haven, CT: Yale University Press, 1981). See also V. O. Key, Jr., *The Responsible Electorate* (Cambridge, MA: Harvard University Press, 1966).

[18] Layman and Carsey present evidence of voters changing their partisanship to reflect new or altered party positions, but also demonstrate that some voters alter their own positions to match the altered or new positions of the party they already identify with. Geoffrey C. Layman and Thomas M. Carsey, "Party Polarization and Party Structuring of Policy Attitudes: A Comparison of Three NES Panel Studies," *Political Behavior* 24 (2002), 199–236; Geoffrey C. Layman and Thomas M. Carsey, "Party Polarization and 'Conflict Extension' in the American Electorate," *American Journal of Political Science* 46 (2002), 786–802; Thomas M. Carsey and Geoffrey C. Layman, "Changing Sides or Changing Minds? Party Identification and Policy Preferences in the American Electorate," *American Journal of Political Science* 50 (2006), 464–77.

DIFFERING PERSPECTIVES IN INTERPRETING CHANGE
AND THE PLAN OF THE BOOK

These differing notions of how political changes unfold have had great significance for interpreting what is occurring in politics. Those who thought change came about primarily from abrupt, critical realignment interpreted a decline in attachment to or identification with parties that emerged in the 1960s and 1970s as party decline or dealignment.[19] No clear and abrupt change in party loyalties occurred. Those looking for such changes did not turn to the secular realignment perspective because they were expecting to see abrupt instead of gradual change. When party identification began to increase in the late 1900s and party polarization emerged, the secular realignment perspective became useful in explaining the changes that were occurring.[20]

This book's thesis is that both abrupt and gradual changes have characterized American political history. There are moments when abrupt change occurs; for example, the Democratic Party substantially increased

[19] Paul Allen Beck, "Partisan Dealignment in the Postwar South," *American Political Science Review* 71 (June 1977), 477–96; Paul Allen Beck, "The Electoral Cycle and Patterns of American Politics," *British Journal of Political Science* 9 (April 1979), 129–56; David S. Broder, *The Party's Over: The Failure of Politics in America* (New York: Harper and Row, 1972); Walter Dean Burnham, *Critical Elections and the Mainsprings of American Politics* (New York: W.W. Norton, 1970); Norman H. Nie, Sidney Verba, and John R. Petrocik, *The Changing American Voter* (Cambridge, MA: Harvard University Press, 1976); Martin P. Wattenberg, *The Decline of American Political Parties, 1952–1996* (Cambridge, MA: Harvard University Press, 1998).

[20] For work detailing the resurgence of partisanship, see Larry M. Bartels, "Partisanship and Voting Behavior, 1952–1996," *American Journal of Political Science* 44 (2000), 35–50; Marc J. Hetherington, "Resurgent Mass Partisanship: The Role of Elite Polarization," *American Political Science Review* 95 (2001), 619–31; Jeffrey M. Stonecash, *Political Parties Matter: Realignment and the Return of Partisan Voting* (Boulder, CO: Lynne Rienner, 2006). For discussions of the increasing polarization in American politics, see Alan Abramowitz and Kyle Saunders, "Why Can't We All just Get Along? The Reality of a Polarized America," *The Forum* 3 (2005); Jon R. Bond and Richard Fleisher (eds.), *Polarized Politics: Congress and the President in a Partisan Era* (Washington, DC: CQ Press, 2000); Mark D. Brewer and Jeffrey M. Stonecash, *Split: Class and Cultural Divides in American Politics* (Washington, DC: CQ Press, 2007); Thomas B. Edsall, *Building Red America: The Conservative Coalition and the Drive for Permanent Power* (New York: Basic Books, 2006); Gary C. Jacobson, *A Divider, Not a Uniter: George W. Bush and the American People* (New York: Pearson/Longman, 2007); Geoffrey C. Layman, Thomas M. Carsey, and Juliana Menasce Horowitz, "Party Polarization in American Politics: Characteristics, Causes, and Consequences," *Annual Review of Political Science* 9 (2006), 83–110. For dissenting views on the existence of polarization, see Wayne Baker, *America's Crisis of Values: Reality and Perception* (Princeton, NJ: Princeton University Press, 2005); Morris P. Fiorina, with Samuel J. Abrams and Jeremy C. Pope, *Culture War? The Myth of a Polarized America*, second edition (New York: Pearson/Longman, 2006).

its electoral base in 1932, and much of that change has persisted through to the present.[21] However, as David Mayhew so effectively demonstrated, critical realignment theory has many shortcomings and ultimately fails to adequately explain political change in all but a handful of instances.[22]

Therefore, we argue that the primary changes in American politics are more gradual in nature, and that political change in American electoral politics is best understood through the lens of secular realignment. In our view, no work has managed to discredit this theory of political change. We concur with Theodore Rosenof and his detailed study of realignment theory: There is a good deal of value in the concept of gradual change if properly utilized.[23] Social and economic changes are constantly unfolding. Parties and their political candidates continually propose ideas and policies as social and economic changes develop. They try to assess which constituency will be attracted to or alienated by their ideas and policies. At times, parties and their candidates will gamble and articulate a position not previously expressed to try to increase their electoral base; at other times, social and economic changes force parties and candidates to shift gears to survive.

This does not mean that candidates and parties abandon their core positions as raw opportunists. Principle matters and politicians are reluctant to abandon prior positions to gain votes. That will lead to charges of being a "flip-flopper" or a candidate without principles and convictions. Rather parties are always looking for what to emphasize or deemphasize about their views as they struggle with a shifting electoral arena. These calculations and pursuits are rarely, if ever, without risk. Uncertainty rules and intraparty conflict rages as different factions and groups within the parties debate the proper course(s) of action and battle it out for control of the party.[24] Parties can never be sure how their strategic maneuvers will play

---

[21] Even here it could be argued that 1932 represented the culmination of an already ongoing secular realignment as much as it did a critical realignment. See Jerome M. Clubb and Howard W. Allen, "The Cities and the Election of 1928: Partisan Realignment?," *American Historical Review* 74 (1969), 1205–20; Samuel Lubell, *The Future of American Politics*, second edition, revised (Garden City, NY: Doubleday Anchor Books, 1956); Alan Ware, *The Democratic Party Heads North, 1877–1962*. It should be noted here that Ware would more likely say that 1932 was in the middle of the secular realignment rather than its culmination.

[22] David R. Mayhew, *Electoral Realignments: A Critique of Am American Genre* (New Haven, CT: Yale University Press, 2002).

[23] Theodore Rosenof, *Realignment: The Theory that Changed the Way We Think about American Politics* (Lanham, MD: Rowman and Littlefield, 2003).

[24] Once again we feel we must repeat a statement made in the first paragraph of this chapter – change is not inevitable. As David Plotke makes clear, social and economic

out, and even when it appears that a certain strategy has been successful party leaders are unclear about how long apparent success will last.
Change unfolds slowly, in fits and starts.

The combination of social change and candidate and party assessments
create change in party positions, shifts in which groups support each
party, and change in which party controls government. The end result
is an interaction between citizens and politicians that creates representation. Citizens seek expression of their concerns, whereas politicians seek
votes and generally share the concerns of those they seek to represent.
Parties simplify and organize the process and create representation.

Our emphasis on presidents and presidential candidates does not
imply a candidate-centered view of American politics. Although we see
presidential candidates as the primary spokespeople for the American
people on the subject of politics, remember that they are the spokespeople and representatives of their respective parties first. Presidential
candidates result from intraparty debate and conflict over who the
parties should present to the public as their representative for the highest
office in the land. Presidential candidates and their policies reflect a
party's decision regarding what it wants to communicate to voters.
The politics of presidential elections is about assembling a winning
coalition out of the various groups and constituencies that make up the
American electorate. We agree with John Petrocik that changes in the
group components of partisan coalitions are critical to the concept of
realignment.[25] Because presidential elections are the ultimate exercise
in partisan coalition building in the United States, they are central to our
analysis.

---

change only provide the opportunity for political change, not political change itself. Parties and partisan politicians must take advantage of these opportunities in order for political change to actually occur, as Plotke demonstrates in his study of the assembly of the
New Deal coalition. Sydney Milkis and Alan Ware also emphasize this point in their
respective analyses of the same subject. See Sidney M. Milkis, *The President and the Parties:
The Transformation of the American Party System Since the New Deal* (New York: Oxford University Press, 1993); David Plotke, *Building a Democratic Political Order: Reshaping American
Liberalism in the 1930s and 1940s*; Alan Ware, *The Democratic Party Heads North, 1877–1962*.
As Jerome Clubb and his colleagues put it, "Whether or not a new and lasting distribution
of partisan loyalties is formed and whether the dominance of the temporarily advantaged
party is perpetuated – whether or not, in other words, the process of political realignment
is consummated – depends on the degree to which this opportunity for effective policy
action is fulfilled." Jerome M. Clubb, William H. Flanigan, and Nancy H. Zingale, *Partisan Realignment: Voters, Parties, and Government in American History* (Beverly Hills, CA: Sage
Publications, 1980), p. 12.

[25] John R. Petrocik, *Party Coalitions: Realignment and the Decline of the New Deal Party System*
(Chicago: University of Chicago Press, 1981).

It should also be noted that our focus on parties and their presidential candidates does not constitute a simple elite-driven or top-down model of partisan and electoral change such as that outlined by John Zaller and to a lesser extent by Geoffrey Layman and Thomas Carsey.[26] Our understanding of secular realignment is more aligned with the model of partisan change offered by John Aldrich – a feedback loop of sorts.[27] Conditions change in the electorate; as parties and their politicians pick up on these changes, they react to them in some cases. This may lead to further partisan shifts in the electorate, which the parties once again must react to. The process is ongoing and feeds off of itself.

The dynamic nature of this interaction and process of change over the last several decades has led to the current polarization in American politics. In the last decade, party voting has steadily increased. The Democrats increasingly vote together and against the Republicans while the Republicans vote together and against the Democrats. *Moderates*, or members who hold positions between liberals and conservatives, are disappearing.[28] While defining whether voters are entirely polarized is a matter of dispute it is clear that voters are steadily moving in the direction of being more divided about economic issues and the role of government in affecting social issues.[29] As this has occurred, the divisions between the parties have grown.

Understanding how we got to this point in American politics requires comprehending broad historical changes. The current situation is a product of changes that began long ago, a series of evolutions that have been decades in the making. Party divisions did not just randomly decline and then reemerge. The Democrats have gradually become a party

---

[26] John R. Zaller, *The Nature and Origins of Mass Opinion* (New York: Cambridge University Press, 1992); Geoffrey C. Layman and Thomas M. Carsey, "Party Polarization and Party Structuring of Policy Attitudes: A Comparison of Three NES Panels"; Geoffrey C. Layman and Thomas M. Carsey, "Party Polarization and 'Conflict Extension' in the American Electorate"; Thomas M. Carsey and Geoffrey C. Layman, "Changing Sides or Changing Minds? Party Identification and Policy Preferences in the American Electorate."

[27] John Aldrich, "Electoral Democracy During Politics as Usual – and Unusual," in Michael B. MacKuen and George Rabinowitz (eds.), *Electoral Democracy* (Ann Arbor: University of Michigan Press, 2003), 279–310.

[28] Jon R. Bond, Richard Fleisher, and Jeffrey M. Stonecash, "The Rise and Decline of Moderates in the House, 1876–2004," prepared for the conference on *Going to Extremes: The Fate of the Political Center in American Politics*, Rockefeller Center for Public Policy and the Social Sciences, Dartmouth College, Hanover, New Hampshire, June 19–21, 2008.

[29] Alan Abramowitz, "The Disappearing Center: Political Engagement and Polarization in the American Electorate," prepared for the conference on *Going to Extremes: The Fate of the Political Center in American Politics*, Rockefeller Center for Public Policy and the Social Sciences, Dartmouth College, Hanover, New Hampshire, June 19–21, 2008.

dominated by liberals; they are now forceful advocates of liberal concerns. These changes attracted some new constituents and alienated others. The Republicans have gradually attracted more conservatives and they are now forceful advocates of lower taxes and traditional morals. As change occurred and voters moved from one party to another, it appeared that the parties differed less. This was a phase in which transitions created more diverse parties and some ambiguity in the images of each party. The result is that parties are further apart and more polarized than in decades. The story of these changes is a complicated one, which we hope to detail in this book.

Chapter 2 is an overview of change that describes the big picture before tracking the more specific dynamics of change. With the broad changes established, we then move to a chronological approach. Our emphasis will be largely on the post–Civil War era to the present. Events, gradual changes, and responses weave together to create a dynamic that has slowly transformed the electoral bases of the parties and shaped public debates within American politics.

2   Overview: Social Change and Shifting Party Bases

Political parties face a continuing challenge as they seek to create a majority. American society is always changing and they must respond. Yet fundamental issues endure and they must represent them. Parties have an existing base but they may need to seek new constituents as society changes. The challenge is to retain as much of the older base as possible while adding in new constituents. It is not an easy balancing act.

The enduring concerns have been economic, involving issues of promoting economic growth, fairness, and opportunity. Over time, the Republican Party has been the conservative party, arguing against government activity. Republicans believe that individuals can and should make it on their own. Too much government intrusion is bad for the economy and stifles growth. Democrats argue that class background, inequalities in opportunity, and the condition of the economy often affect the ability of individuals to succeed. They believe the government needs to take steps to increase equality of opportunity and provide some protection to individuals from the harm that could be done to them by corporations that often give a low priority to working conditions and employee well-being.[1] Other issues, such as immigration, race, and moral and cultural concerns, have flared periodically, creating pressures for both parties to respond and address these concerns as well.

The challenge in understanding American political parties over time is to sort out how there could be continuity of many concerns while at the same time the composition of each party's electoral base has shifted significantly. Economic concerns have always been with us, but who the

---

[1] John Gerring, *Party Ideologies in America, 1828–1996* (New York: Cambridge University Press, 1998); Keith T. Poole and Howard Rosenthal, *Congress: A Political-Economic History of Roll Call Voting* (New York: Oxford University Press, 1997).

prosperous and less prosperous are and where they reside have shifted over time. As the parties have adapted to change and sought new constituents (while at the same time holding on to their old ones), their decisions have resulted in a dramatic transformation in their sources of support.

From the end of Reconstruction through the early decades of the twentieth century, the Democratic Party was largely based in the South, with some isolated and generally small areas of strength outside of the region. Democratic leaders argued that farmers in the South and West were being dominated and exploited by Eastern-owned railroads and banks, reflecting the primary concerns of the party's largely rural constituency. The party sought changes in the monetary and transportation systems to make it easier for farmers and other rural interests to borrow money and ship goods. The party we now see as dominated by urban constituencies was once primarily rural. A century after the battles of the late 1800s, Democrats still derive a good deal of their support from the less affluent; however, today's have-not portion of the Democratic base is much more likely to come from urban areas filled with minorities and the less affluent who are concerned about equality of opportunity. The cast of characters who make up the rank-and-file of the Democratic Party has changed, but the party's concern with fairness for those not faring as well as others persists.

Republicans have experienced equally significant change. From their founding in the 1850s through at least the early 1960s the party drew the bulk of its support from areas in the Northeast and upper Midwest The party did well in urban and rural areas in these parts of the country. Beginning in the 1960s, the parts of the nation that found the Republican message most appealing began to change. As populations, affluence, and suburbs grew in the South and the Mountain West, the party found a new base in these areas among those who did not see a great need for government. Indeed, many saw dangers to economic growth in an expanded government role. In addition, the party has exchanged the bulk of its former urban base for support in the suburban and rural areas of the United States. The Republicans' electoral base has changed as the location and distribution of economic interests in American society have shifted.

Since the end of the Civil War, both the Republicans and the Democrats have somehow adapted to the endless change within American society. Although both parties have lost some constituents and attracted others, they have retained their status as viable (at some times more viable than at others) options for attaining power at the federal level. The parties have done this by consistently representing different ideas about what government should and should not do, even while their electoral bases have changed. These processes of change in America have been lengthy and hard to decipher at times. During recent decades, there have been times when it appeared that political parties were on the decline; instead, a gradual and complicated realignment was occurring. The transitions have often become evident only in retrospect. Once enough time has passed, the evolution of the major parties and the results of the inexorable resorting of the electorate can be seen in response to the social and partisan changes occurring.

Part of the difficulty in tracking the process of realignment as it unfolds is because it does not proceed smoothly. As society changes, party leaders are often slow in recognizing or responding to the change. A response to changing conditions may be delayed because newcomers to the party argue for the need to change policy positions, but existing incumbents and interests resist change. And when responses do come, they are not always clear. New issues emerge that are not about economic divisions and the parties are not sure how to respond. After World War II the issue of racial justice became a central issue. Beginning in the 1960s cultural issues emerged. In both cases these new issues became part of the political agenda but initially muddied the partisan waters before eventually becoming clear sources of party division. The rise of new issues – emerging from social and economic changes and voter concern about them – enormously complicates each party's decisions about whom and what they should represent. However, eventually the time comes – sometimes quickly, sometimes slowly – when the parties make a decision and adopt clear positions. Voters then respond, and this combination of party action and subsequent voter reaction goes a long way in determining the direction and amount of partisan change that ultimately comes to pass.

PRESIDENTIAL CANDIDATES AND INITIATING CHANGE

The ambitions of presidential candidates have driven much of this change. House and Senate candidates care about the overall party situation and formulate strategies to expand their base, but their primary concern as candidates is to create majorities in their jurisdictions. Presidential candidates, as noted in the prior chapter, have to create a majority in the Electoral College if they are to win, which forces them to create a broader base. If a party is confined to minority status, this challenge can be

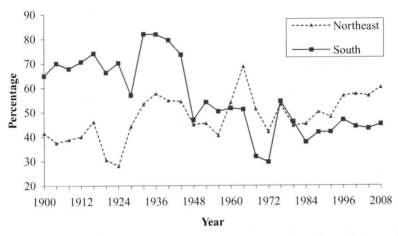

FIGURE 2.1. Percentage voting for Democratic presidential candidates within regions, 1900–2008

particularly important in producing changes in where and among what kinds of voters the party finds support.

The most significant changes in the parties' presidential coalitions in recent years involve the lengthy reversal of partisan support patterns in the Northeast and the South.[2] Other regions have fluctuated between the two parties over time. Together, the Northeast and South include roughly 50 percent of all voters in recent decades. Figure 2.1 presents the percentage of the vote received by Democratic presidential candidates since 1900 in the two regions. The Northeast was once the stronghold of the Republican Party, whereas the South was regarded as automatically Democratic. The problem facing the Democrats was that this base was not large enough to produce a national Democratic presidential candidate victory. The party knew it had to do well outside the South. It was able to do so in 1932 when Franklin Roosevelt won, but FDR knew he had to then reach out to and represent the new constituents he had attracted. His administration enacted considerable legislation intended to help those in urban areas, especially the less affluent and industrial laborers. The efforts of the party eventually created greater and relatively stable support in Midwest and Northeast urban areas. As a result of the 1930s,

[2] Northeast is defined as New England plus New Jersey, Delaware, Maryland, West Virginia, Pennsylvania, and New York. Although including West Virginia and Maryland as part of the Northeast may be questioned, they follow the same pattern as the other states included – gradual movement from Republican to Democrat – so they are included. The South is defined as Alabama, Florida, Georgia, Kentucky, Louisiana, Mississippi, North Carolina, South Carolina, Tennessee, Texas, and Virginia.

the party had a larger electoral base comprised of the New Deal Coalition of white Southerners, Northern city dwellers, Roman Catholics, and union households.

However, there was a price for this shifted emphasis. The party gained seats in relatively liberal Northern cities and the more liberal concerns expressed by this new wing alienated the South and eventually provided an opening for the Republicans. These gains by Democrats in the North in turn had consequences for Republicans. By the 1950s and 1960s, Republican presidential candidates were finding their Northeast base eroding and knew they had to do better in the growing South to have a chance to win. GOP candidates shifted their focus to emphasize more conservative positions, campaigned in the South, and gradually improved their success in that region. Today the South is a solid source of votes for Republican candidates. The Northeast, where only 40 percent voted Democratic in the early 1900s, has moved to be strongly and consistently supportive of Democratic presidential candidates. Issues involving economic divisions have endured, but the geographical bases of support for each party have changed. For the Democrats farmers who felt harmed by eastern bankers and railroads were replaced by Northern laborers who felt mistreated. Since then the party has added minorities and the urban less affluent. The issues of unfairness and the need for government assistance have persisted, but involving a different cast of characters. Republicans have continued to defend free markets and limited government, but their base has sifted from the urban North to rural areas, the suburbs, and the booming areas of the Sunbelt.

The result has been a dramatic shift in where presidential candidates get their Electoral College votes from, as shown in Figure 2.2. With some fluctuations (remember that the rules are winner-takes-all within states, so small shifts in percentages within states can create large shifts in which candidate gets state electoral votes), Democrats got substantial percentages of their electoral votes from the South until 1960. Since then, they have consistently received fewer votes from that region. Republicans have also reversed their success. They received few Electoral College votes in the South, but in recent elections have won all of them and now build from that solid base.

This shift in policy priorities and electoral bases, prompted by presidential candidates, eventually affected the congressional party in two major ways. First, it led to a disconnection and then reconnection between presidential and congressional electoral bases. That disconnection resulted in an increase in divided government – with one party controlling the

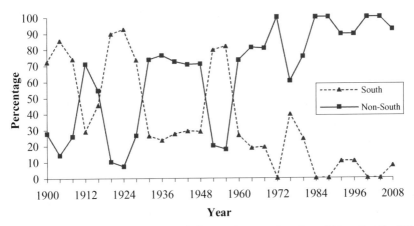

FIGURE 2.2. Democratic source of electoral votes, South and Non-South, 1900–2008. *Source:* 1900–1996: Results presented in Rusk, *A Statistical History of the American Electorate*, Table 4–3; 2000–2008 were taken from newspaper reports

presidency and the other party having a majority in the Congress. This process of transition, with divided government occurring more than in the past, made it difficult to interpret what was occurring for some time. Second, the evolving agendas of each party were not accepted by all members within the congressional parties, leading to more policy disagreements within parties, lower party unity, and diminished differences between the parties. As realignment continued from the 1980s through the 2000s, this divisiveness has declined, resulting in greater homogeneity within each party, greater party unity, and the extent of polarization that now exists between the parties.

DISCONNECTING AND RECONNECTING PRESIDENTIAL AND CONGRESSIONAL ELECTORAL BASES

Presidential candidates created changes in partisan voting in specific areas of the country before they occurred in congressional elections. In elections for the House and Senate, most elections are dominated by incumbents. Such officeholders have built up some visibility and positive evaluations by the local electorate. They are able to survive even while the nature of presidential outcomes in their district is changing.

The pattern of presidential success before congressional success has occurred regularly as realignment has unfolded. In the early 1900s, both Democratic presidential and House candidates in the Northeast averaged about 40 percent of the vote. Franklin Roosevelt was able to make

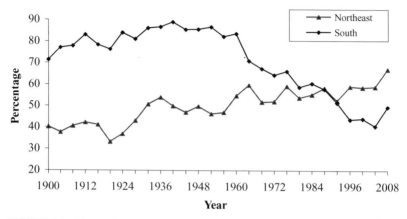

FIGURE 2.3. House Democratic voting percentages, by region, 1900–2008

greater inroads into the Northeast than his congressional party from 1932–1944. House Democrats were able to achieve some success in the Northeast in the 1930s, but their sustained success did come until 1958 and thereafter.[3]

For Republicans their presidential candidates also lead the process of change. As the Democratic Party became more responsive to Northern concerns, it provided an opening for Republican presidential candidates to make inroads into new areas. In 1948, President Harry Truman took a stand in favor of some limited civil rights for Blacks in the South. The Democratic presidential percentage in the South dropped that year and never came back up to its prior level again. Dwight Eisenhower, the successful Republican presidential candidate in 1952 and 1956, was able to do fairly well in the South in the 1950s, but House Republican candidates did not experience significant gains in the South until 1964, as shown in Figure 2.3. In both the Northeast and South presidential candidates disrupted the partisan status quo and results in both the House and the Senate eventually followed.

This difference in partisan voting in presidential and congressional results created a disconnect between partisan voting in House districts and states. In the early 1900s, a House district's partisan vote for a presidential and House candidate was generally highly associated. A strong vote for a Republican presidential candidate was accompanied by a strong vote for a Republican House candidate. The changes just described disrupted

[3] Howard L. Reiter, "Counter-Realignment: Electoral Trends in the Northeast, 1900–2004," delivered at the Social Science History Association Meetings, Chicago, Illinois, November 15–18, 2007; Howard L. Reiter, "Partisan Realignment in the Northeast," presented at the 2008 American Political Science Association Meetings, Boston, August, 2008.

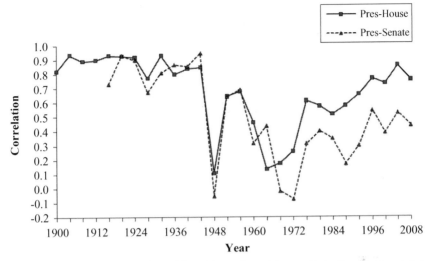

FIGURE 2.4. Correlation of presidential results, with results in Senate (by state) and House (by district), 1900–2008

this pattern. Southern House districts in the 1950s increasingly voted for a Republican presidential candidate while supporting Democratic House candidates. Northern House districts in the 1960s voted in growing numbers for a Democratic presidential candidate, yet retained Republican House candidates. These divergent outcomes (called *split-outcomes*) created a consistent decline in the association of presidential-congressional election results in states and House districts.

This decline in the consistency of results can be seen in the association of presidential results with House results over time. We can calculate the *correlation*, or degree of association, of presidential and House results across House districts. If high Democratic presidential percentages are accompanied by high Democratic House results, and low with low, then the correlation will be high. If the two have little association, the correlation will be low. Figure 2.4 indicates the correlation between the percentage vote for Democratic presidential and House candidates across House districts since 1900 for years of a presidential election. During the 1930s, there was a movement to the Democratic Party in presidential and House elections, and the correlation between the two results continued at .8 to .9. In 1948, with Truman having alienated the South, a major disruption occurred and the correlation between the two sets of results plummeted to .11. The correlation recovered somewhat in 1952 and 1956, but then dropped again in 1960 and 1964. Following the 1964 election, the association between results began to increase and by the

2000s, it returned to the level of the early 1900s. The process of change took almost fifty years (from 1948 to 2000) before the results for presidential and House results were strongly associated again.

The association between presidential and Senate election results has followed essentially the same pattern. In this case, the correlation is between state presidential percentages and those received by Senate candidates running in that year. Only one-third of Senate seats are up for election in any one year, which could make the association much more erratic depending on the states involved. Even with that, the pattern shown in Figure 2.4 is roughly the same as for president–House results. The association is high until 1948. The relationship returns to a relatively high level in 1952 and 1956 and then declines to nothing in the 1960s. Since then, with retirements and realignment occurring, the association has been increasing steadily.

This disconnect between presidential and congressional election results led to considerable uncertainty about the state of parties in the 1970s and 1980s. Surveys indicated that more voters saw themselves as independents and thus not attached to a major party. It was easy to speculate that maybe parties were on the decline within the electorate.[4] In reality, the era was one of transition of party bases.

This realignment process did not affect just the association between election results. It also created a prolonged period in which there was an increase in split-outcomes, or the partisan winner of House and Senate elections was different from which presidential candidate won the district or the state. Presidential candidates led the process of change, yet congressional incumbents persisted. Figure 2.5 indicates the percentage of House districts in which the winners of the presidential and House candidates were from the same party. During the first half of the 1900s, the percentage of districts in which partisan winners were the same was very high. Beginning with the 1948 election, there was a steady decline in unified partisan winners. This culminated in the 1984 election when only 54 percent of districts had the same party winning both contests in House districts. Since then, there has been a sustained increase of the same party winning presidential and House elections within districts.

The same process of change has affected the Senate. This pattern is evident even though only one-third of senators are elected in any election

[4] For examples, see Norman H. Nie, Sidney Verba, and John R. Petrocik, *The Changing American Voter* (Cambridge, MA: Harvard University Press, 1976); Martin P. Wattenberg, *The Decline of American Political Parties, 1952–1996* (Cambridge, MA: Harvard University Press, 1998).

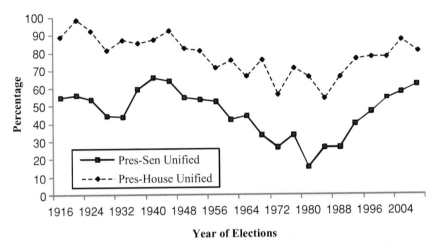

FIGURE 2.5. Percent of districts and states with same party winning presidential and congressional elections, 1916–2008

year. Figure 2.5 indicates the percentage of states in which the partisan presidential outcome was the same as the partisanship of the Senate delegation. The partisanship of the Senate delegation is determined by the outcome of any election held that year plus the party of the senator continuing in office that year. For example, if a Republican presidential candidate won the state but two Democratic senators continued in office, the result is no unified partisan outcome. If a Republican presidential candidate won the state and a Republican senator continues in office and another Republican wins a seat up for election, the outcome is unified. The concern here is with whether the outcome is unified. Because only one-third of Senate seats are up for reelection each election year, the degree of unity is certain to be less than for the House, with elections every year, and that has proven to be the case.

The decline in unified outcomes began in the 1940s and reached a low point in 1980. In that year, only 15 percent of the states had the same party winning the presidential election and holding both Senate seats after the election was held. Since 1980, there has been a sustained and rapid increase in the overlap of partisan presidential and Senate results.

The presence of unified partisan delegations – regardless of presidential results – has followed the same pattern. Seventy to 80 percent of state delegations were unified until the mid-1950s. Then a decline set in, plummeting to 46 percent in 1980. Since then it has increased, and following the 2008 elections 72 percent of state delegations were unified.

The decline in unified outcomes that occurred through the 1980s made interpreting the status of parties difficult. It created an increase in divided government, with one party holding the presidency and another controlling one or both houses of Congress. It created a strong need for presidents to work with the opposing party. Many attempted to explain this occurrence as perhaps a product of what voters wanted – balanced government – as a means of creating a moderate government.[5] In reality, the rise in divided government that occurred from 1950 through 2000 was a by-product of the uneven pace of realignment in presidential and congressional elections. Although this was difficult to see while change was occurring, it became clearer with the passage of time.

INTERNAL PARTY CONFLICTS

The other major impact of the shifting agendas prompted by presidential candidates was that some existing members were reluctant to accept the changes, creating more divisiveness within each party. When Franklin Roosevelt was elected president in 1932, he and the Northern wing of the party pushed for federal programs that provided direct benefits to individuals. He also supported greater federal management of the economy. Southern Democrats, who had embraced federal action to help farmers and regulate railroads and banks, did not want to expand the federal role that much. They had been liberal in the sense that government should help agriculture, but were reluctant to accept this broader notion of liberalism to help individuals and intrude into the economy.[6] The Southern wing gradually moved to more moderate positions, thus reducing the unity of the party. Figure 2.6 provides an indication of the broad changes that occurred. It indicates what percentage of Senate Democratic Party members had liberal, moderate, and conservative voting records.[7] This rise and decline in party diversity also unfolded within the House Democratic Party.

With Democratic presidents pushing a more liberal agenda and the Northern wing of the party supporting this, Southern Democrats became a source of disunity. Eventually, as realignment unfolded, Southern

[5] Gary C. Jacobson, *The Electoral Origins of Divided Government* (Boulder, CO: Westview, 1990); and Morris P. Fiorina, *Divided Government* (Boston: Allyn and Bacon, 1996).
[6] Bond, Fleisher, and Stonecash, "The Decline of Moderates in the House of Representatives, 1876–2004."
[7] These classifications are determined using analyses of voting records by Keith Poole and Howard Rosenthal.

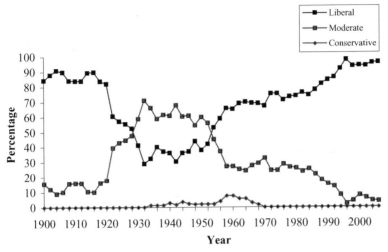

FIGURE 2.6. Distribution of Senate Democratic members' voting records, 1900–2006

Democrats were replaced by Republicans with more conservative voting records or liberal Democrats.

Within the Republican Party, dissent developed later and more slowly because change within the party developed later. Gradually, as shown in Figure 2.7, the party acquired more members who were opposed to all the liberal legislation passed by the Democrats, first in the 1930s and

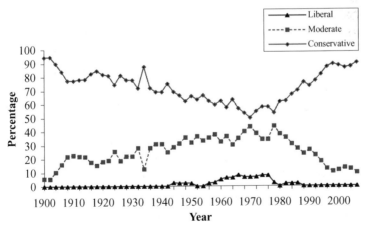

FIGURE 2.7. Distribution of Senate Republican members' voting records, 1900–2006. *Source:* Presidential election results compiled by the author; DW-Nominate scores taken from the Web page of Keith Poole, at: http://voteview.com/dwnl.htm

then in the 1960s. The conservative wing of the party began to push for more conservative positions. Some Senate Republicans, and particularly those from the more moderate Northeast, were more inclined to accept at least some of the liberal legislation. They became the moderates and reduced Republican Party unity as they voted with Northern Democrats for various pieces of liberal legislation. Again, the same pattern prevailed in the House. As realignment unfolded, these moderates were eventually replaced by liberal Democrats or more conservative Republicans, and the divisiveness within the party declined.

THE CONSEQUENCES FOR PARTY UNITY

The disconnection between presidential and House results had enormous consequences for party unity and image. As the separation of presidential and congressional results unfolded, more and more representatives and senators found themselves in situations where their state or district was being won by a presidential candidate from the other party. If presidential results are taken as an indication of the partisan and policy inclinations of states and districts, many legislators were running in a state or district that was becoming less inclined to support the presidential candidates of the party. In the 1950s through much of the 1980s, many Southern Democrats were defecting from their party because their districts were not liberal. Northern Republicans were defecting from their party because their districts were not willing to support the conservative candidates and positions being adopted by the party's presidential candidates. This resulted in a decline in the unity of party voting within the Senate and the House.

Figure 2.8 indicates what happened in the Senate, with the House following the same pattern. The lines track the average percentage of times that Democrats voted with their party and the average percentage of times that Republicans voted with their party. Party unity ranged from 80 to 90 percent from 1870 through the 1920s, but dropped for both parties into the low 70s during the 1970s. More senators were voting with the opposing party. The internal divisiveness of each party made unity difficult for many years. Party unity was not only a problem for the congressional parties. Presidents also needed to build coalitions that were bipartisan. They had to approach Democrats and Republicans to create a majority for their legislative agenda. Much of the significant legislation that presidents initiated and passed during the 1960s and 1970s was

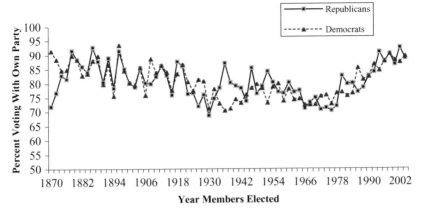

FIGURE 2.8. Average party unity score by party, Senate, 1870–2006

supported by both Democrats and Republicans.[8] Cross-party coalitions became more prevalent.

However, beginning in the 1980s the realignment process changed that. Existing members were defeated or retired and were replaced by members who were more sympathetic to the policy directions each party was taking. As previously shown in Figures 2.4 and 2.5, presidential and congressional outcomes came into greater congruity. The party that was winning presidential and congressional elections within states and House districts became the same, so that party members increasingly shared the same electoral base as their presidential candidates. More party members found that they had an electoral base similar to other congressional party members. Party unity became easier to achieve. Recent presidents (George W. Bush in particular) have focused on creating support within their party and paid far less attention to reaching out to the other party because of their shared electoral base. Because of this, bipartisan voting has declined and polarized parties have become the norm in the 2000s.

These changes over time have affected the differences between the parties. Using a measure of how liberal or conservative a member's voting record is, it is possible to calculate an average score for each party over time and then the difference between the two parties.[9] This can be

---

[8] David R. Mayhew, *Divided We Govern: Party Control, Lawmaking, and Investigations, 1946–1990* (New Haven, CT: Yale University Press, 1991).

[9] These data are taken from work done by Keith Poole. He has analyzed the voting records of members of the Senate and House and derived measures of the placement of members relative to others within the respective houses of the Congress. For those interested in

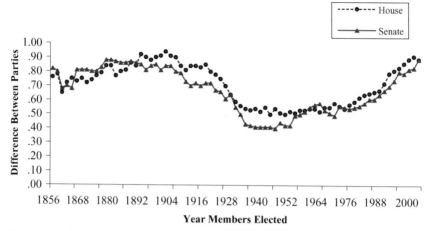

FIGURE 2.9. Average congressional party differences, 1856–2006

done for the Senate and the House, and the results are presented in Figure 2.9. In the early 1900s, the parties in Congress had very different voting records. As change created more diversity within each party, the average differences between the parties declined. As the sorting-out process continued, the diversity within each party in each House declined and the differences began to increase again.

PARTY CHANGE AND PARTY IMAGES

Political parties are presumed to play a major role in a democracy. Many voters are trying to sort out which party, if any, best represents their concerns. Voters are more likely to have a sense that parties differ and what each party stands for when elected officials within one party take relatively similar positions and act as unified entities, and opposing party officials advocate different positions. During the 1970s, it was clear that such a situation did not exist. The process of change created considerable diversity within parties and diminished the differences between them.

The result was that it was not always clear to voters that parties differed significantly. The diversity within parties – and the cross-party coalitions that occurred in the 1950s through the 1970s – diminished any sense of

these data, see: http://voteview.com/dwnl.htm. The derivation of these data is complicated, but essentially the process compares how much a member lines up with his party. Whether this measures ideology or the degree to which a member agrees with a position taken by his or her party, the measure captures differences in position taking and the average captures differences in position taking between the parties.

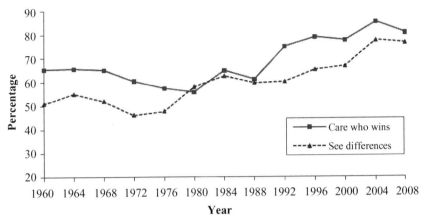

FIGURE 2.10. Voter awareness of party differences, 1960–2008. *Source:* NES Cumulative File, 1948–2004, NES 2008 Time Series Study

difference between the parties. To many Americans, the claim of Alabama Governor George Wallace that there wasn't "a dime's worth of difference" between the Democrats and Republicans appeared to be somewhat accurate. For many years, a bipartisan coalition of Southern Democrats and Northern Republicans regularly dominated Congress, blocking a considerable amount of legislation that liberals wanted. When presidents were able to pass liberal legislation, it was often done with bipartisan coalitions of liberals and moderates pulled from both parties. The Democratic Party contained liberals and conservatives, and the Republican Party also contained considerable diversity. Determining just how different the parties were could not have been easy.

That diversity has declined in recent decades. Each party now presents a clear and different image. During the last decade Republicans have strongly supported the Iraq War, tax cuts, and fewer government regulations in a wide array of policy areas. Most Democrats opposed the war, tax cuts, and have wanted the government to do more to enforce regulations on the private sector. These changes have made it easier for voters to see differences between the parties. Figure 2.10 tracks the reactions of voters to party differences from 1952 to 2008. Voters were asked if they care which party wins the presidency and whether they see a difference between the parties. In the 1960s and 1970s, about 50 percent of those voting saw a difference between the parties. Beginning in the 1980s, the perception of party differences began to increase and in 2004 it reached 78 percent and in 2008 it was 77 percent. The same pattern prevailed for concern about which party wins the presidency. As both parties have lost their moderate bloc and increasingly differ in their policy proposals, voters have come to see the differences between the parties.

THE PROCESS OF CHANGE

The lengthy process of change has created the polarization we are now experiencing. Parties that once derived large percentages of their supporters and seats from one region of the country sought to add new constituents to their electoral bases. Presidential candidates were particularly important to this process. They sought to add voters to create a majority and win. As they pursued their ideals and majorities, the congressional parties added members in new areas, sometimes creating new tensions within their party as the composition and concerns of the party adjusted. The process of change was lengthy, gradual, and sometimes erratic, but it eventually transformed the parties. It took voters considerable time to recognize how much the parties differ, but now they do.

Our goal in subsequent chapters is to explain how and why these changes in party bases occurred, why the changes created diversity within each party, and why the eventual outcome has been very different parties. It is a process of change that seems clear only in retrospect. To those involved as change occurred, where the process would end up was very uncertain. There were disputes about whether changing policy priorities would pay off by attracting new voters. There were anxieties about interpreting results. There were party defeats that led members to question the directions and strategies being pursued. Uncertainty was ever present in the process. The struggle to pursue policy and political goals and build majorities in a democracy is not a simple process, but it is a fascinating story of how parties seek to represent concerns within a democracy.

3 Taking Shape: Party Coalitions in the Post-Bellum Nineteenth Century

We begin examining the evolution of American political parties in the post-bellum nineteenth century, starting with the 1876 election cycle. By 1876, *Reconstruction* (the efforts of the North to regulate the South and create a society where blacks had some rights) was ending as Northerners tired of the conflict the issue was creating. Furthermore, a deal had been struck in Congress: In exchange for accepting Republican Rutherford Hayes as the winner of the disputed 1876 presidential election, southerners were promised an end to Reconstruction. The result was that the national playing field had largely returned to normal by 1876. All of the former Confederate states had been readmitted to the Union,[1] and almost all former Confederate soldiers and officials had regained full political privileges.[2] We will end this chapter with a discussion of the 1892 election cycle, the final year in what can be described as a twenty-year dead heat in American electoral politics, at least as aggregated to the national level. The 1892 elections were also the final round of federal contests before the party alignment underwent a relatively dramatic change in favor of the Republican Party, which is the subject of the next chapter. This chapter focuses on the period from 1876 to 1892 and how the parties tried to construct winning coalitions for themselves during these years.

PARTISAN CONFLICT IN THE POST-BELLUM NINETEENTH CENTURY

As Joel Silbey describes it, political conflict in the United States from the late 1830s through the early 1890s was almost entirely organized and

---

[1] Georgia was the final state of the former Confederacy to be readmitted, on July 15, 1870.

[2] C. Vann Woodward, *Reunion and Reaction: The Compromise of 1877 and the End of Reconstruction* (Boston: Little, Brown, & Company, 1951).

expressed through the political parties: "Political parties were serious, and Americans took them seriously."[3] Such seriousness was present with good reason. Electoral competition between the parties from 1876–1892 was incredibly close, at least when the individual district and state contests for federal office were aggregated to the national level. In the words of Walter Dean Burnham, during these years "there was in fact no national majority for either party."[4] The presidential elections of this period speak to the closeness of partisan divisions. The Republicans and the Democrats were separated in the popular vote in three of the five presidential elections from 1876–1892 by less than one percentage point, and in the other two the difference was a mere three percentage points. Even the Electoral College vote, which tends to produce much larger margins for the winner than does the popular vote, was close during this time. Only in 1892 did the difference in electoral votes exceed 100 votes, and in the disputed election of 1876, the difference was one electoral vote. Even if this closeness in presidential elections was largely the product of only a handful of states, as Ware notes, outcomes were always in doubt, often right until Election Day (and in the case of 1876 far beyond).[5] Citizens were highly concerned with these outcomes, and responded with very high levels of participation.[6]

Some scholars argue that this intense partisan conflict of the late nineteenth century was largely devoid of substance. In this view, partisan conflict was still driven largely by the Civil War, and both the Republican and Democratic Parties inspired and mobilized their supporters by "waving the bloody shirt" and urging voters to "remember the

---

[3] Joel H. Silbey, *The American Political Nation, 1838–1893* (Stanford, CA: Stanford University Press, 1991). Quote on p. 146.

[4] Walter Dean Burnham, *Critical Elections and the Mainsprings of American Politics* (New York: W.W. Norton, 1970), 32.

[5] Alan Ware, *The Democratic Party Heads North, 1877–1962* (New York: Cambridge University Press, 2006). For more on the closeness of post-Reconstruction nineteenth-century elections, see Paul Kleppner, *The Cross of Culture: A Social Analysis of Midwestern Politics, 1850–1900* (New York: The Free Press, 1970); Paul Kleppner, *The Third Electoral System, 1853–1892* (Chapel Hill: University of North Carolina Press, 1979); Gretchen Ritter, *Goldbugs and Greenbacks: The Antimonopoly Tradition and the Politics of Finance in America, 1865–1896* (New York: Cambridge University Press, 1997); and Stephen Skowronek, *Building a New American State: The Expansion of National Administrative Capacities, 1877–1920* (New York: Cambridge University Press, 1982).

[6] Paul Kleppner, "Partisanship and Ethnoreligious Conflict: The Third Electoral System, 1853–1892," in Paul Kleppner (ed.), *The Evolution of American Electoral Systems* (Westport, CT: Greenwood Press, 1981), 114–46; Michael E. McGerr, *The Decline of Popular Politics* (New York: Oxford University Press, 1986).

lost cause."[7] However, portraying partisan conflict from 1876 to 1892 as without issues is incorrect. Certainly the Civil War remained fresh in voters' minds, and partisan battles during this period contained a strong sectional component. Yet there was more to the contest between the parties than Civil War grudges and animosities. There were major differences between the parties, and these differences were meaningful and salient.[8] In addition to the sectional divide left over from the Civil War (in reality already in place before the war, as will be discussed momentarily), conflict between the Republican and Democratic Parties also involved significant cleavages centered on issues of religion and ethnicity and also an industrial/urban and agrarian/rural divide.

SECTIONAL DIVISIONS

Although the North–South division was not the only cleavage in postbellum nineteenth-century American politics, it certainly was an important one, and a case can be made that any examination of partisan combat during this period needs to begin with a focus on geography. Even after the Civil War and Reconstruction ended, the Republicans and the Democrats continued to clash over war- and Reconstruction-related issues. These clashes combined with still intense hostility over the war itself to create a strong sectional division between the parties.[9] In fact, this division was in many ways present in the last few election cycles leading up to the Civil War, and reappeared in an even stronger fashion as normalcy gradually reappeared in the nation's politics in the 1870s.[10]

It is not surprising that the Civil War – a conflict that pitted American against American, was fought within U.S. boundaries, and resulted in the most military fatalities of any conflict in the history of American military involvement – would remain politically potent even after its conclusion.[11] Both parties – the Republicans in the states that remained in the Union

[7] For examples of such an analysis, see Lawrence Goodwyn, *Democratic Promise: The Populist Moment in America* (New York: Oxford University Press, 1976); James L. Sundquist, *Dynamics of the Party System: Alignment and Realignment of Political Parties in the United States*, revised edition (Washington, DC: Brookings Institution Press, 1983).

[8] Silbey, *The American Political Nation, 1838–1893*.

[9] Sundquist, *Dynamics of the Party System*.

[10] Kleppner, *The Third Electoral System, 1853–1892*; Ware, *The Democratic Party Heads North, 1877–1962*.

[11] Hannah Fischer, Kim Klarman, and Mari-Jana Oboroceanu, "American War and Military Operations Casualties: Lists and Statistics" (Washington, DC: Congressional Research Service), June 29, 2007.

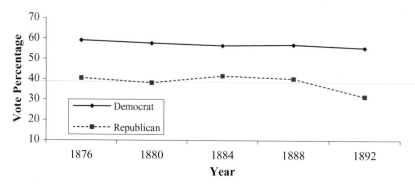

FIGURE 3.1. Democratic and Republican presidential candidates vote percentages, South, 1876–1892

and the Democrats in the former Confederate states – eagerly and often utilized the politics of "waving the bloody shirt," or, in other words, rallying their supporters on the basis of Southern secession or Northern aggression as appropriate.[12] The political importance of this episode in American history did not end with General Lee's surrender at the Appomattox Courthouse in 1865 or with the formal end of Reconstruction in 1877; its impact was still pronounced throughout the rest of the nineteenth century, and in some parts of the United States, far into the twentieth century as well.

Civil War-related themes were used successfully by both parties in all regions of the country, but the political aftereffects of the war were strongest in the South. In many ways the South came out of the Civil War and Reconstruction as a more separate and distinct region than it was before the conflict began.[13] This political distinctness is shown in Figures 3.1 and 3.2.[14] Figure 3.1 presents the percentage of the vote won in

[12] Mark Wahlgren Summers, *Rum, Romanism, and Rebellion: The Making of a President, 1884* (Chapel Hill: University of North Carolina Press, 2000).

[13] C. Vann Woodward, *Origins of the New South, 1877–1913* (Baton Rouge: Louisiana State University Press, 1951).

[14] All aggregate data for both presidential and House elections used in this book come from Jerrold G. Rusk, *A Statistical History of the American Electorate* (Washington, DC: CQ Press, 2001) (years 1876–1998) and Richard M. Scammon, Alice V. McGillivray, and Rhodes Cook, *America Votes 24* (Washington, DC: CQ Press, 2001) (year 2000); Scammon, McGillivray, and Cook, *America Votes 25* (year 2002); Scammon, McGillivray, and Cook, *America Votes 26* (year 2004); and Cook, McGillivray, and Scammon, *America Votes 26* (year 2006). In the nineteenth century, it was not unusual for states to elect members of the House in both at-large and district-based elections. When this is the case, we follow Rusk's decision and use only the at-large results to determine the state vote by party. Rusk provides an alternate measure using the district votes in Appendix B of his work. Also, no special elections are included in the House data.

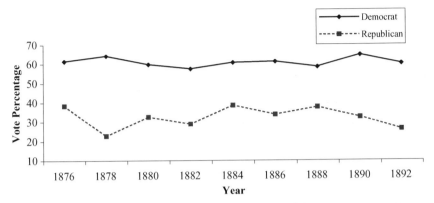

FIGURE 3.2. Democratic and Republican House candidates vote percentages, South, 1876–1892

presidential elections for Democratic and Republican presidential candidates in the South from 1876 to 1892, whereas Figure 3.2 presents the vote percentages for party candidates for House seats during this same period in the South.[15]

For both presidential and House elections, Democrats held a large advantage over Republicans in the South during these years. Democratic dominance in the South is even more pronounced if one examines Electoral College results. After 1876, when the Republicans were judged to have won the disputed electoral votes of Florida, Louisiana, and South Carolina, the GOP did not win a single electoral vote in any of the Southern states from 1880 to 1892. Many white Southerners did indeed "vote as they shot" in post–Civil War, nineteenth-century elections. The legacy of the Civil War also extended to areas outside the South, with Republicans regularly trying to tie Democrats outside the South to the taint of Southern rebellion.[16]

In two other regions of the country, this lopsided advantage for one party did not prevail. In the Northeast and Midwest, elections were very close. The partisan vote percentages for 1876–1892 in the Northeast are shown in Figures 3.3 and 3.4, and those for the Midwest are in Figures 3.5

[15] We roughly use the Mason-Dixon Line to define the states that make up the South. Although in some instances we utilize only the eleven states of the former Confederacy when discussing the South, we also make sure to note this distinction. Unless otherwise indicated, the South as defined in this study is comprised of: Alabama, Arkansas, Florida, Georgia, Louisiana, Mississippi, North Carolina, South Carolina, Tennessee, Texas, Virginia, District of Columbia (for presidential elections only once the District becomes eligible to participate in the Electoral College), Kentucky, Maryland, Missouri, Oklahoma, and West Virginia.

[16] Summers, *Rum, Romanism, and Rebellion: The Making of a President, 1884.*

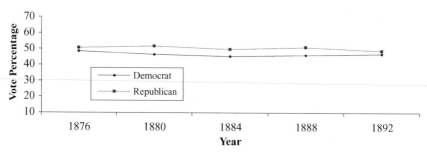

FIGURE 3.3. Democratic and Republican presidential candidates vote percentages, Northeast, 1876–1892

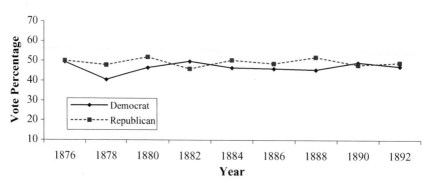

FIGURE 3.4. Democratic and Republican House candidates vote percentages, Northeast, 1876–1892

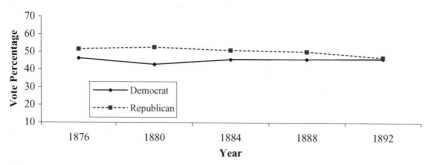

FIGURE 3.5. Democratic and Republican presidential candidates vote percentages, Midwest, 1876–1892

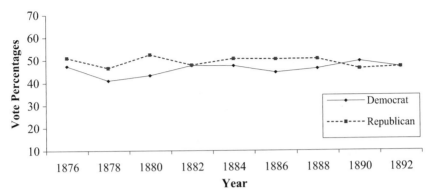

FIGURE 3.6. Democratic and Republican House candidates' percentage of the total vote in the Midwest, 1876–1892

and 3.6.[17] Although elections were closer in these two regions, the GOP slightly outpolled the Democrats on Election Day in the majority of election cycles from 1876 to 1892. At least part of this slim Republican advantage can be ascribed to the fact that they were the party of the Union and abolition, whereas the Democrats were the party of the Confederacy and slavery.

Although Republicans lost badly in the South and faced close elections in the Northeast and Midwest, they regularly did well in the West, offsetting the South to some extent. As Figures 3.7 and 3.8 indicate, Republicans consistently had a substantial advantage over Democrats in the West. The overall effect of these regional situations was to produce very competitive national outcomes. Democrats dominated the South, Republicans the West, and the two areas containing most of the population – the Northeast and Midwest – consistently had close elections, but with Republicans generally holding a slight edge over Democrats.

ETHNO-RELIGIOUS DIVISIONS

Whereas the Republican Party was the party of preference outside the South from 1876 to 1892, the GOP's edge over the Democrats was relatively slim in the Northeast and the Midwest. It is clear that not everyone

[17] The Northeast is defined here as Connecticut, Delaware, Maine, Massachusetts, New Hampshire, New Jersey, New York, Pennsylvania, Rhode Island, and Vermont. The Midwest is defined as Illinois, Indiana, Iowa, Michigan, Minnesota, Ohio, and Wisconsin. The West is defined as Arizona, Colorado, Idaho, Kansas, Montana, Nebraska, Nevada, New Mexico, North Dakota, South Dakota, Utah, Wyoming, Alaska, California, Hawaii, Oregon, and Washington.

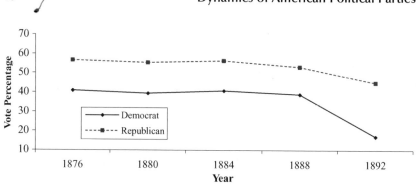

FIGURE 3.7. Democratic and Republican presidential candidates vote percentages, West, 1876–1892

outside of the South was driven into the arms of the Republican Party because of the Democrats' association with the South and the former Confederacy.[18] Many Americans outside of the South were voting Democratic in presidential and House elections. The important question is why were they doing so?

At least part of the answer has to do with issues surrounding religion and ethnicity. Starting in the 1830s, American society was fundamentally altered by an almost one-hundred-year period of immigration unlike that seen by any other nation in modern history. For decades, wave after wave of immigrants landed on America's shores, each one altering the composition of American society. In the first half of this period of immigration, the bulk of the new arrivals came from Northern and Western Europe, whereas in the second half the majority of immigrants came from Southern and Eastern Europe. Regardless of where in Europe the immigrants originated, many of them were Roman Catholic.[19] This religious identity, along with their ethnicity, served to mark them as distinct and different from the majority of those who already called the United States home. As is often the case in politics, this distinctiveness translated into political and eventually partisan conflict. The roots of this conflict can be found in nativism and anti-Catholicism.

Anti-Catholicism has a long history in the United States, and was incredibly widespread in nineteenth-century America. In Billington's words, "The average Protestant American of the 1850s had been trained

---

[18] Ware, *The Democratic Party Heads North, 1877–1962*.

[19] Maldwyn Allen Jones, *American Immigration*, second edition (Chicago: University of Chicago Press, 1992).

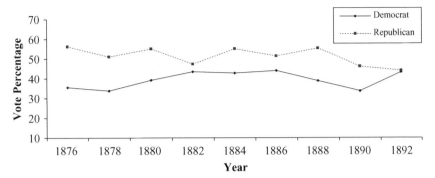

FIGURE 3.8. Democratic and Republican House candidates' percentage of the total vote in the West, 1876–1892

from birth to hate Catholicism."[20] *Nativism*, or hostility toward immigrants because they lack the so-called proper character, also has a long history in the United States. Because many of the immigrants arriving in America were Catholic, nativism and anti-Catholicism soon became inextricably linked during the nineteenth century.[21] By the 1850s, a powerful political movement known as the *Know-Nothings* had developed to push issues of nativism and anti-Catholicism to the forefront of American politics. The Know-Nothings collapsed by the middle of the decade because of internal disputes over slavery, but many former members eventually found their way into the newly formed Republican Party by the end of the decade.[22] So while the GOP has its origins in the abolition of slavery, it also was identified with anti-immigrant and anti-Catholic sentiment as well.[23] This would prove critical to post-bellum nineteenth-century conflict between the parties.

[20] Ray Allen Billington, *The Protestant Crusade 1800–1860: A Study of the Origins of American Nativism* (New York: Macmillan, 1938), quote on p. 345.

[21] Billington, *The Protestant Crusade 1800–1860*. See also Jay P. Dolan, *The American Catholic Experience: A History from Colonial Times to the Present* (Notre Dame, IN: University of Notre Dame Press, 1992).

[22] Tyler Anbinder, *Nativism and Slavery: The Northern Know Nothings and the Politics of the 1850s* (New York: Oxford University Press, 1992); William E. Gienapp, "Nativism and the Creation of a Republican Majority in the North before the Civil War," *Journal of American History* 72 (December 1985): 529–59. The Republicans were also closely tied to the popular anti-Catholic organization of the late 1880s and early 1890s, the American Protective Association (APA). For more on the connections between the GOP and the APA, see Donald L. Kinzer, *An Episode in Anti-Catholicism: The American Protective Association* (Seattle: University of Washington Press, 1964).

[23] Joel H. Silbey, *The Transformation of American Politics, 1840–1860* (Englewood Cliffs, NJ: Prentice Hall, 1967).

The Republican Party from its very outset saw itself as the defender of morality in American society, the vehicle of grand moral reform in American politics. In nineteenth-century America, this meant abolishing slavery, but it also entailed support for keeping Protestantism in public schools and preventing public money from going to Catholic schools, creating and enforcing laws that preserved the sanctity of the Sabbath, and working toward restrictions on and eventually prohibition of alcohol. The GOP was in favor of using the power of the federal government to enforce proper social behaviors. The Democrats, on the other hand, were the party of liberty, at least for white male citizens. They were strongly opposed to an active and powerful national government, instead believing that issues of morality and personal behavior should be left to the state governments or to individuals themselves. This was central to their stand on the issue of slavery, but it is also highly relevant to the other issues outlined earlier. In short, the Republican Party wanted to use federal power to enforce what it saw as proper moral behavior, whereas the Democrats opposed such actions.[24]

These matters played out in post–Civil War nineteenth-century politics in a relatively predictable manner, at least outside of the South. As the party more strongly identified with nativist and anti-Catholic views, efforts to curb immigration, and willingness to use federal power to enforce morality, the Republicans attracted the support of so-called old-stock Protestants, particularly those Protestants belonging to denominations that Jensen and Kleppner label "pietistic," meaning in part that they believed in efforts to change a sinful world into something more in line with what God had in mind. In the eyes of pietists government action which supported establishing proper moral behavior would be a fine way to create a more moral society.

As for the Democrats, their opposition to federal government intervention in state and individual affairs, combined with their image outside of the South as the party more sympathetic to Catholics and immigrants, served to attract some immigrants, Catholics, and also Protestants who belonged to denominations that were more "liturgical" (Jensen's term) or "ritualistic" (Kleppner's term). Holders of a liturgical or ritualistic perspective place a greater emphasis on following historical church doctrine and formalized ritual practices. For these individuals and for Catholics as

[24] John Gerring, *Party Ideologies in America, 1828–1996* (New York: Cambridge University Press, 1998); Mark Wahlgren Summers, *Party Games: Getting, Keeping, and Using Power in Gilded Age Politics* (Chapel Hill: University of North Carolina Press, 2004).

well, the government should have a very limited role in personal behavior. The world may be a sinful place, but the government has no place in remedying the situation. Such efforts are properly left to the church or to the individual.[25] These partisan differences set up a powerful ethno-religious cleavage in American politics of this period (again, except in the South), the results of which can be seen in Figures 3.3 through 3.8. In those regions of the country where Catholics, Protestants, old-stock, and newer immigrants were relatively evenly matched (e.g., the Northeast and the Midwest), partisan competition was quite evenly balanced. Only in the West, where there were fewer Catholics and fewer immigrants, did the GOP enjoy a relatively substantial edge.

THE URBAN/INDUSTRIAL AND RURAL/AGRARIAN DIVIDE

One additional cleavage existed alongside sectionalism and ethno-religious issues: a division between the rapidly growing urban and industrial America and the declining rural and agrarian America. The debate over which of these models American society should follow has a long history. The question of whether the United States should be a nation of small farmers and small towns or a nation of large cities booming with the business activities of manufacturing and trade go back at least to the debates between Thomas Jefferson and his supporters and Alexander Hamilton and his supporters. However, in the late nineteenth century, the debate began to take on an increased urgency, even though for all intents and purposes the question had already been settled.

Then, just as now, the Republican Party was the party of business. Northern industrialists had profited handsomely from the Civil War and the Republican policies during this period, and they were more supportive of the party.[26] The GOP strongly believed in using the power of the federal government to promote increased industrialization and economic growth, while opposing the use of government power to regulate markets or firms that would harm business. In the words of Gerring, "If ever there was a time when the business of America was business, it was the

---

[25] Richard Jensen, *The Winning of the Midwest* (Chicago: University of Chicago Press, 1971); Kleppner, *The Cross of Culture*; Kleppner, *The Third Electoral System, 1853–1892*. See also Mark D. Brewer, *Relevant No More? The Catholic/Protestant Divide in American Electoral Politics* (Lanham, MD: Lexington Books, 2003), Ch. 2.

[26] Everett Carll Ladd, Jr., *American Political Parties: Social Change and Political Response* (New York: W.W. Norton, 1970); Sundquist, *Dynamics of the Party System*.

post-Civil War period. And the Republican Party was preeminently the party of business."[27]

The most important policy issue in American politics after the Civil War was the tariff. The Republicans were firmly in favor of a high protective tariff designed to insulate American business from foreign competition. The tariff served several crucial purposes for the party. It protected American businesses from international competition by raising the price of foreign goods. It provided revenue for the national government without having to impose taxes on individuals. It specifically provided revenue to fund pensions for Union Civil War veterans, which increased their loyalty to the Republican Party.[28]

Yet the Republicans were not just the party of business. The GOP also did fairly well among the urban working class. Republican leaders and platforms of this period regularly extolled the virtues of workers and an honest day's work, arguing that workers were the backbone of the party and also of the nation. The Republican Party also pointed to its high tariff stance, telling workers that this policy kept out cheap foreign goods that if let into the country duty-free would cost them their jobs. Even if the jobs of urban workers weren't the greatest, a job always beats no job. So many urban workers in the industrial areas of the Northeast and Midwest, especially non-Catholic ones, threw their support behind the GOP.[29] Thus, outside of the South, the Republican Party was the party of industrialization and economic growth. The party argued that promoting economic growth would be good for everyone and government should do what it could to support the growth of business. According to GOP wisdom, if business did well, workers would do well, and ultimately America would do well.

On the urban/industrial and rural/agrarian question, the Democrats were a coalition of conflicting interests that prevented them from taking a clear set of positions. The Democrats had an Eastern wing of the party that was supportive of business and industrialization in almost the same way the Republicans were. However, the Democrats were also overwhelmingly the party of the South. This gave the party a strong rural,

---

[27] Gerring, *Party Ideologies in America, 1828–1996*, p. 78. See also Summers, *Party Games: Getting, Keeping, and Using Power in Gilded Age Politics*.

[28] Richard F. Bensel, *The Political Economy of American Industrialization, 1877–1900* (New York: Cambridge University Press, 2000); Theda Skocpol, *Protecting Soldiers and Mothers: The Political Origins of Social Policy in the United States* (Cambridge, MA: Harvard University Press, 1992).

[29] Gerring, *Party Ideologies in America, 1828–1996*.

agrarian element to it as well. Then there was the party's burgeoning strength among the increasing immigrant, largely Catholic populations of the Northeastern and Midwestern cities. Soon the tensions between supporting both rural and urban concerns left the party with an image more muddled than that of the Republicans, an issue that we will explore more fully in the next chapter.[30] While this muddled image existed, the dominant faction within the Democratic fold defended the interests of agrarians and extolled the virtues of small town and rural life. Historian Robert Wiebe does an excellent job in describing the burning desire on the part of this faction of the Democratic Party to hang onto a society that was slipping away before its very eyes.[31] This faction within the party supported a "utopia that looked backward to the republic as it stood in 1789 rather than forward to the twentieth century."[32]

INTRAPARTY TENSIONS IN AN ENVIRONMENT OF PARTISAN STALEMATE

After the dust had settled and the results were in for the 1892 elections, the parties found themselves essentially where they had been in 1876. The Democrats controlled the presidency and both houses of Congress, but this control was delivered by tiny margins. Nationally, Democrat Grover Cleveland had defeated Republican incumbent Benjamin Harrison in the popular vote 46 to 43 percent. Regionally, the Republican presidential candidate Harrison took the popular vote in the Northeast 49 to 47 percent, the Midwest 47 to 46 percent, and the West 45 to 37 percent. Only in the South did Cleveland win at least a plurality of the popular vote, 55 to 32 percent. The popular vote totals in House elections by region were even closer. The Republicans claimed the Northeast 49 to 47 percent and the West 44 to 43 percent. The Midwest was a dead heat at 47 to 47 percent, and the Democrats came out ahead in the South at 60 to 26 percent. Neither party had a clear advantage over the other in the contest for national power, but both had plenty of motivation to expand their electoral coalitions. Both parties had opportunities as well, largely due to the one region that has received the least attention thus far: the West.

---

[30] Gerring, *Party Ideologies in America, 1828–1996*; Goodwyn, *The Populist Moment in America*; Ralph M. Goodman, *Search for Consensus: The Story of the Democratic Party* (Philadelphia: Temple University Press, 1979); Ritter, *Goldbugs and Greenbacks*; Summers, *Party Games*.
[31] Robert H. Wiebe, *The Search For Order, 1877–1920* (New York: Hill and Wang, 1967).
[32] Gerring, *Party Ideologies in America, 1828–1996*, p. 162.

As the nineteenth century progressed in the years after the Civil War, the West began to rise in importance in American politics.[33] As Americans flocked toward the Pacific and new states were rapidly added to the Union, both parties were presented with the challenges and opportunities provided by a quickly evolving electoral landscape. The opportunity in the West was the chance to attract new voters and gain more Electoral College votes and seats in the House of Representatives. The challenge was that as time passed, it became increasingly clear that the political views and interests of the West did not match up perfectly with establishment views of either party.

As the West became more populated, the initial beneficiary was the Republican Party. As seen in Figures 3.7 and 3.8, the West tended to be relatively Republican in both presidential and House elections in the 1870s. Yet while the GOP never lost this region to the Democrats during the period under examination in this chapter, their percentage of the vote did begin to decline, first in House races and then in presidential elections. Increasingly, agrarian and mining interests in the West were becoming unhappy with what they saw as the Republican Party's protection of big corporations at their expense. Tensions over the issue of gold versus silver being used to back American currency – an issue that will get much more attention in the next chapter – grew particularly heated, and many Western interests increasingly called for change, in many instances radical political and economic change.[34] This was potentially problematic for the Republican Party, who recognized that with no hope of winning in the South they had to have at least some success in the West.[35]

Some Democrats saw the growing discontent in the West as an opportunity for the party to expand its coalition. After all, the party already had a large agrarian wing in the South that shared much of the West's anger at Northeastern banks and railroads.[36] However, the Democrats also found themselves in a bit of a conundrum as they contemplated winning the West. The party still had its Northeastern wing, which was closely affiliated with the same corporate and financial interests the West was railing against. In fact, the current Democratic president – Grover

---

[33] Ware, *The Democratic Party Heads North, 1877–1962.*

[34] Goodwyn, *Democratic Promise: The Populist Moment in America*; Ritter, *Goldbugs and Greenbacks*; Sundquist, *Dynamics of the Party System*; and Wiebe, *The Search for Order.*

[35] Summers, *Rum, Romanism, and Rebellion.*

[36] Sundquist, *Dynamics of the Party System.*

Cleveland – was firmly in the camp of this faction.[37] Then there was the immigrant/Catholic wing of the party located in the Northeast and the Midwest. This faction also failed to mesh closely with Cleveland and the Eastern corporate wing, and it was at best unclear how this faction would react to a party that reached out to the West.

The culmination of the 1892 election season found America's two major parties in an uneasy stalemate. Both could attain power nationally, and both had at least a chance to win elections in every region except for the South, where the Democrats were firmly in control. But each could also just as easily lose elections and power. Uncertainty existed for both the Democrats and Republicans, contributing further to the close partisan divide. This stalemate would not last much longer. By 1896, both events and decisions on the part of leaders in both parties had combined to dramatically alter the partisan alignment.

---

[37] Alan Nevins, *Grover Cleveland: A Study in Courage* (New York: Dodd, Mead, and Company, 1932); Rexford G. Tugwell, *Grover Cleveland* (New York: Macmillan, 1968); Robert E. Welch, Jr., *The Presidencies of Grover Cleveland* (Lawrence, KS: University Press of Kansas, 1988).

4 Republican Ascendancy and Democratic Efforts to Respond, 1896–1928

As the Democrats reflected on the results of the 1892 election cycle, they had reason to be relatively pleased with themselves. They had captured the presidency, and although Grover Cleveland's three percentage point margin in the popular vote is not large by historical standards, it was larger than average in presidential elections from 1876–1892. Cleveland's 133-vote margin in the Electoral College was also a healthy one for this period. In addition, the Democrats controlled both Houses of Congress. Although the party did lose seventeen seats in the House because of the 1892 elections, it still had a comfortable ninety-one-seat edge over the Republicans. The Democrats recaptured the Senate for the first time since 1878, turning an eight-seat GOP advantage into a four-seat edge for themselves.[1] All in all, Democratic Party leaders and officeholders likely were relatively pleased with their performance at the ballot box in 1892.

This satisfaction, however, was short-lived for the Democrats. Change was in the air, and a combination of events and decisions made by the Democratic Party was about to transform the relatively balanced partisan battle of post-Reconstruction nineteenth-century America into a prolonged era of Republican domination at the national level.

A TIME OF TROUBLE: THE DEMOCRATS IN 1893 AND 1894

When he was inaugurated for his second term as president in March 1893, Grover Cleveland was already being warned by some of his economic advisors and various business leaders that trouble was brewing in

---

[1] Information on election results and seat divisions taken from Jerrold G. Rusk, *A Statistical History of the American Electorate* (Washington, DC: CQ Press, 2001; Office of the Clerk, U.S. House of Representatives; and U.S. Senate Historical Office.

the nation's economy.[2] By May 1893, it was clear that these voices were correct, and the United States had entered into a significant economic downturn. What became known as the *Panic of 1893* would devastate the American economy on virtually all fronts. By the end of 1893, the stock market had crashed, approximately five hundred banks had failed, and more than sixteen hundred businesses had closed their doors. During the winter of 1893–1894, some estimates placed national unemployment at 20 percent. Historical analysis would determine that the Panic of 1893 was the worst economic crisis that the United States had endured to that point in its history (today it ranks second only to the Great Depression in terms of national economic troubles, although this ranking could change as economists study the economic downturn of 2008–2009).[3] By the end of 1893, the national economy was in full meltdown, and Americans across the nation clamored for something to be done.

Cleveland was sure he knew what needed to be done. He was a hard money man, thoroughly committed to the gold standard and adamantly opposed to any place for silver in the American monetary system. Cleveland viewed gold as the only legitimate basis for a sound currency, and believed that adding silver as a base to the monetary system would only create inflation. Perhaps more important, he thought adding silver would increase uncertainty and fear among America's business and financial leaders, and that these two reactions were the primary causes of the nation's economic troubles. As such, one of Cleveland's first moves of his second term as president was the calling of a special session of Congress with the goal of repealing the Sherman Silver Purchase Act of 1890. This law required the federal government to purchase four million ounces of silver per month with Treasury notes. These notes were redeemable in gold, and Cleveland blamed the Silver Purchase Act for undermining the gold standard and sending the economy into a tailspin.[4]

---

[2] Richard E. Welch, Jr., *The Presidencies of Grover Cleveland* (Lawrence: University Press of Kansas, 1988).

[3] Charles Hoffmann, "The Depression of the Nineties," *Journal of Economic History* 16 (June 1956), 137–64; Gretchen Ritter, *Goldbugs and Greenbacks: The Antimonopoly Tradition and the Politics of Finance in America* (New York: Cambridge University Press, 1997); Welch, *The Presidencies of Grover Cleveland*.

[4] It is difficult for us today to see what all the tension and conflict was about in the debate over gold versus silver. However, we need to keep in mind that the question was hotly debated in the United States from the 1870s–1990s, and not just by financial and government elites. Average Americans had a prime role in the discussion as well. In addition to the economic implications of silver or gold, there was significant symbolism surrounding the currency question related to what type of nation the United States should be. For

In October 1893, Cleveland prevailed; the Senate repealed the Silver Purchase Act, matching the action taken earlier by the House. However, in taking the course he viewed as essential to preserving the gold standard and thus rescuing the American economy, Cleveland tore apart the Democratic Party. Many congressional Democrats, especially those in the South and the West, were strong supporters of some role for silver in America's monetary system, believing that it would make credit more easily available and life significantly better for their constituents.

Although seemingly an arcane question of how to manage a nation's money supply, the issue involved a fundamental economic division. Following the Civil War, a major issue emerged about managing how much money was available in the American economy. The battle pitted creditors from the East against farmers and other agrarian interests in the South and West.[5] Many wealthy individuals had loaned the Union large amounts of money to fund the war effort. They presumed they would be paid back, but were worried that the money supply would be increased, creating inflation. If the money supply doubled, *inflation* would run rampant, meaning for example that all goods that had been $1.00 would suddenly cost $2.00 (assuming the production of goods remained the same). If that happened and creditors were repaid only the $1.00 they had originally loaned, they would in reality be getting back fifty cents on a dollar (in purchasing power), or only half of their original investment. Creditors wanted a tight rein on growth in the money supply, and were actually able to get the government to shrink the money supply over time.

Farmers, who had to borrow money, were vehemently opposed to such a course of action. If a farmer borrowed $1,000 and prices suddenly increased due to the expanded money supply and resulting inflation, then they could pay back the $1,000 much easier, in dollars that were not worth as much as when they borrowed them. They wanted inflation, but were getting deflation, which meant that paying back loans was costing them more in terms of "real" dollar values. That made credit for farmers in the South and West more expensive. This credit was largely supplied by Eastern banks and the increasing cost of acquiring it had

more on this issue, see Ritter, *Goldbugs and Greenbacks*; Robert H. Wiebe, *The Search for Order, 1877–1920* (New York: Hill and Wang, 1967).

[5] For overviews of these developments, see Richard F. Bensel, *The Political Economy of American Industrialization, 1877–1900* (New York: Cambridge University Press, 2000); Ritter, *Goldbugs and Greenbacks*; Elizabeth Sanders, *Roots of Reform: Famers, Workers, and the American State, 1877–1917* (Chicago: University of Chicago Press, 1999); James L. Sundquist, *Dynamics of the Party System: Alignment and Dealignment of Political Parties in the United States*, revised edition (Washington, DC: Brookings Institution Press, 1983).

angered Westerners and Southerners. Because of where creditors and debtors were located, the issue accentuated regional conflicts.

The solution for many farmers was to increase the money supply by adding silver as a basis for issuing money. For decades, gold had been the sole basis for issuing money. After a prolonged battle, the proponents of expanding the money supply were able to enact the Sherman Silver Purchase Act in 1890, which added silver to the money supply. They strongly opposed repeal. Cleveland's ardor and tenacity (he ruthlessly used his control of federal patronage to get his way) in the repeal of the Silver Purchase Act alienated Democrats outside of the Northeast, many of whom already bitterly viewed him as nothing more than a tool of the nation's business and financial elite. This bitterness only intensified when Cleveland's administration brokered a deal in 1895 with the banking house of J. P. Morgan to purchase federal government bonds in return for gold to replenish the federal government's Treasury reserve.[6]

The Silver Purchase Act was repealed, but the weak economy remained. Nothing Cleveland's administration did seemed to improve the situation, and if anything, the economy appeared to get worse. Animosity toward the Democrats in general rose, and anger with Cleveland in particular mounted, even among his fellow Democrats. This anger was most intense in the South and West, where agrarian interests had been suffering for some time. They saw themselves as unfairly manipulated and taken advantage of by Eastern financial elites, the same elites they believed controlled Grover Cleveland. As Southern and especially Western discontent roiled, Cleveland further angered a portion of have-not America by using federal troops to crush the Pullman Strike in Chicago in July 1894.[7] Most of the labor movement was in urban areas and his opposition to labor hurt the party's prospects there. By any account, Cleveland experienced a difficult first two years of his second term as president.

---

[6] For discussions of Cleveland, the repeal of the Sherman Silver Purchase Act of 1890, and the resulting tensions, see Paul Kleppner, *Continuity and Change in Electoral Politics, 1893–1928* (Westport, CT: Greenwood Press, 1987); Allan Nevins, *Grover Cleveland: A Study in Courage* (New York: Dodd, Mead, and Company, 1932); James L. Sundquist, *Dynamics of the Party System*, revised edition (Washington, DC: The Brookings Institution, 1983); Ritter, *Goldbugs and Greenbacks*; Rexford G. Tugwell, *Grover Cleveland* (New York: Macmillan, 1968); Alan Ware, *The Democratic Party Heads North, 1877–1962* (New York: Cambridge University Press, 2006); Welch, *The Presidencies of Grover Cleveland*.

[7] For accounts of Cleveland's actions during the Pullman Strike, see Nevins, *Grover Cleveland: A Study in Courage*; Tugwell, *Grover Cleveland*; Welch, *The Presidencies of Grover Cleveland*.

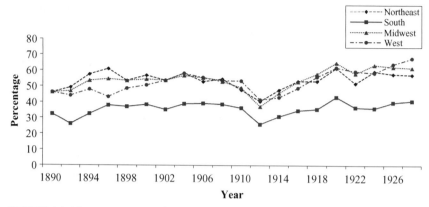

FIGURE 4.1. Vote percentage for House Republican candidates by region, 1890–1928

This rough patch did not translate well for Cleveland's party in the 1894 congressional elections. As is always the case for the party in control when economic hard times set in, the electorate placed a good deal of blame on the Democrats for the Panic of 1893, which was still going full force in 1894.[8] In addition to the economic downturn that occurred during their watch, the Democrats were also saddled with Cleveland, who had managed to alienate Western and Southern agrarian interests, silver supporters, and urban labor. Thus, it is not surprising that the Democrats suffered serious setbacks at the ballot box in 1894. The party lost control of the House of Representatives with a staggering loss of 114 seats in 1894, and also lost control of the Senate. As Figure 4.1 shows, Republicans made significant gains in the Northeast and Midwest. In the West, their percentage remained flat, but went up in subsequent years. Only in the South were the Democrats able to maintain a majority of the total popular vote for the House in 1894; in the Northeast, Midwest, and especially the West, the party's vote total declined dramatically from 1892 to 1894. The 1894 elections were devastating for Democrats.

THE PRESIDENTIAL ELECTION OF 1896: PARTIES AND CHOICES

The 1894 congressional election results should have made the Democratic Party take notice. After all, the 114-seat loss in the House was then and

---

[8] Paul Kleppner, *The Cross of Culture: A Sociological Analysis of Midwestern Politics, 1850–1900* (New York: The Free Press, 1970); Kleppner, *Continuity and Change in Electoral Politics, 1893–1928.*

remains today the single largest loss of seats by any party in a House election cycle. As the 1896 presidential election approached, the Democrats could not have been feeling too bullish about their prospects for victory, especially given Cleveland's lack of popularity and the ongoing economic troubles.[9] At first glance, it would appear that 1896 was shaping up as a Republican year.

But sometimes first glances can be deceiving, or at least some can convince themselves of this fact. It is important to remember that – the big GOP success in 1894 aside – the Democrats and Republicans had been relatively evenly matched nationally since the end of Reconstruction. The Democrats' loss of seats in 1894 was enormous, but the Republicans only had to go back two election cycles to 1890 to recall a seventy-seven-seat loss that gave the Democrats control of the House. One must also keep in mind the amount of volatility present in the party system of the period; both inside and outside of the two major parties. Both parties had internal divisions focused around industrial/agrarian and East/West cleavages, and the Democrats had an additional fissure between recent immigrants and old-stock Americans. Significant third-party movements were popping up, starting with the Greenback Party and then later the People's (better known as the Populist) Party. These third parties were particularly attractive to those in the West, who to a certain degree thought both major parties were opposed to their interests. The West was also growing as westward expansion was adding new states to the Union and creating a rapidly expanding and evolving electorate in that part of the nation. Immigration continued unabated, and over time those immigrants naturalized and became eligible to vote. Urbanization was exploding. Change was everywhere, and such rapid change inevitably creates uncertainty among politicians and party leaders.

Uncertainty can be unnerving, but can also present opportunity. Given how close election outcomes were over the prior twenty years, each party was looking for opportunities to expand its coalition and establish itself as the clear majority party in the United States. As mentioned in the introductory chapter, such periods of uncertainty and opportunity are often those that produce change. Examining the wreckage of 1894, it was the Democrats who acted first. Most Democrats saw the incredibly unpopular Grover Cleveland as representative of the Eastern elite wing of the party, and thus wanted to take the party in a different direction in 1896.

---

[9] Hoffmann argues that the Panic of 1893 did not start to abate until 1897, and that full recovery did not occur until 1900. Hoffmann, "The Depression of the Nineties."

During the House debate on Cleveland's proposed repeal of the Silver Purchase Act in 1892, a young Nebraska Democrat had delivered a three-hour diatribe against the "goldbugs" who were primarily interested in oppressing American farmers and lining the pockets of Eastern bankers and financiers.[10] That young congressman was William Jennings Bryan, and as the 1896 Democratic Convention approached, he was becoming an increasingly prominent face of the party's agrarian wing. The 1896 Convention saw a heated battle between the Eastern and Western wings of the party, and given the Eastern wing's ties to Cleveland and that they were seen as responsible for the party's putrid performance in 1894, it is not surprising that the Western faction of the party, with the support of the South, won out in the end. Bryan got the presidential nomination, and the party looked toward the South and the West for success. The Democratic Party was under new management.[11]

Today we often see the presidential election of 1896 portrayed as a lopsided defeat for the Democratic Party, and the party's strategy in that election described as foolhardy. Such depictions, however, are inaccurate. First, William Jennings Bryan did not lose to William McKinley by an overwhelming margin. More will be said on this later in the chapter, but the 1896 contest ranks relatively low on the scale of presidential election landslides in American history. Second, and perhaps for our purposes more important, the Democrats' strategy for electoral success in 1896 seemed sound at the time. Even today, with the benefit of more than 100 years of hindsight, one can easily see why the Democrats felt their plan gave them a plausible chance to win the presidency. As noted in Chapter 3, the West was rapidly rising in political importance in the latter part of the nineteenth century. The Republicans were generally successful in the region, but the interests of the West often went against those held by the Eastern establishment in control of the GOP. This tension within the party certainly gave the Democrats reason to believe that they could wrest control of the region from the Republicans, if they played their cards right.[12]

The nomination of Bryan was central to the Democrats' plan. The 1890s had seen the Populist Party do very well in elections in the West, largely because of agrarian discontent and the Populist stand for free silver. Farmers and ranchers were angry, and the Populists benefited from this anger.

---

[10] Welch, *The Presidencies of Grover Cleveland*.

[11] Kleppner, *Continuity and Change in Electoral Politics, 1893–1928*; Ware, *The Democratic Party Heads North, 1877–1962*.

[12] Sundquist, *Dynamics of the Party System*, revised edition.

The Democrats saw no reason why they too could not benefit from this discontent. Significant factions within the party shared the Populists' disdain for Eastern business and financial elites. The Democrats proposed a fusion arrangement to the Populist Party, where the Democrats would offer a platform amenable to the Populist program and the fused parties would nominate Bryan for president.[13] The Democrats' reasoning was relatively compelling; simply put, the party planned to run a haves versus have-nots campaign, presenting themselves clearly as the party of the have-nots.

In theory, this idea made a good deal of sense. By fusing with the Populist Party, the Democrats envisioned taking the West away from the Republicans. They could do this without hurting themselves at all in the South. The South was agrarian as well, and as Woodward makes clear, agrarian discontent actually started in the South before moving westward.[14] Finally, the Democrats were counting on being able to craft a truly inclusive have-not coalition by melding together poor agrarians and the poor urban working class of the Northeast and the Midwest. Such an arrangement was not that far-fetched; the early Farmers Alliance groups that eventually formed the core of the Populist Party had ties to the early labor movement in the United States, and the two groups had many similar complaints against the haves of American society. Besides, the Democrats had long been the party more sympathetic to the interests of newly arriving immigrant groups, and it was these groups that made up the bulk of the urban working class. Many of these Northeastern and Midwestern cities were increasingly governed by political machines, many of these machines were Democratic, and these machines were supported by the urban immigrant working class. On paper, the strategy made sense.

Sound Democratic strategy notwithstanding, the Republican Party must have approached the 1896 presidential election with at least some degree of confidence. After all, the GOP tended to be the more popular party outside of the South, they were coming off huge victories in the 1894 congressional contests, and perhaps most important, the economic downturn that began on the Democrats' watch was still going strong. The Republicans nominated William McKinley, former congressman and governor of Ohio, as their candidate for president. McKinley was a firm

---

[13] Lawrence Goodwyn, *Democratic Promise: The Populist Moment in America* (New York: Oxford University Press, 1976); John D. Hicks, *The Populist Revolt* (Minneapolis: University of Minnesota Press, 1931).

[14] C. Vann Woodward, *Origins of the New South, 1877–1913* (Baton Rouge: Louisiana State University Press, 1951).

advocate for the gold standard, and one of the leading Republican voices for the necessity of high protective tariffs. McKinley also had solid backing in the business and financial community, partly because of the connections of his campaign manager, business leader and fellow Republican Mark Hanna.

The GOP viewed McKinley as a strong candidate in an election that they should be able to win, but the party did have some concerns. Republican leaders were worried that their strong defense of the gold standard combined with McKinley's close ties to the industrial and financial elite would hurt them in the West. It turns out that such concerns were justified; McKinley carried only five states (including Minnesota) west of the Mississippi River. The Republican Party was convinced that victory in the former Confederate states was out of the question, although they believed that they could be competitive in the border South states. In light of these concerns about the West and the South, McKinley and Hanna designed a Republican strategy focused on wringing every last vote – electoral and popular – that they could out of their strongholds in the Northeast and the Midwest, contesting the border South, and doing the best they could in the West and perhaps picking up a few states in that region.

At first glance, such a strategy might appear problematic; many of the states in the Northeast and Midwest had large and rapidly growing cities, teeming with recent immigrants working in relatively low-paying industrial jobs. McKinley and the GOP would not seem to be a match for these voters, especially given the Democratic plan to heavily target the have-nots of American society. Yet again, things are not always as they at first appear. As mentioned in the previous chapter, the Republican Party presented itself as the party of labor during the nineteenth and early twentieth centuries, and more important such a presentation was accepted by a good many workers.[15] This image was only reinforced in 1896 by the anti-labor actions of the Democratic Cleveland administration. In addition, McKinley's years of contesting and winning elections in Ohio had taught him the necessity of the immigrant and Catholic vote, and he was much more receptive to courting such voters than were many of his fellow Republicans. In fact, McKinley recognized early on that these voters were central to the Republican strategy in the Northeast and Midwest,

---

[15] John Gerring, *Party Ideologies in America, 1828–1996* (New York: Cambridge University Press, 1998); Everett Carll Ladd, Jr., *American Political Parties: Social Change and Political Response* (New York: W.W. Norton, 1970).

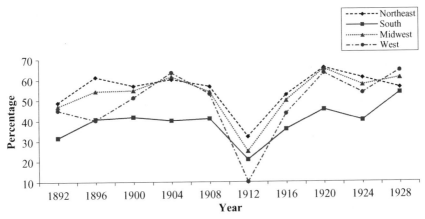

FIGURE 4.2. Vote percentage for Republican presidential candidates by region, 1892–1928

and he pushed his party to drop the antagonism toward these groups that had often characterized the GOP in the past.[16]

In the end, of course, the Republicans prevailed in the presidential election of 1896. William McKinley defeated William Jennings Bryan by a margin of 50 to 46 percent in the popular vote and 271 to 176 in the Electoral College, neither of which is indicative of a landslide.[17] As shown in Figure 4.2, McKinley won the popular vote in the Northeast and the Midwest (his gain over 1892 in the Northeast is particularly impressive), while losing the South and the West to Bryan.

The heavily populated (and thus rich in electoral votes) states of the Northeast and Midwest were crucial to the outcome, and it is perhaps in these states where the Democrats made their biggest strategic error in the 1896 election. This error involved the proposed coalition of the have-nots. Aiming for such a coalition was not a bad idea; not too far in the future such a coalition would serve Franklin Roosevelt and the Democrats quite well. The error in this case had more to do with the policies presented and the salesperson selected to peddle such a coalition. The Democrats attempted to unite the have-not agrarians of the West and South with the have-not urban workers of the Midwest and Northeast primarily through

[16] Kleppner, *The Cross of Culture*; Kleppner, *Change and Continuity in Electoral Politics, 1893–1928*; Sundquist, *Dynamics of the Party System*, revised edition.

[17] For more on the closeness of the 1896 presidential election, see Sanders, *Roots of Reform*; Ware, *The Democratic Party Heads North, 1877–1962*.

promises of free and unlimited coinage of silver and a low protective tariff. These issue positions were highly attractive to farmers and others connected to the agrarian way of life. Free silver would produce easier credit and inflationary pressures, which would enable farmers to borrow more easily and possibly pay back old debts with newly inflated dollars. Low tariffs meant lower prices for the manufactured goods that they needed to buy, and also suggested that more of their agricultural products could be exported if other nations lowered their tariffs in response to America's lowering of duties.

These issues did not, however, hold the same appeal to urban workers. The question of gold versus silver meant very little to them. Most of them purchased very little on credit, and if anything, the inflationary nature of silver meant that their paychecks would suddenly be worth less. Low tariffs were another matter. The jobs of urban workers may have been low-paying, but they were jobs and they did pay. In a message that Republicans never tired of repeating, lower tariffs meant more foreign competition, which meant trouble for American manufacturers and ultimately fewer jobs. When McKinley campaigned with the message that his stand on the tariff would protect workers' jobs and result in the "full dinner pail," many workers had no problem accepting his claims.

The final matter here deals with the selection of Bryan as the Democratic pitchperson for the coalition of the have-nots. Bryan was a son of the plains; he was the epitome of agrarian, small-town, evangelical Protestant America and presented himself as such. This played very well in the South and the West, but was not nearly as well received in the melting-pot industrial cities of the Northeast and Midwest.[18] As Ladd phrased it, "Bryan the Populist was Bryan the religious fundamentalist, Bryan the prohibitionist, Bryan the provincial."[19] As such, it is not at all surprising that Bryan and the Democrats did not do as well as they needed to in Northeastern and Midwestern cities to carry the election.

The 1896 election cycle is one of the most analyzed and discussed in American history. Some see 1896 as a critical election, one of a handful of elections in which the nature of American electoral politics is fundamentally altered.[20] Others argue that the 1896 election cycle was nothing out of the ordinary; the 1896 results were really not that different

[18] Kleppner, *The Cross of Culture*; Kleppner, *Change and Continuity in Electoral Politics, 1893–1928*; Sundquist, *Dynamics of the Party System*, revised edition.

[19] Ladd, *American Political Parties: Social Change and Political Response*, p. 123.

[20] Walter Dean Burnham, *Critical Elections and the Mainsprings of American Politics* (New York: W.W. Norton, 1970); E. E. Schattschneider, *The Semisovereign People: A Realist's View of*

from those that came before or those that would come after.[21] However, what is clear is that in the years after the elections of 1894 and 1896, the American party system went from two relatively closely matched parties (outside of the South) to an arrangement where the Republicans were dominant in the Northeast and Midwest, and slowly but surely would regain at least a slight edge in the West as well. The Democrats were left with the South. At the national level, the Democrats would not retake control of the House of Representatives until the 1910 election cycle, and would have to wait until 1912 for the presidency and the Senate. The data presented in Figures 4.1 and 4.2 do not lie; after the 1896 election cycle, it was clear that the post-Reconstruction stalemate had been broken. The Republicans were now the majority party in the United States.

A good deal of the newfound Republican edge in 1896 and in the years immediately following had to do with the party's increased success in the Northeast and the Midwest, especially in urban areas. As was noted earlier, Bryan and the Democrats' celebration of rural life and agrarian populism did not go over well in urban America.[22] Bryan expounded on the virtues of the agrarian life in his famous "Cross of Gold" speech at the 1896 Democratic Convention. This speech was widely credited with securing him his party's presidential nomination.

> You come to us and tell us that the great cities are in favor of the gold standard. I tell you that the great cities rest upon these broad and fertile prairies. Burn down your cities and leave our farms, and your cities will spring up again as if by magic. But destroy our farms and the grass will grow in the streets of every city in the country.[23]

One can imagine urban America rolling its eyes in contempt or shaking its head in disgust. As McCormick notes, agrarian populist themes appealed

---

Democracy in America (New York: Holt, Rinehart, and Winston, 1960); Sundquist, *Dynamics of the Party System*, revised edition.

[21] David R. Mayhew, *Electoral Realignments: A Critique of an American Genre* (New Haven, CT: Yale University Press, 2002); Ware, *The Democratic Party Heads North, 1877–1962*; Jeffrey M. Stonecash and Everita Silina, "The 1896 Realignment: A Reassessment," *American Politics Research* 33 (January 2005): 3–32.

[22] David Burner, *The Politics of Provincialism: The Democratic Party in Transition, 1918–1932* (New York: Alfred A. Knopf, 1968); Walter Dean Burnham, "The Changing Shape of the American Political Universe," *American Political Science Review* 59 (March 1965): 7–28; Burnham, *Critical Elections and the Mainsprings of American Politics*; Kleppner, *The Cross of Culture*; Kleppner, *Continuity and Change in Electoral Politics, 1893–1928*; Ladd, *American Political Parties: Social Change and Political Response*; Sundquist, *Dynamics of the Party System*, revised edition.

[23] William Jennings Bryan, "Cross of Gold," speech delivered at the Democratic National Convention, Chicago, IL, July 9, 1896.

to farmers, but generally frightened the rest of the nation.[24] In choosing to recast their party in a more Populist image, the Democrats were hitching themselves to a horse that in the long term simply could not win the race. By 1896, it was clear that an industrial America was the way of the future; small town and rural life, although certainly not in danger of completely disappearing, was also certainly not the wave of the future. Political power was going to continue to move toward industrial America, with its large cities and equally large factories.[25] In this way, the rural/agrarian strategy that the Democrats had bet on in 1896 was not just a loss for that election cycle; it was perhaps an even bigger loss for those election cycles that would immediately follow. Election results bear this out; the decade from 1900 to 1910 was a barren period for the Democrats, except of course in the South. Democratic electoral success was hard to come by.

THE WILSON INTERMEZZO: 1912–1920

Fortunately for the Democrats, the Republican Party and the national economy were about to present them with an opportunity for revival. The economic opening came first in the form of the *Panic of 1907*. Although not as devastating as the depression of the 1890s, the Panic of 1907 was a significant economic downturn. Manufacturing declined and business failures rose, as did consumer prices. Unemployment topped 16 percent in 1908, and stayed in double figures through 1912.[26] The Republicans were the party in charge in 1907, and while they were spared the wrath of the electorate in 1908 (the party lost only four seats from its majority in the House and Taft defeated Bryan by almost nine percentage points in the presidential election), the length of the economic downturn almost dictated that the GOP would eventually have to pay at the ballot box. Such payment began in the congressional elections of 1910. The Republicans lost fifty-two seats in the House and control of the chamber returned to the Democrats for the first time since the 53rd Congress of 1893–1895. The GOP retained control of the Senate, but the Democrats did pick up twelve seats, indicative of their increased success at the state level as well.

---

[24] Richard L. McCormick, *The Party Period and Public Policy: American Politics from the Age of Jackson to the Progressive Era* (New York: Oxford University Press, 1986).

[25] Lewis L. Gould, "The Republicans Under Roosevelt and Taft," in Lewis L. Gould (ed.), *The Progressive Era* (Syracuse, NY: Syracuse University Press, 1974), 55–82; Richard Hofstadter, *The Age of Reform: From Bryan to F.D.R.* (New York: Vintage Books, 1960); Wiebe, *The Search for Order, 1877–1920.*

[26] Kleppner, *Continuity and Change in Electoral Politics, 1893–1928.*

It is debatable whether economic troubles alone would have been enough to propel the Democrats to victory in the 1912 presidential election.[27] However, the party did not have to rely on economic hard times alone. The fracturing of the Republican Party suddenly gave the Democrats their best chance at winning the presidency in twenty years. After winning a landslide victory in 1904 and serving out his term, popular Republican Theodore Roosevelt left office and anointed William Howard Taft as his preferred successor. Taft won the presidency in 1908, but by 1910, Roosevelt was very vocally and publicly unhappy with Taft. Both Roosevelt and Taft put themselves forward as candidates for the GOP presidential nomination in 1912. Taft won the nomination, and the disgruntled Roosevelt left the Republican Party to launch an independent bid for the White House.

Technically, Roosevelt did not run as an independent in 1912. He ran under the banner of the Progressive Party, which is appropriate because it was the Progressive movement that splintered the GOP in the first place. The Progressive movement was a major reform effort that began in the early 1900s and ended with America's entrance into World War I. It was not a unified movement; individuals joined the effort for many reasons. Some Progressives were worried about corruption in urban political machines and wanted a *civil service system* – government workers appointed through competency tests and protected from political interference as they executed their responsibilities. Others wanted to change the electoral system to create a focus on individuals instead of parties. Another group wanted scientific policy responses to developing social problems. Goals varied from region to region, but one thing did unify the Progressives, as Sundquist noted: "They were dissatisfied."[28]

Both parties had their Progressive supporters during this period, but the intraparty tension between the Progressives and their non-Progressive party brethren was highest in the Republican Party. Taft had angered Republican Progressives with his conservative governance as president; Roosevelt was only too happy to fan the flames of this Progressive discontent in his hope of winning the presidency in 1912. Once the party split, many Progressive Republicans followed Roosevelt away from the GOP, while old guard non-Progressive party members remained solidly behind Taft. The Democrats, on the other hand, were relatively united in

---

[27] For a good discussion of this question, see Ware, *The Democratic Party Heads North, 1877– 1962*.
[28] Sundquist, *Dynamics of the Party System*, revised edition, p. 172.

1912 and awarded their presidential nomination to New Jersey governor and former Princeton University president Woodrow Wilson.[29]

With the Republicans badly split, Wilson and the Democrats won in 1912. Wilson received an impressive 435 votes in the Electoral College (to Roosevelt's 88 and Taft's 8 votes). The Democrats added fifty-three seats to their majority in the House and also regained control of the Senate. On its face, the 1912 election cycle signified a fully revived and highly competitive Democratic Party. However, even with the success of 1912, Democratic leaders had reason to be concerned. Wilson had won with only 42 percent of the popular vote, whereas Roosevelt and Taft combined received 51 percent. These figures pointed to potential trouble if the Republican Party could heal its wounds and reunite. Even the impressive gains in the House in both 1910 and 1912 gave cause for concern if examined carefully. As Figure 4.1 shows, it was only in the South that Democratic House candidates far outpaced their Republican opponents in total House votes. Republican candidates topped Democratic ones in the other three regions in 1910, and in 1912, the parties essentially tied in the Northeast, the Democrats came out narrowly on top in the Midwest, and the Republicans did the same in the West. So although the Democrats had a 134-seat advantage in the House after the 1912 elections, their comfort level for similar levels of success in the near future could not have been terribly high.

The reversal of Democratic fortunes began quickly. In 1914, the Republicans began to increase their advantage over the Democrats in House voting in all regions except the South. The Democrats lost forty-three House seats in 1914 and another twenty-one in 1916, keeping control of the chamber in 1916 only because the few minor party members in the House caucused with them. The presidential election of 1916 was kinder to the Democrats, but still pointed to weaknesses in the party. Wilson did win reelection in 1916, but only by a small margin of 3 percent in the popular vote and twenty-three votes in the Electoral College. Wilson maintained his huge popular vote advantage in the South and also took the popular vote in the West, but the nomination of Supreme Court Justice and former New York Governor Charles Evans Hughes had

---

[29] John Morton Blum, *The Progressive Presidents: Roosevelt, Wilson, Roosevelt, Johnson* (New York: W.W. Norton, 1980); Kleppner, *Continuity and Change in Electoral Politics, 1893–1928*; Arthur S. Link, *Woodrow Wilson and the Progressive Era, 1910–1917* (New York: Harper & Brothers, 1954); Sundquist, *Dynamics of the Party System*, revised edition; Wiebe, *The Search for Order, 1877–1920*.

reunited the Republican Party, and Hughes won more votes than Wilson in the Northeast and the Midwest. In this sense, the regional base of the Democrats in 1916 was very similar to what it was in 1896.[30] In fact, if one were to look at the Electoral College maps of 1896 and 1916, Wilson's victorious collection of states in 1916 would look much like Bryan's losing collection of 1896. Both Wilson and Bryan did very well in the South and the West. Wilson was able to win California (Bryan lost there in 1896), and he also won the three states that participated in 1916 that had not in 1896 – Arizona, New Mexico, and Oklahoma. On the other hand, both Wilson and Bryan did poorly in the Northeast (Bryan was shut out and Wilson won only New Hampshire) and the Midwest (Bryan was again shut out and Wilson took only Ohio). In fact, had Wilson lost Ohio's twenty-four electoral votes (and Wilson in both 1912 and 1916 was the only Democrat to win Ohio from 1896–1928) he would have lost the election.

Wilson won a second term in 1916, but it was clear that he had not succeeded in two of his other goals: reshaping the Democratic Party's coalition and establishing the Democrats as the clear national majority party. As the Democrats examined the results of the 1916 election cycle, it was clear that the party's base was still largely rural and Southern. They had control of Congress and the presidency, but in terms of the party's coalition, they were in essentially the same place they were in 1896. Wilson's reelection was due in large part to the appeal of his claim that he had kept the United States out of World War I, and when this claim was no longer true after 1917, party leaders were quite concerned about their prospects in upcoming elections.

These fears were soon borne out. The Democrats lost control of both Houses of Congress in 1918 (the Senate was now being decided by direct election as well). The year 1920 was even worse for the party; Republican Warren Harding defeated Democrat James Cox for the presidency 61 to 34 percent in the popular vote, the Democrats lost another fifty-nine seats in the House, and an additional ten in the Senate. In less than eight years, the Democrats had gone from unified control of the national government to losing that control in a series of electoral thrashings. It is important not to place too much of the blame for this at the hands of Woodrow Wilson. As both Blum and James point out, Wilson was at a disadvantage not faced by most presidents who win elections. Rather

---

[30] Burner, *The Politics of Provincialism*; Ware, *The Democratic Party Heads North, 1877–1962*.

than trying to maintain an already successful electoral coalition, Wilson was instead trying to build one on the fly.[31] He recognized that the old Bryan Democratic base was not enough for this party to win on a regular basis, and tried hard to expand the Democratic coalition. In the end, Wilson was unable to do so.[32]

REPUBLICAN RETURN TO DOMINANCE

The 1920 election cycle ushered in a decade of remarkable electoral success for the Republican Party, and a decade of misery for the Democrats. The GOP won all three presidential elections in the 1920s, and the Democratic performances in these races represent the worst consecutive performances in a three-presidential election series of any major party in American history. The Republicans maintained their control of Congress as well, although the Democrats did perform reasonably well in the 1922 House elections and the 1926 contests for both chambers. Yet even in these instances, the Republicans came out on top. Republican control of the national government was absolute in the 1920s, and at the time it seemed that such control could go on forever. In addition to being relatively few in number and largely shut out from power other than in the South, the Democrats were bitterly divided.[33]

However, as is often the case in American electoral politics, the 1920s did provide the Democratic Party with several opportunities for future success. The Republican Party of the 1920s was all about meeting the needs and granting the wishes of American business.[34] In the words of William Leuchtenburg:

> By the end of the Harding administration, the Republican Party was firmly committed to single-interest government. By allying with business, the Republican believed that they were benefiting the entire nation. Hamilton was the patron saint of the decade. The 1920s represent

---

[31] John Morton Blum, *Woodrow Wilson and the Politics of Morality* (Boston: Little, Brown, and Company, 1956); Scott C. James, *Presidents, Parties, and the State: A Party System Perspective on Democratic Regulatory Choice, 1884–1936* (New York: Cambridge University Press, 2000).

[32] Burner, *The Politics of Provincialism*; Ware, *The Democratic Party Heads North, 1877–1962*.

[33] John M. Allswang, *The New Deal and American Politics: A Study in Political Change* (New York: John Wiley and Sons, 1978); Burner, *The Politics of Provincialism*.

[34] John D. Hicks, *Republican Ascendancy, 1921–1933* (New York: Harper & Row, 1960); John D. Hicks, *Normalcy and Reaction 1921–1933: An Age of Disillusionment* (Washington, DC: Service Center for Teachers of History, 1960); William E. Leuchtenburg, *The Perils of Prosperity, 1914–1932* (Chicago: University of Chicago Press, 1958).

not the high tide of laissez faire but of Hamiltonianism, of a hierarchical concept of society with a deliberate pursuit by the government most favorable to large business interests. No political party, no national administration could conceivably have been more cooperative with business interests.[35]

At the same time that the GOP was catering to business, American society was continuing to evolve. It was in the 1920s that the United States completed its transformation from a rural to an urban nation.[36] The growth of the nation was taking place in the large cities of the Northeast and the Midwest. Industrial growth occurred at a furious pace, and the size of the urban labor force grew right alongside it. However, as labor grew in size, its treatment by both management and government became worse.[37] Immigration was largely ended by statute in 1921 and 1923, but the large wave of immigrants who had arrived before 1923 continued to reshape American society as they themselves became citizens through the naturalization process and also as their children grew to adulthood.[38] Economic inequality rose to astronomical levels, and the gulf between the haves and the have-nots reached epic proportions.[39] All of these developments provided the Democrats with the opportunity to change their electoral fortunes. This new wave of voters – the urban masses, ethnic immigrants and their offspring, labor, the have-nots – was being largely ignored by the Republican Party. If the Democrats could appeal to these voters and add them to their coalition without losing its current support, success would be possible. They began this process in 1928. The Democratic presidential candidate that year, Al Smith, lost badly to incumbent Republican President Herbert Hoover. Yet in that defeat were the seeds of future Democratic success.

---

[35] Leuchtenburg, *The Perils of Prosperity, 1914–1932*, p. 103.

[36] Hofstadter, *The Age of Reform*; Samuel Lubell, *The Future of American Politics*, third edition, Revised. (New York: Harper and Row, 1965).

[37] Leuchtenburg, *The Perils of Prosperity, 1914–1932*.

[38] Kristi Andersen, *The Creation of a Democratic Majority, 1928–1936* (Chicago: University of Chicago Press, 1979).

[39] Robert D. Plotnick, Eugene Smolensky, Eirik Evenhouse, and Siobhan Reilly, "The Twentieth-Century Record of Inequality and Poverty in the United States," in Stanley Engerman and Robert Gallman (eds.), *The Cambridge Economic History of the United States, Vol. 3: The Twentieth Century* (New York: Cambridge University Press, 2000), 249–99.

5 Tables Turn: The New Deal Era and Democratic Dominance, 1932–1948

AL SMITH AND THE PRESIDENTIAL ELECTION OF 1928

The year 1928 did not appear to be a good year for the Democratic Party. The party's presidential candidate, former New York Governor Al Smith, lost to Republican incumbent Herbert Hoover in landslide fashion in the popular vote (58 to 41 percent), failing even to perform up to par in the Democratic base of the former Confederacy (Smith won only six of the eleven Southern states).Already in the minority in both the House and the Senate, the Democrats lost another thirty-two seats in the lower chamber and seven more in the upper chamber, along with losing a vacant seat election to the GOP.

Although Democrats were soundly thrashed in the 1928 election cycle, some results did offer the party a few rays of hope. Smith received only 41 percent of the popular vote, but this figure was significantly higher than the 34 percent received by Democratic candidate James Cox in 1920 and the 29 percent received by Democrat John Davis in 1924.[1] In addition, Smith may have carried only eight states, but two of them – Massachusetts and Rhode Island – were states that the Democrats had managed to win only once before (1912) since 1876. These facts provided the Democrats with a little silver lining to the dark cloud that was the 1928 election cycle.

There are additional reasons to see 1928 as a step in the right direction for the Democratic Party. In many ways, the nomination of Al Smith in 1928 can be seen as the end of what Ware called a "civil war" within

---

[1] This figure represents the lowest percentage received by a presidential candidate of a major party since the inception of meaningful two-party competition in 1828 with the exception of 1912, when Republican William Howard Taft received 23 percent of the popular vote.

the party, or at the very least the establishment of a truce that would last until 1948.[2] The tension and conflict between the rural and urban factions of the Democratic Party described in previous chapters simmered in the first two decades of the twentieth century, and reached full boil in the 1920s. The urban and rural wings of the Democratic Party had clashed bitterly throughout much of the decade as they battled for control of the party. The two sides fought viciously at the 1924 Democratic Convention, where each side prevented the other from seeing its preferred candidate (Al Smith for the urban wing, William Gibbs McAdoo for the rural wing) gain the party's presidential nomination. Finally a draw was called, and after 102 votes that produced no convention nominee, the nomination was given to compromise candidate John Davis on the 103rd ballot. The relatively easy nomination of Smith in 1928 signaled a reduction of tension within the party, and also a shift in power toward the urban wing of the party.[3]

Tension may have been reduced but not eliminated. After all, five states of the former Confederacy – a crucial part of the Democrats' rural wing – abandoned the party in 1928 and cast their electoral votes for Republican Herbert Hoover. Nonetheless, Smith's performance did represent an improvement for the Democrats in comparison to their two previous presidential efforts, and he did particularly well among some groups that would soon become crucial to the success of the party. Smith was the grandson of immigrants and was proud of his immigrant lineage. He was born in New York City, and got his start in politics in New York's notorious Tammany Hall political machine. Smith had little formal education, and worked a number of menial jobs before devoting full attention to politics. He was a proud Roman Catholic, and kept a photo of the Pope over his desk while he was governor of New York.[4] Because of his background

---

[2] Alan Ware, *The Democratic Party Heads North, 1877–1962* (New York: Cambridge University Press, 2006), 147.

[3] John M. Allswang, *A House for All Peoples: Ethnic Politics in Chicago, 1890–1936* (Lexington: University Press of Kentucky, 1971); John M. Allswang, *The New Deal and American Politics: A Study in Political Change* (New York: John Wiley & Sons, 1978); David Burner, *The Politics of Provincialism: The Democratic Party in Transition, 1918–1932* (New York: Alfred A. Knopf, 1968); Ralph M. Goldman, *Search for Consensus: The Story of the Democratic Party* (Philadelphia: Temple University Press, 1979); Ware, *The Democratic Party Heads North, 1877–1962*. Talk of a possible brokered convention for the Democrats in 2008 brought some renewed attention to the 1924 convention; Peter Carlson, "The Ballot Brawl of 1924," *Washington Post*, March 4, 2008, p. C01.

[4] Oscar Handlin, *Al Smith and His America* (Boston: Little, Brown, and Company, 1958); Matthew Josephson and Hannah Josephson, *Al Smith: Hero of the Cities* (Boston: Houghton Mifflin, 1969).

and upbringing, Smith was well positioned to appeal to the very groups –
the urban masses, ethnic immigrants and their offspring, labor, the have-
nots – that were being largely ignored by the Republican Party. Although
he lost the election badly, Smith did deliver on his potential and attracted
a good portion of each of these groups to the Democratic ticket in 1928.[5]
This is why Smith's victories in Massachusetts and Rhode Island are so
important. These two states were longtime GOP strongholds in 1928, but
they were also heavily urban, Catholic, immigrant, and blue collar. Smith
brought them into the Democratic presidential fold in 1928. Each state
has only left the Democratic Party four times since.[6]

THE DEMOCRATS' COMEBACK: FDR AND THE NEW DEAL

Al Smith and the Democrats were soundly defeated in 1928, but that election cycle offered important hints on possible future success for the party
to anyone paying careful attention. Franklin Delano Roosevelt (FDR)
was paying attention. Famous today for his unprecedented four presidential election victories, FDR was a heavyweight in Democratic circles
well before he sat behind the desk in the Oval Office. Roosevelt's activities with the Democratic Party began more than twenty years before he
became the party's nominee for president in 1932. He was elected as
a Democrat to the New York State Senate in 1910, and left that position in 1913 after Democratic President Woodrow Wilson appointed him
Assistant Secretary of the Navy. Roosevelt was the party's vice presidential candidate in 1920, and despite being stricken with polio in 1921,
remained very active in party affairs, both in New York State and nationally. The volume of FDR's correspondence with leading Democrats during
this period is legendary. He worked to gain the party's presidential nomination for Al Smith in both 1924 and 1928, offering Smith for nomination

---

[5] Allswang, *A House for All Peoples*; Kristi Andersen, *The Creation of a Democratic Majority,
1928–1936* (Chicago: University of Chicago Press, 1979); Burner, *The Politics of Provincial-
ism*; Jerome M. Clubb and Howard W. Allen, "The Cities and the Election of 1928: Partisan Realignment?" *American Historical Review* 74 (April 1969); John D. Hicks, *Republican
Ascendancy, 1921–1933* (New York: Harper & Row, 1960); William E. Leuchtenburg, *The
Perils of Prosperity, 1914–1932* (Chicago: University of Chicago Press, 1958), pp. 1205–20;
Samuel Lubell, *The Future of American Politics*, second edition, revised (Garden City, NY:
Doubleday Anchor Books, 1956); James L. Sundquist, *Dynamics of the Party System: Align-
ment and Realignment of Political Parties in the United States*, revised edition (Washington,
DC: The Brookings Institution, 1983).

[6] Massachusetts favored the Republican candidate in 1952, 1956, 1980, and 1984, while
Rhode Island went Republican in 1952, 1956, 1972, and 1984. All of these elections were
large Republican victories nationally.

in both years and giving Smith his nickname of the "Happy Warrior." He ran for governor of New York himself in 1928, winning the election while Smith lost the state in that year's presidential election. FDR was easily reelected governor in 1930, and by then was clearly seen as presidential material by many within the Democratic Party.

Franklin Roosevelt studied the 1928 election results carefully. He had been considering the plight of the Democratic Party for more than twenty years. As former Roosevelt aide Rexford Tugwell noted in his biography of FDR, in 1908 Roosevelt had told his fellow clerks at a Wall Street law firm that he would be elected president someday, and explained to them how he would do it.[7] Even at age twenty-six, FDR had his eyes on the White House. One of the things that Roosevelt took away from the 1928 contest was the importance of the cities to future Democratic success. He knew that in order to win a presidential election, a Democratic candidate would have to attract high levels of support from those in the cities, Catholics, immigrant-stock individuals, and blue-collar workers. After his impressive reelection as governor of New York in 1930, FDR believed he was the front-runner for the Democratic nomination in 1932,[8] and he set about analyzing how he could win the votes of the urban population.

The America of the 1930s had indeed become an urban America. In the words of Richard Hofstadter, "The United States was born in the country and has moved to the city."[9] As Lubell makes clear, this urbanization of America was crucial to the election and the three-time reelection of Franklin Roosevelt.[10] Although he recognized the importance of the city, FDR knew that he could not rely solely on urban America to put him and his party in the White House. Roosevelt recognized that he would need to win the South as well, and because he did not share Al Smith's Roman Catholicism, he assumed he would do that. He also realized that he would have to attract some support in the rural areas of the Midwest and particularly the West. Through his careful analysis, FDR envisioned his coalition as the one Bryan wished for but was unable to construct in 1896, and as the one that Wilson was able to temporarily cobble together in 1916. FDR, however, envisioned his as broader, larger, and ultimately more enduring.

---

[7] Rexford G. Tugwell, *The Democratic Roosevelt: A Biography of Franklin D. Roosevelt* (Garden City, NY: Doubleday and Company, 1957).

[8] Rexford G. Tugwell, *FDR: Architect of an Era* (New York: Macmillan, 1967).

[9] Richard Hofstadter, *The Age of Reform: From Bryan to F.D.R.* (New York: Vintage Books, 1960), 23.

[10] Lubell, *The Future of American Politics*, second edition, revised.

For all the years of his careful strategizing about how he would lead the Democratic Party to victory in a presidential election, FDR did not have to rely on much of it in winning the 1932 presidential election. Republican presidents had presided over a remarkable period of economic prosperity in the 1920s, and thus it was unlikely that any Democratic candidate could have defeated the Republican Hoover in 1928.[11] To many, it seemed as these economic good times would continue without end.[12] Of course they did not. When the stock market crashed in October 1929, the worst economic crisis in the history of the United States began. The economic downturn that became known as the *Great Depression* would (as was the case for all previous economic downturns) extract a price from the presiding party. In 1929, that party was, of course, the Republican Party. As the Depression dragged on and worsened in 1930, 1931, and 1932, it became more likely that a desperate and disgruntled electorate would turn the keys to national power over to the Democrats. As Sundquist put it, "It probably did not matter what kind of campaign Roosevelt conducted [in 1932]. . . . When unemployment stands at 24 percent, as it did in 1932, an incumbent president is not reelected."[13]

The first signs of a Democratic upturn came in the 1930 congressional elections. The Democrats picked up fifty-one seats in the House of Representatives, and were actually able to take control of the chamber because of special elections that occurred after the November general elections. They gained eight seats in the Senate, although they were still in the minority in the upper chamber. The party also improved somewhat in terms of total House of Representatives vote in all four regions of the nation, as Figure 5.1 indicates. However, it was in 1932 that the big gains were achieved by the Democrats. They won another one hundred seats in the House to control that chamber by a huge margin and they added twelve seats in the Senate, enabling the Democrats to control that body as well. Democratic House candidates outpolled their Republican opponents in all regions of the country. The big prize, of course, was the presidency, which the Democrats also captured easily. FDR defeated Hoover 57 to 40 percent in the popular vote and 472 to 59 in the Electoral College, limiting the Republican incumbent to victories in only six states. Roosevelt beat Hoover in the popular vote in all four regions of the

---

[11] Burner, *The Politics of Provincialism*, pp. 178–80, 217.
[12] Leuchtenburg, *The Perils of Prosperity, 1914–1932*; Arthur M. Schlesinger, Jr., *The Crisis of the Old Order, 1919–1933* (Boston: Houghton Mifflin, 1957).
[13] Sundquist, *Dynamics of the Party System*, revised edition, p. 210.

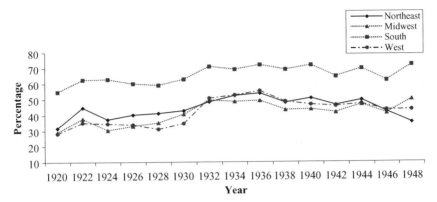

FIGURE 5.1. Democratic House candidates' percentage of the vote by region, 1920–1948

nation, as shown in Figure 5.2, and it was close only in the Northeast. After a miserable twelve-year run as the minority party, the Democrats were back in control.

Whereas much of the political change in American politics has involved a gradual secular realignment, the elections of 1930 and 1932 are a clear case of abrupt change and critical realignment. There was an across-the-board movement of voters toward the Democratic Party, and the movement persisted for some time. FDR and the Democrats won easily and convincingly in 1932. Yet when it comes to the issue of ascribing meaning to these victories, we must be careful. After all, 1932 was a daunting year to be a Republican office seeker. As Schlesinger notes, it is difficult to overstate the magnitude of the economic collapse that was the Great Depression, and also the depth of the suffering that broad segments of the

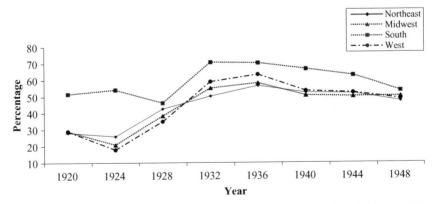

FIGURE 5.2. Democratic presidential candidates' percentage of the vote by region, 1920–1948

American public were enduring.[14] The GOP was the party in charge at the outset of the Depression, and thus was viewed by the majority of Americans as responsible for the economic misfortune they were experiencing. In retrospect, it is hard to imagine Hoover being reelected in 1932, or the Republicans being able to win control of Congress in that year.

Another reason to be cautious about reading too much into Democratic success in 1932 was that Roosevelt and his party did not present to voters much in terms of a substantive plan during the 1932 campaign. FDR had been active in attempting to deal with the Depression during his tenure as governor of New York.[15] In addition, Roosevelt regularly emphasized his intention to do something about the nation's economic woes if he was elected president, but he was not clear exactly what that something would be.[16] It has often been said that Roosevelt ran in 1932 on the promise of hope; for many Americans in that election cycle, hope was enough.

In spite of Roosevelt being less than forthcoming with the specifics of how he would address the nation's economic misery, this does not mean that he was lacking ideas. In fact, he had plenty of ideas. To economist and FDR advisor Rexford Tugwell, it seemed at times in 1932 and 1933 that Roosevelt might have had too many different plans and ideas on what government could or should do.[17] Roosevelt generated some of these policy options on his own; some he got from his famous set of advisors known as his *Brains Trust*; others he picked up from reading the work of academics or other policy experts; still others appeared to come from nowhere in particular.[18] Regardless of where they came from, Roosevelt had policies aplenty when he took the oath of office in March 1933. He wasted little time in putting them into action, both unilaterally and with the assistance of the new Democratic Congress. Roosevelt's

---

[14] Arthur M. Schlesinger, Jr., *The Coming of the New Deal* (Boston: Houghton Mifflin, 1959).

[15] Burner, *The Politics of Provincialism*.

[16] William E. Leuchtenburg, *Franklin D. Roosevelt and the New Deal, 1932–1940* (New York: Harper & Row, 1963); David Plotke, *Building a Democratic Political Order: Reshaping American Liberalism in the 1930s and 1940s* (New York: Cambridge University Press, 1996); Schlesinger, *The Crisis of the Old Order*; Rexford G. Tugwell, *Roosevelt's Revolution* (New York: Macmillan, 1977). Tugwell expresses nicely the dual reasons to be careful in interpreting FDR's win in 1932: "Roosevelt suddenly became a savior found in the electoral processes Americans believed in. What made this seem strange was that obviously Hoover had been voted out of office and Roosevelt only incidentally voted in. Moreover, the campaign had revealed almost nothing the president-elect actually meant to do" (p. 3).

[17] Rexford G. Tugwell, *In Search of Roosevelt* (Cambridge, MA: Harvard University Press, 1972).

[18] Rexford G. Tugwell, *The Brains Trust* (New York: Viking Press, 1968).

first "100 Days" are still famous for the sheer magnitude of policies that were enacted during that period, and while the pace did slow a bit as the administration entered the summer of its first year, the enactment of public policy to ameliorate the impact of the Great Depression moved steadily along throughout 1933 and 1934.[19] In many ways, the Roosevelt of these years can be seen as the ultimate experimenter: He threw an inordinate amount of policy against the wall, and then waited to see what stuck.[20]

It can be argued that the electorate reacted well to the early efforts of FDR and his fellow Democrats. In breaking with the normal pattern, the president's party gained seats in the 1934 midterm congressional elections. The Democrats added eight seats to their already impressive majority in the House and ten seats in the Senate, bringing their total in the upper chamber to sixty-nine. However, the policies enacted were somewhat of a mixed bag in many ways. Some were viewed as successful; others were not. Some policies were liked by Roosevelt's fellow Democrats in Congress; others were not. The general public, while strongly approving of Roosevelt himself, saw some of his policies in a much more favorable light than others. Even FDR himself was conflicted, having a much higher regard for some of his handiwork than he did for other efforts he had undertaken in his first two years in office. Even before the Supreme Court began invalidating parts of the so-called First New Deal (1933–1934) in 1935, FDR was reevaluating how the federal government should address the problems and challenges the nation faced.[21] The results of this reevaluation process were a dramatic shift in the policies put forward and backed by the administration (labeled the Second New Deal), and perhaps more important a fundamental restructuring of the Democratic Party's electoral coalition.

Alan Ware has an enlightening view of what the Great Depression did for the Democratic Party. According to Ware, the Depression provided the Democrats with "breathing space" that allowed the party time to redesign itself at the same time that it remained in power.[22] This is an important matter. Instead of trying to construct a majority coalition on the fly, as Wilson was forced to do after his victory in 1912, or struggling

---

[19] Leuchtenburg, *Franklin D. Roosevelt and the New Deal, 1932–1940*; Arthur M. Schlesinger, Jr., *The Coming of the New Deal* (Boston: Houghton Mifflin, 1959).

[20] Schlesinger, *The Coming of the New Deal*; Tugwell, *In Search of Roosevelt*.

[21] Leuchtenburg, *Franklin D. Roosevelt and the New Deal, 1932–1940*; Schlesinger, *The Coming of the New Deal*; Tugwell, *FDR: Architect of an Era*.

[22] Ware, *The Democratic Party Heads North, 1877–1962*, p. 166.

to hold a divided base together, as the Democrats did after Cleveland's victory in 1892, FDR and the Democrats found themselves in an advantageous position after their victories in 1932. They had won easily in 1932, and had done even better in 1934. More important, the party had an unprecedented opportunity to use public policy to expand and solidify the party's base. Given FDR's popularity, the huge majorities they possessed in Congress, and the wide open policy window presented by the Great Depression, the Democratic Party could be reshaped in the electorate. FDR was very much interested in taking advantage of this opportunity, not only for his own personal success, but also for the long-term good of the party. He wanted to construct a Democratic Party that would be America's majority party far into the future.[23] Roosevelt began this process in earnest in 1935.

In addition to his own desire to reshape the Democratic Party, FDR was also motivated to shift his policy direction by a number of outside forces. As noted earlier, the Supreme Court invalidated significant elements of the First New Deal in 1935, including most prominently the National Industrial Recovery Act in the famous *Schechter* case, forcing Roosevelt to look for alternatives. In addition, the business community – somewhat accepting if not content with Roosevelt in 1933–1934 – began to turn against him in 1935.[24] This enabled FDR to move more to the left and act in a more progressive fashion, if he chose to do so. Finally, other political actors on the American stage were nudging – if not shoving – Roosevelt in just such a leftward direction. By 1935, three prominent public figures – Father Charles Coughlin, Senator Huey Long, and Dr. Francis Townsend – had reached the height of their considerable popularity, and each of these men was using their large public pulpits to argue for policy significantly to the left of what the Roosevelt administration had offered to that point. Coughlin, the immensely popular radio priest from Michigan, was particularly important. Early on he was a strong backer of FDR and the New Deal, but by 1935, he had become clearly opposed. Coughlin increasingly attacked capitalism, and regularly called for inflationary policies,

---

[23] Sidney M. Milkis, *The President and the Parties: The Transformation of the American Party System Since the New Deal* (New York: Oxford University Press, 1993); Arthur M. Schlesinger, Jr., *The Politics of Upheaval* (Boston: Houghton Mifflin, 1960).

[24] Scott C. James, *Presidents, Parties, and the State: A Party System Perspective on Democratic Regulatory Choice, 1884–1936* (New York: Cambridge University Press, 2000); Everett Carll Ladd, Jr., *American Political Parties: Social Change and Political Response* (New York: Norton, 1970) ; Leuchtenburg, *Franklin D. Roosevelt and the New Deal, 1932–1940*; Raymond Moley, *After Seven Years* (New York: Harper and Brothers, 1939); Plotke, *Building a Democratic Political Order*; Schlesinger, Jr., *The Coming of the New Deal*.

including reviving the old Bryan/Populist plan of monetizing silver. In 1934, Coughlin received more mail than any other person in the United States (including FDR), so his voice was clearly being heard. Long, the incredibly dynamic and popular former governor and then senator (some would say that for all practical purposes he was really both at the same time) from Louisiana, had a radical plan he called "Share Our Wealth." Under Long's plan, all personal wealth over a certain amount would be taken by the federal government, and redistributed to all families in the United States. Townsend, a doctor from California, was an exponent of an old-age pension plan that would give citizens over age sixty a $200 per month pension, as long as the individual agreed to not work for pay and spend the entire sum each month. Townsend argued that this would open up jobs for the younger unemployed, and also serve to stimulate the economy through consumer spending.[25]

Roosevelt firmly believed that all three men were nothing more than demagogues, but he also recognized that they and their various plans were quite popular. Roosevelt was particularly concerned with Long, and during 1935, he increasingly thought about how he could neutralize the flamboyant senator from Louisiana.[26] As FDR advisor and, for a time, chief speech writer Raymond Moley related, at one point in the spring of 1935 Roosevelt actually outlined various ways in which he might "steal Long's thunder" in a conversation with Moley and some other advisors.[27] The president was not alone in his focus on Long. Other Democratic Party leaders were concerned about how many votes Long would attract if he chose to run for president as an independent in 1936. Some party officials were even more worried that Long would mount a serious challenge for the Democratic nomination in 1940.[28]

It is not clear why FDR moved significantly to the left in his policy offerings in 1935. It could have been primarily due to the evolution of his own views, as Tugwell seems to believe. Or it could be because of the threat of the popularity of radicals like Long, as Leuchtenburg hints at, or due to his desire to reshape his electoral coalition, as Moley and Milkis argue. It is likely that all three factors were relevant. What is important

[25] Leuchtenburg, *Franklin D. Roosevelt and the New Deal, 1932–1940*; Schlesinger, *The Politics of Upheaval.*

[26] Leuchtenburg, *Franklin D. Roosevelt and the New Deal, 1932–1940*, p. 96.

[27] Moley, *After Seven Years*, p. 305.

[28] James, *Presidents, Parties, and the State*; Leuchtenburg, *Franklin D. Roosevelt and the New Deal, 1932–1940*; Moley, *After Seven Years*; Raymond Moley, *27 Masters of Politics* (Westport, CT: Greenwood Press, 1949 [1979]); Schlesinger, *The Politics of Upheaval.*

is that he did move,[29] and he ultimately brought a good portion of the Democratic Party with him. The Second New Deal that began in 1935 saw Roosevelt and at least some of his Democratic majority in Congress push through such liberal measures as the Social Security Act, which established a retirement income program for the elderly and disabled; the Wagner Act, which guaranteed labor the right to organize and bargain collectively; and the so-called "Soak the Rich" tax bill, which among other things raised the estate tax to 70 percent and set the top personal income tax rate at 75 percent. There were additional measures as well, all of which were well to the left of what FDR had proposed in 1933 and 1934.[30] By the 1936 election cycle, it was clear to most Americans that the Democratic Party under the leadership of Franklin Roosevelt was significantly more liberal (at least outside of the South) than it had been before he had assumed control.[31] In the eyes of some, Roosevelt's Second New Deal represented the full flowering of populism in American politics.[32]

There is little doubt that FDR's moves paid off at the ballot box for both him and his party in 1936. Not only was the 1936 election cycle the apex of Democratic success during the New Deal,[33] it is also the most successful the Democratic Party has ever been in its long history of contesting American elections. Roosevelt defeated Republican Alf Landon 61 to 37 percent in the popular vote and 523 to 8 in the Electoral College, limiting Landon to wins in only Maine and Vermont. Amazingly, the Democratic edge in Congress – already substantial – increased even more. Democrats gained thirteen additional seats in the House and seven seats in the Senate. These gains gave the party a 335 to 89 edge in the lower chamber and a 76 to 16 advantage in upper chamber. As Figures 5.1 and 5.2 indicate, 1936 is the high point in Democratic popular vote in all regions (with the exception of a relative tie with 1932 for presidential popular vote in the South). The only comparable round of Democratic

[29] Leuchtenburg, *Franklin D. Roosevelt and the New Deal, 1932–1940*; Milkis, *The President and the Parties*; Moley, *After Seven Years*; Tugwell, *FDR: Architect of an Era*.

[30] James, *Presidents, Parties, and the State*; Leuchtenburg, *Franklin D. Roosevelt and the New Deal, 1932–1940*; Schlesinger, *The Politics of Upheaval*.

[31] Ladd, *American Political Parties*; Everett Carll Ladd, Jr., with Charles D. Hadley, *Transformations of the American Party System* (New York: W.W. Norton, 1975).

[32] John Gerring, *Party Ideologies in America, 1828–1996* (New York: Cambridge University Press, 1998); James, *Presidents, Parties, and the State*; Plotke, *Building a Democratic Political Order*.

[33] Plotke, *Building a Democratic Political Order*; Sundquist, *Dynamics of the Party System*, revised edition.

success is 1964, and even then the party did not match its 1936 success in the Electoral College or in the congressional elections.

Not only was 1936 an incredible electoral success for FDR and the Democratic Party, it also represented Roosevelt's successful remaking of the Democratic Party. The famous New Deal coalition that is often seen as embodying the party's golden era first appears in 1936. In winning the presidency in 1936, FDR was able to attract high levels of support from the less affluent, organized labor, urban dwellers, Roman Catholics, white ethnics, Northern blacks, women, and younger voters.[34] He was able to attract these groups without losing support in the South, where he was very careful not to antagonize voters on the issue of race.[35] With his efforts from 1933 to 1936 (and continuing at least through 1938), Franklin Roosevelt was able to use public policy to reshape the Democratic Party coalition, and to fundamentally alter the nature of partisan competition in the United States.[36] In the words of Raymond Moley, FDR "realized that he could – by cementing the labor vote by the privileges and powers of the Wagner Act, by unemployment and old-age benefits, by the liberal use of relief money and by class appeals in his speeches – win the solid support of the great masses in the larger northern cities."[37]

The result of these efforts was that Democrats were able to make sustained gains in urban areas. Figure 5.3 indicates just how significant that change was. House districts in the Northeast are grouped by the number of people per square mile.[38] From 1900 to 1924, Democrats could not win 50 percent of seats in any category of districts. In 1928, the party

---

[34] An incredible amount of scholarship has been devoted to the New Deal coalition. For some of the highlights of this work, see Allswang, *The New Deal and American Politics*; Kristi Andersen, *The Creation of a Democratic Majority, 1928–1936* (Chicago: University of Chicago Press, 1979); John Morton Blum, *The Progressive Presidents: Roosevelt, Wilson, Roosevelt, Johnson* (New York: W.W. Norton, 1980); Ladd, *American Political Parties*; Everett Carll Ladd, Jr., with Charles D. Hadley, *Transformations of the American Party System*; Leuchtenburg, *Franklin D. Roosevelt and the New Deal, 1932–1940*; Lubell, *The Future of American Politics*, second edition; John R. Petrocik, *Party Coalitions: Realignments and the Decline of the New Deal Party System* (Chicago: University of Chicago Press, 1981); Plotke, *Building a Democratic Political Order*; Schlesinger, *The Politics of Upheaval*; Sundquist, *Dynamics of the Party System*, revised edition.

[35] William E. Leuchtenburg, *The White House Looks South: Franklin D. Roosevelt, Harry S. Truman, and Lyndon B. Johnson* (Baton Rouge: Louisiana State University Press, 2005).

[36] Leuchtenburg, *Franklin D. Roosevelt and the New Deal, 1932–1940*; Milkis, *The President and the Parties*; Plotke, *Building a Democratic Political Order*; Schlesinger, *The Politics of Upheaval*; Martin Shefter, *Political Parties and the State: The American Historical Experience* (Princeton, NJ: Princeton University Press, 1994); Ware, *The Democratic Party Moves North, 1877–1962*.

[37] Moley, *27 Masters of Politics*, p. 40.

[38] The variations are: low equals 0–59, medium equals 60–999, and high equals 1,000 or greater. The vote percentages are the average Democratic House vote by type of district.

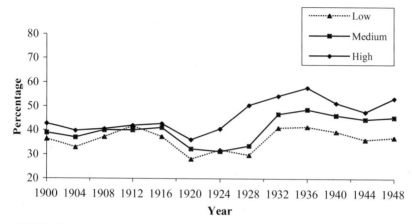

FIGURE 5.3. Democratic House percentages by population density of districts, Northeast, 1900–1948

improved its fortunes in the more urban districts. In 1932 and 1936, it was able to make significant gains in the most urban districts and even in those with medium density. Some of these gains were lost in the 1940s, but the party was still in a stronger position than before the 1930s.

Being able to attract a more diverse coalition while maintaining a stranglehold on the South established the Democratic Party as the clear majority party in American politics. FDR and the Democrats had opportunities to expand their electoral coalition, and they acted aggressively to take advantage of them. Their moves paid off handsomely, and thus the party was able to exercise government power and control the direction of public policy for years to come.

REPUBLICAN REACTION TO THE NEW DEAL

Republicans were roundly defeated in the 1936 election cycle, but it is important to note that the party began to recover from this debacle rather quickly. Indeed, as Ware points out, although the years 1932–1946 are regularly portrayed as a bleak and uncompetitive period for the Republican Party, the truth is actually very different.[39] Although the GOP did continue to be the minority party nationally from 1936 to 1946, a closer inspection of electoral results during this period reveals that the Republicans were not in as dire straits as is commonly asserted. Indeed, the GOP as the out-party during this time was far better off than the Democrats

[39] Ware, *The Democratic Party Heads North, 1877–1962.*

were when they were the minority party during the 1920s. Looking at Figures 5.1 and 5.2, outside of the South – where the Democrats maintained a huge advantage – the Republican Party began a slow but steady upward march in terms of popular vote percentage after 1936 in both presidential and House elections. By 1940, FDR and Republican candidate Wendell Wilkie were close in the popular vote in the Northeast and virtually tied in the Midwest. Roosevelt had a small edge in the West, but the only region where he had a big advantage was in the South.

The distance between the parties narrowed even further in the 1944 presidential contest between Roosevelt and New York Governor Thomas Dewey. A similar pattern is seen in the vote percentages of the parties in House elections, but here the GOP rebound is even more apparent. By 1938, Democrats had dipped to 50 percent or less in the regions outside the South, giving Republicans a tie or the electoral advantage, a pattern that held after 1938. In terms of congressional seats, the Republicans added seventy-three in the House and seven in the Senate in 1938. This improved success finally culminated with the GOP retaking both Houses of Congress after the 1946 election cycle. It could also be argued that for the Democrats success in both winning the presidency and controlling Congress was heavily dependent on the large margins the party regularly received in the South. As we will see later, the conservatism of that region created tensions within the party and limits on what the party could pursue.

At least in terms of electoral results, the Republican Party had reasons for hope in the late 1930s and early 1940s. Other signs pointed to opportunity for the GOP as well. By mid-1937, a number of conservative Democrats in Congress had become disillusioned enough with FDR and the New Deal to begin voting against the president in Congress. Aligned with the Republican members, this alliance came to be known as the *Conservative Coalition*, and from 1937 forward, FDR and the liberal Democrats were much less successful in getting their preferred policies through Congress.[40] Perhaps more important, many of these conservative congressional Democrats were from the South, and their increased unhappiness with the larger Democratic Party in many ways reflected that of their constituents. As the 1940s progressed, the Democrats would meet with increasing difficulties in this crucial region. Beginning in 1940,

[40] Leuchtenburg, *Franklin D. Roosevelt and the New Deal, 1932–1940*; Milkis, *The President and the Parties*; James T. Patterson, *Congressional Conservatism and the New Deal: The Growth of the Conservative Coalition in Congress, 1933–1939* (Lexington: University of Kentucky Press, 1967); Schlesinger, *The Politics of Upheaval*.

the Republican presidential vote in the South began to rise significantly.[41]
The pace of Republican gains – at least at the presidential level – picked
up substantially after the conclusion of World War II. A good deal of this
is because the Democrats were increasingly confronted with internal conflict relating to the issue of race.[42]

As noted earlier, FDR had been able to finesse attracting Northern
African Americans to the Democratic Party, on the one hand, while holding on tight to the Southern white vote, on the other. Roosevelt's successor as president, Harry Truman, did not have the same touch. It could
also be argued that Truman did not share Roosevelt's caution on the issue
of race. Certainly some of his actions support such a conclusion. Truman
created a presidential committee on civil rights in 1946, became the first
president to ever address the National Association for the Advancement
of Colored People (NAACP) in 1947, and desegregated the American military by executive order in 1948. The 1948 Democratic platform also contained a strong civil rights plank (which actually went a bit too far for
Truman's liking), and Truman went to Harlem in search of votes, another
presidential first.

These actions served to solidify black support for the Democratic Party,
but they also served to seriously anger Southern Democrats.[43] Despite
the formation of the segregationist Dixiecrat Party (officially the States'
Rights Democratic Party) headed by presidential candidate Strom Thurmond, Truman and the Democrats were able to hold on to the presidency
in 1948. However, it was a narrow victory, and the Republicans came
closer to capturing the White House than they had in years. The GOP had
opportunities to regain the majority. The question, as is always the case,
was could a minority party take advantage? That would take some time.

---

[41] Lubell, *The Future of American Politics*, second edition.

[42] Plotke, *Building a Democratic Political Order*.

[43] Edward G. Carmines and James A. Stimson, *Issue Evolution: Race and the Transformation of American Politics* (Princeton, NJ: Princeton University Press, 1989); Michael K. Fauntroy, *Republicans and the Black Vote* (Boulder, CO: Lynne Reinner, 2007); Leuchtenburg, *The White House Looks South*; Sundquist, *Dynamics of the Party System*, revised edition.

6 The Democratic Drive to the Great Society

The New Deal dramatically changed the role of the federal government in the United States. The Social Security Act of 1935 established a national program to provide for the elderly and the disabled. For the first time, the federal government assumed some responsibility for the unemployed by making it attractive for states to implement unemployment insurance. Federal expenditures on and responsibility for public works programs of all shapes and sizes increased exponentially. Regulation and oversight of financial markets and other important segments of the economy expanded significantly, and in a long-sought victory by labor activists, the federal government used its coercive power to ensure workers the right to organize and bargain collectively.

Taxation expanded as well in order to fund all of this new government activity. Franklin Roosevelt and his fellow Democrats in Congress responded to the Great Depression and made federal government action legitimate and even desirable, at least to most Americans. World War II further expanded the role of the national government. Tax levels increased again, and still more federal agencies were established. To many it seemed clear that the political dialogue, and indeed the public mood itself, had shifted to the left.[1] Government was not a destroyer of freedom, but rather a source of assistance and an actor to make sure that no interest had undue influence and that no American was unduly left behind.[2] It is difficult to overstate the magnitude of this change in the view of government, and the situation of the parties most certainly reflected this shift.

---

[1] For a discussion of the concept of public mood, see James A. Stimson, *Public Opinion in America: Moods, Cycles, and Swings*, second edition (Boulder, CO: Westview Press, 1999); James A. Stimson, *Tides of Consent: How Public Opinion Shapes American Politics* (New York: Cambridge University Press, 2004).

[2] Eric Foner, *The Story of American Freedom* (New York: W.W. Norton, 1998), 195–218.

REPUBLICAN FRUSTRATIONS

As the 1950s began, most Republicans saw their situation as worse off than that of the Democrats. Although there were some reasons for optimism, as discussed in the last chapter, the facts on the ground were unavoidable and unavoidably ugly for the GOP. Republicans had not won the presidency since 1928. Thomas Dewey, presumably a top-quality candidate, lost in 1948 when he was expected to win. The party held a majority in the House only once since the 1932 election, in 1947–1948. In the Senate, the party had also been in the minority for the last twenty years, except for 1947–1948. There were many in the party who thought they had to accept New Deal programs and carve out a position of moderation with some conservative elements. For these Republicans, it seemed that a large, activist federal government was here to stay. Perhaps the best that could be done was to conduct government more efficiently and keep it from expanding further.

The political situation Republicans faced is shown in Table 6.1. By the early 1950s, surveys of the American public were asking if they generally identified with the Democratic or Republican Party. Those who said they were independent were then asked if they leaned toward either party. Those who say they are independent but leaning to a party can be added with those initially indicating a party preference to indicate the general distribution of party identification.[3] In the early 1950s, Democrats had a twenty-point national lead in party identification. Part of their edge stemmed from their huge advantage in the Southern states[4] (72 to

---

[3] Research has shown that these leaners tend to behave in much the same way as self-identified "weak" partisans, although they are less partisan than self-identified "strong" partisans. See Bruce E. Keith, David B. Magleby, Candice J. Nelson, Elizabeth Orr, Mark C. Westlye, and Raymond E. Wolfinger, *The Myth of the Independent Voter* (Berkeley, CA: University of California Press, 1992).

[4] What constitutes the South has been a source of some disagreement. For the analysis that follows, the focus is on the eleven states that formed the Confederacy during the Civil War. We focus on these states because they are the ones that became so solidly Democratic following the Civil War and became such a reliable base for the party. These states and their concerns also subsequently created problems for the party because these states were largely rural until the 1970s, and these representatives struggled with accepting a more urban agenda. They were also concerned about preserving state autonomy so segregation would not be affected. This is the same grouping Jerald Rusk uses in his very valuable *A Statistical History of the American Electorate* (Washington, DC: CQ Press, 2001), and we find his data very useful to document change. While using this, we also recognize that other groupings have been used and have their own merits. Indeed, in earlier chapters we have used a more inclusive grouping, such as the National Election study uses. However, for our purposes here, it is the role and transition of these eleven states that has been so important in American politics.

TABLE 6.1. Party identification in the early 1950s

	Year	
	1952	1954
Entire nation (without leaners)		
Democrat	47	47
Republican	27	27
Entire nation (with leaners)		
Democrat	57	56
Republican	34	33
South (with leaners)		
Democrats	72	
Republicans	18	
Non-South (with leaners)		
Democrats	52	
Republicans	40	

Note: The South/non-South distinction is not available for 1954.

Source: NES Cumulative file, 1948–2004. For this analysis, the focus is on the Solid South as a base of the Democratic Party compared to the rest of the nation. The South is defined as Alabama, Arkansas, Florida, Georgia, Kentucky, Louisiana, Mississippi, North Carolina, South Carolina, Tennessee, and Texas.

18 percent in 1952), but they also had a significant advantage outside the South, where 52 percent identified with the Democratic Party and 40 percent with the Republican Party.

Many Republicans concluded that the Democratic Party's argument that government, and particularly the national government, should play a strong and active role in society had triumphed. Democrats appeared to have a solid grip on the South (as long as they stayed away from nominating Catholics for president and didn't talk too much about civil rights for blacks) and were doing well enough outside the South to be difficult to beat. There were, of course, forceful dissenters within the Republican Party. As we will see Chapter 7, committed conservatives had not given up in their efforts to make a case against an expanded government.[5] Yet for much of the 1940s and 1950s, conservatives within the GOP could not persuade the rest of their party that a sustained attack on the size and scope of the federal government would pay off. It took a long run of liberal activism and social change to provide an opportunity for conservatives to finally make a convincing case. For a time, conservatives had to

[5] For an early example of this, see Herbert Hoover's impassioned critique of activist government, *The Challenge to Liberty* (New York: Charles Scribner's Sons, 1934).

be content to make their arguments and wait for the tide to turn in their favor.

The issue of whether Republicans should move in a more conservative direction emerged immediately as the 1952 party convention approached. Senator Robert Taft from Ohio had a consistent conservative record and had been denied the nomination in 1948 by moderates within the party who much preferred New York Governor Thomas Dewey. After Dewey's defeat, conservatives felt they deserved a candidate in 1952. Moderates within the party, seeing the trends of the last two decades, believed that a conservative nominee would do nothing more than guarantee defeat. A moderate candidate was the only way to victory; after all, Dewey had come excruciatingly close to winning in 1948. These moderates within the party approached Dwight Eisenhower, who had commanded U.S. forces during World War II, to consider being a candidate. He accepted and a divided convention chose Eisenhower over Taft. Eisenhower went on to defeat the Democratic candidate Senator Adlai Stevenson of Illinois, convincing many Republicans that they had done the right thing in steering a moderate course. Eisenhower presented himself as a pragmatist, largely accepting the New Deal and its expanded federal role.[6] The sense that the party had to largely accept the Democratic position was solidified by the 1954 elections. Republicans had taken the majority in both chambers of Congress in the 1952 elections, but lost it in 1954, putting them back in the minority in each House in 1955. It was difficult for many Republicans to accept an argument that moving toward more conservative values would put them in the majority when voters kept putting Democrats in office.

DEMOCRATS: SUCCESS WITH A GROWING SENSE OF UNEASE

Democrats, in contrast, appeared be in a reasonably good situation. They had dominated national government for two decades. They continued to hold together their coalition of Southern whites and working-class ethnics of Italians, Irish, Poles, and others from the urban areas of the Northeast and Midwest. However, all was not well within the party. The Democrats have always been a relatively fractious bunch, and by the mid-1940s (if not earlier), tensions were on the rise within the party.

---

[6] Sidney M. Milkis, *The President and the Parties: The Transformation of the American Party System since the New Deal* (New York: Oxford University Press, 1993); David Plotke, *Building a Democratic Political Order: Reshaping American Liberalism in the 1930s and 1940s* (New York: Cambridge University Press, 1996).

The Southern wing was still not entirely supportive of many government social programs, and was suspicious of an activist federal government.[7] As pointed out at the end of Chapter 5, many (if not most) white Southerners were especially opposed to the national government intruding into segregation practices within their region. Southern voters had moved away from Harry Truman in 1948 because of his actions supporting civil rights for African Americans.[8] They did not come back entirely to the Democratic Party in 1952 and 1956 (as they had in 1932), giving Eisenhower 48 and 49 percent of the popular vote in the two elections, respectively.[9] The rise of the civil rights movement was troubling to many Southerners who did not want any more activism by the national government in this area or in the area of legislation making it easier for labor unions to form. The Southern delegation of the Democratic Party was becoming more conservative and increasingly resisted many of the party's initiatives during the late 1930s and 1940s.[10]

The Northern wing of the party had a different agenda. Blacks had been moving to Northern and Midwest urban areas for decades, and they were increasingly registering to vote.[11] Democratic members of Congress were being elected from districts with substantial percentages of nonwhites and these members were more liberal. The labor movement was strong in the Northeast and parts of the Midwest, and unions provided crucial campaign support by providing volunteers and contributions. Blacks wanted more attention paid to issues of segregation and congressional legislation to ensure equal rights. Unions wanted modifications in existing labor law. During the 1930s, Democrats had passed legislation making it easier for unions to organize workers. Republicans held power in Congress in 1947–1948 and they passed the Taft-Hartley Act, which made it much more

[7] Kari Frederickson, *The Dixiecrat Revolt and the End of the Solid South, 1932–1968* (Chapel Hill: University of North Carolina Press, 2001).
[8] Edward G. Carmines and James A. Stimson, *Issue Evolution: Race and the Transformation of American Politics* (Princeton, NJ: Princeton University Press, 1989); Michael K. Fauntroy, *Republicans and the Black Vote* (Boulder, CO: Lynne Rienner, 2007); Michael Gardner, *Harry Truman and Civil Rights: Moral Courage and Political Risks* (Carbondale: Southern Illinois University Press, 2003); William E. Leuchtenburg, *The White House Looks South: Franklin D. Roosevelt, Harry S. Truman, and Lyndon B. Johnson* (Baton Rouge: Louisiana State University Press, 2005).
[9] Jerrold G. Rusk, *A Statistical History of the American Electorate* (Washington, DC: CQ Press, 2001), 140.
[10] James T. Patterson, *Congressional Conservatism and the New Deal: The Growth of the Conservative Coalition in Congress, 1933–1939* (Lexington: University of Kentucky Press, 1967); Howard L. Reiter, "The Building of a Bifactional Structure: The Democrats in the 1940s," *Political Science Quarterly* 116 (Spring 2001): 107–29.
[11] Nicholas Lemann, *The Promised Land* (New York: Alfred A. Knopf, 1991).

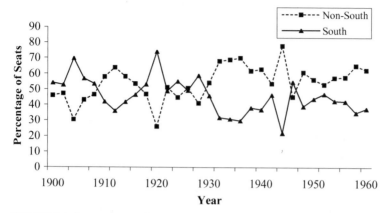

FIGURE 6.1. Percentage of Democratic House seats derived from regions, 1900–1960. *Source:* Data compiled by the authors; South is defined here as in Table 6.1

difficult for unions to operate. The act shifted the definition of unfair labor practices from management treating workers badly to unions harming firms. The law prohibited wildcat strikes (spontaneous, short strikes that disrupted production), strikes in solidarity with other unions, some picketing, and rules that workers had to join a union.

Furthermore, the party now realized that it was less dependent on its Southern base than it had been in years past. Democrats increased their electoral success in northern urban areas in the 1932 elections and that success had persisted.[12] Figure 6.1 indicates the percentage of House Democrats from the South & elsewhere from 1900–1960. Table 6.2 also indicates the percentage of House Democrats from the South and the non-South from 1900 to 1960. From 1900 to 1928, a majority of Democratic House members were usually from the South. Beginning in 1930, the majority usually came from outside the South, and the non-Southern portion of the party was more liberal. This liberal wing was watching Southern members join with Republicans to form the *Conservative*

---

[12] Samuel J. Eldersveld, "The Influence of Metropolitan Party Pluralities in Presidential Elections since 1920: A Study of Twelve Key Cities," *American Political Science Review* 43 (December 1949), 1189–1206; Samuel Lubell, *The Future of American Politics*, second edition, revised (Garden City, NY: Doubleday Anchor Books, 1956); Carl N. Degler, "American Political Parties and the Rise of the City: An Interpretation," *Journal of American History* 51 (June 1964), 41–59; Kristi Andersen, *The Creation of a Democratic Majority 1928–1936* (Chicago: University of Chicago Press, 1979); Julius Turner and Edward V. Schneier, *Party and Constituency: Pressures on Congress*, revised edition (Baltimore: Johns Hopkins Press, 1970).

TABLE 6.2. Democratic success in House elections, 1928–1960

Year	Nation			Non-South			South		
	D	R	D%	D	R	D%	D	R	D%
1928	165	269	38.0	68	262	20.6	97	7	93.3
1930	216	217	49.9	117	213	35.5	99	4	96.1
1932	313	117	72.8	213	115	64.9	100	2	98.0
1934	322	103	75.8	221	101	68.7	100	2	98.0
1936	335	89	79.0	235	87	73.0	100	2	98.0
1938	262	170	60.7	162	168	49.1	100	2	98.0
1940	267	163	62.1	168	161	51.1	99	2	98.0
1942	222	210	51.4	119	208	36.4	103	2	98.1
1944	242	191	55.9	139	189	42.4	103	2	98.1
1946	188	246	43.3	85	244	25.8	103	2	98.1
1948	263	171	60.6	160	169	48.6	103	2	98.1
1950	235	199	54.2	132	197	40.1	103	2	98.1
1952	213	221	49.1	113	215	34.5	100	6	94.3
1954	232	203	53.3	133	196	40.4	99	7	93.4
1956	234	201	53.8	135	194	41.0	99	7	93.4
1958	283	153	64.9	184	146	55.8	99	7	93.4
1960	263	174	60.2	164	167	49.6	99	7	93.4

Source: Jerrold G. Rusk, *A Statistical History of the American Electorate* (Washington, DC: CQ Press, 2001), 260.

Coalition, which was able to block liberal legislative proposals. Increasingly, the liberals did not like what they saw. The tension within the party focused on how hard the Northern wing would push on issues of segregation, and federal intrusion into state prerogatives steadily increased.

The struggle over the direction of the Democratic Party was pushed in a new direction by the events of 1957–1958. The danger for Northern Democrats – and perhaps the one thing that kept them from making an aggressive push on civil rights – was that the South might go Republican if voters, many of them focused exclusively on segregation issues, saw the Republican Party as an alternative on issues of race. The likelihood of this actually taking place was limited by the reality that congressional Republicans generally had a more liberal civil rights voting record than Democrats did in the 1950s.[13] In 1957, the potential for the South to move Republican on the basis of race was diminished, at least temporarily. In 1954, the Supreme Court issued the historic *Brown v. Board of Education* ruling that public schools must be integrated. The issue of whether

[13] Edward G. Carmines and James A. Stimson, *Issue Evolution: Race and the Transformation of American Politics* (Princeton, NJ: Princeton University Press, 1989).

the ruling would be enforced emerged in 1957 when the courts mandated that schools in Little Rock, Arkansas, had to be integrated. Local officials were reluctant to protect blacks seeking to attend a previously white school, and President Eisenhower was faced with the issue of whether he would protect black students. With some reluctance he decided to do so, sending regular U.S. Army troops into Little Rock to keep the peace while also federalizing the Arkansas National Guard to prevent Governor Orval Faubus from using them to block integration.[14] The result was that any effort to reposition the Republican Party and make it more attractive to white Southerners by portraying the Republican Party as sympathetic to their concerns about integration was diminished. After the events in Little Rock, the possibility of Southern Democrats leaving the party – at least for the GOP – was much reduced.

While 1957 diminished the threat of conservative Southern Democrats embracing the Republican Party as an alternative, the 1958 election cycle emboldened the liberal wing of the party. The problem facing the Democratic Party was that their majorities in Congress rested on their success in the South. Without the South, the Democrats simply could not control Congress. In the 1930s, the party had won more than 50 percent of seats outside the South, but during the 1940s and most of the 1950s they had not been able to achieve that level of success. This, of course, made the South all the more important to the Democrats. Table 6.2 indicates the party's success from 1928 to 1960 for the nation and by region.

Although the party had reacquired the majority in the House in 1954, their margin was slim in that year and also in 1956. This changed in 1958. The 1958 election cycle unfolded during a recession, with many voters blaming a Republican president and therefore voting Democratic for Congress. The results increased the Democratic margin in Congress, with the bulk of this increase being accounted for by an influx of non-Southern liberals. This increased tension within the party and created pressures for the party to pursue a more liberal agenda. Democratic success in winning House seats outside the South jumped to 55.8 percent, the highest since 1936. Analyses of election results indicated that Democrats had come close to doing even better. Republicans lost forty-seven seats, but shifts of five percentage points or less within specific districts could

---

[14] W. H. Lawrence, "Eisenhower 'Deeply Disappointed' in Impasse at Little Rock," *New York Times*, September 20, 1957, p. A1. For more in-depth treatment of this matter, see Elizabeth Jacoway, *Turn Away Thy Son: Little Rock, the Crisis That Shocked the Nation* (New York: The Free Press, 2007); David A. Nichols, *A Matter of Justice: Eisenhower and the Beginning of the Civil Rights Revolution* (New York: Simon & Schuster, 2007).

have cost another sixty-one seats.[15] The Democrats' performance in Senate races was just as impressive, as the party won twenty-six of the thirty-four seats up for election that year. That success changed the overall partisan composition of the Senate from forty-nine Democrats and forty-seven Republicans to sixty-five Democrats and thirty-five Republicans. The crucial matter was who was elected and how the results were interpreted. Those who were elected in 1958 were more liberal than those who had been in office.[16] Liberal Democrats had been frustrated for some time by their inability to enact liberal legislation to further civil rights, raise the minimum wage, help unions, provide housing assistance to those with lower incomes, and provide direct federal aid to local schools. They were regularly being blocked by the Conservative Coalition comprised of Southern Democrats and Northern Republicans, and their patience was wearing thin.[17] Liberal Democrats believed that the 1958 elections were a clear sign that the party should move in a more liberal direction. As the 1959 session began, liberals in the House formed a new group, The Democratic Study Group, to develop liberal legislation. The liberal wing was convinced that the time was ripe for them to push the party in a liberal direction and that this would increase the base of the party.

Although the liberal wing of the Democratic Party thought the 1958 elections signaled that voters were moving their way, conditions were still not conducive for the liberal Democrats to achieve their goals. The Conservative Coalition still dominated Congress. Both houses of Congress relied on *seniority* (length of time in Congress) as a rule for awarding

[15] W. H. Lawrence, "Study of Voting Shows G.O.P. Faces Difficult Task Next Year," *New York Times*, February 1, 1959, p. A1. This did not mean that all Democrats were safe. The study also indicated that forty-seven Democrats won by less than five percentage points and they might be vulnerable.

[16] If we use DW-NOMINATE scores as a guide, the average voting records of new Democratic House members were more liberal ($-.31$) than those who continued from the prior session ($-.22$). A lower score is more liberal. The voting of the new members pushed the average for the Democratic Party from $-.22$ in 1956 to $-.25$ in 1958. In the Senate, the class of Democrats that replaced Republicans was much more liberal than those who had been in office. See Edward G. Carmines and James A Stimson, *Issue Evolution*, 66–72.

[17] For studies of this coalition in the late 1950s, see Congressional Quarterly, "How Big is the North-South Democratic Split?" *Congressional Quarterly Almanac* (Washington, DC: Congressional Quarterly, Inc., 1957), 813–17; Congressional Quarterly, "Basic Democratic Divisions Examined," *Congressional Quarterly Almanac* (Washington, DC: Congressional Quarterly, Inc., 1958), 764–69; Congressional Quarterly, "Extent of North-South Democratic Split Analyzed," *Congressional Quarterly Almanac* (Washington, DC: Congressional Quarterly, Inc., 1959), 135–46. For an overview, see Mack C. Shelley II, *The Permanent Majority: The Conservative Coalition in the United States Congress* (University: University of Alabama Press, 1983).

committee chairmanships, which is where the real power in Congress resided during these years. Conservative Southern Democrats faced little competition, lasted longer in Congress, and controlled the majority of chairmanships. They were able to block liberal legislation and frustrate the ambitions of liberals.[18] The conservatives' stranglehold on key committees made it difficult for liberals to achieve much of their legislative agenda. Frustration mounted, and tensions rose.

For liberals, the 1960 election results confirmed their sense that their base was growing more supportive of a liberal agenda. The party nominated a Catholic politician from the Northeast, John F. Kennedy, as its presidential candidate and won. In 1960, urban Catholics were viewed as strong proponents of a liberal agenda, especially policies that extended the welfare state. Kennedy's win was regarded as historic because the Democrats' last (and to that point, only) Catholic candidate, Al Smith in 1928, had been badly defeated.[19] Many in the party took this change in outcomes as a signal that the public was ready for another round of strong, activist government at the national level. The party slipped somewhat outside the South, but still won almost 50 percent of the seats outside the South and retained 60 percent of all seats in the House. In the Senate, Democrats won twenty of thirty-three seats contested and had a 64–36 overall advantage. The party seemed to have a solid majority and was poised to adopt a clear, activist agenda.

There were also political reasons for Kennedy to pursue an expanded legislative agenda. Kennedy barely won the 1960 race, and he wanted to expand his electoral base in anticipation of a 1964 reelection bid. The question was how to do this. Blacks living in the North were a prime target. Blacks had been moving to the North for years to take jobs in northern urban centers like Chicago, Detroit, Philadelphia, and Pittsburgh.[20] From 1910 to 1970, over six million blacks moved to northern central cities. Blacks were also registering to vote, and they had provided enough votes in Northern urban areas in 1960 to provide Kennedy with his winning margin. In addition to these political concerns, there were also serious social concerns becoming increasingly evident. Most blacks

---

[18] David Rohde, *Parties and Leaders in a Post-Reform House* (Chicago: University of Chicago Press, 1991); Julian E. Zelizer, *On Capitol Hill* (New York: Cambridge University Press, 2004).

[19] To this point, only three Roman Catholics have ever received a major party's presidential nomination, all from the Democrats – Al Smith in 1928, John F. Kennedy in 1960, and John Kerry in 2004.

[20] Lemann, *The Promised Land*.

were poor, lived in ghettos, and were not welcomed by many whites.[21] There were growing concerns about the possibilities of urban conflict, and some saw a need to enact legislation to provide benefits to head off racial unrest and conflict. The challenge for Democrats was how to shore up their support among blacks without pushing civil rights too hard, which would cost the party votes in the South.[22]

There was also a growing sense that it was appropriate for government to take action on the more general issue of poverty and equality of opportunity for blacks and poorer whites. Some saw the growing affluence of the society as providing a basis for addressing the persisting poverty. The median family income in the United States had been rising steadily,[23] and the benefits were being distributed widely. Inequality in the distribution of income had been declining since 1947 because those in the bottom of the income distribution were experiencing greater gains than those at the top.[24] It seemed that economic anxieties were declining and the willingness to help others was rising as incomes grew. This widespread improvement of economic fortunes made a growing number of Americans increasingly confident that the resources were available to improve American society.

There were also a set of ideas emerging that provided rationales for why government action to change society was both possible and desirable. Liberals had become committed to a positive role for the federal government in the 1930s.[25] By the mid-1950s, a host of arguments were emerging about why government could and should do even more. John Kenneth Galbraith published *The Affluent Society* in which he argued that the private sector in America was doing well, but our public infrastructure was impoverished. The Soviets launched the space satellite *Sputnik* in 1957 that made people uneasy that the Russian government was building up its military and surveillance capabilities faster than America. The sense that America was falling behind the Soviets prompted concern that

---

21 Dennis R. Judd and Todd Swanstrom, *City Politics: The Political Economy of Urban America* sixth edition (New York: Pearson-Longman, 2008), 213–20.

22 Frances Fox Piven and Richard A. Cloward, "The Politics of the Great Society," in Sidney M. Milkis and Jerome M. Mileur (eds.), *The Great Society and the High Tide of Liberalism* (Amherst: University of Massachusetts Press, 2006), 257.

23 U.S. Bureau of the Census, Current Population Reports, P6–203, *Measuring 50 Years of Economic Change Using the March Current Population Survey* (Washington, DC: U.S. Government Printing Office, 1998), Table C-10, p. C-19.

24 Sheldon Danziger and Peter Gottschalk, *American Unequal* (Cambridge, MA: Harvard University Press, 1995), 53; Allen, 1999, 57.

25 Foner, *The American Story of Freedom*, 195–218.

the country needed to invest more in public matters such as science and math. Articles appeared regularly in popular magazines such as *Life*, *Look*, and *Esquire*, arguing that it was time for a new energy in government to address problems that had been neglected during the 1950s.[26]

The rising impulse for increased federal action found plenty of potential targets besides the Soviets. There was growing awareness that poverty was not disappearing, even in the face of widespread improvement in economic fortunes. Michael Harrington's *The Other America*, published in 1960, vividly documented the persistence of poverty in America and became a national bestseller.[27] President Kennedy became particularly interested in policy proposals aimed at alleviating poverty and set out to improve the circumstances of the less affluent.[28] He wanted to establish more programs to increase opportunity and provide direct assistance. Furthermore, studies were emerging that documented that the environment – the family and neighborhood – students grew up in had a major impact on their subsequent academic achievement.[29] For liberals, these studies provided all the more reason for the federal government to act to try to reduce poverty.

There was also more pressure to deal with issues of discrimination and denial of basic civil rights in America. In the South, blacks were increasingly pressing for equal rights and the end of segregation in public facilities. In December 1955 in Montgomery, Alabama, Rosa Parks refused to move to the back of a public bus, where blacks were expected to sit when a white person got on the bus. Parks was arrested, and the bus boycott that followed kicked the African American civil rights movement into high gear. Marches to protest segregation sprang up throughout the South, and more and more Americans were watching violent responses by Southern police on their new televisions and growing uncomfortable about the discrepancy between American ideals of equal treatment and the realities of life in the South.

Liberals now had more seats in Congress, poverty was recognized as persisting, protests about racial injustice were increasing, and there was an argument that government could affect the environments of

---

[26] Rick Perlstein, *Before the Storm* (New York: Hill and Wang, 2001), 50.

[27] Michael Harrington, *The Other America* (New York: Macmillan, 1960).

[28] John Kennedy and his brother Robert were powerfully affected by the intense poverty they encountered as they campaigned in 1960. See Daniel Knapp and Kenneth Polk, *Scouting the War on Poverty: Social Reform Politics in the Kennedy Administration* (Lexington, MA: Heath Lexington Books, 1971).

[29] James S. Coleman, *Equality of Educational Opportunity* (Washington, DC: U.S. Department of Health, Education, and Welfare, Office of Education, 1966).

individuals and improve the lives of Americans. In other words, the stage was set for liberal Democrats to enact the activist agenda they had been pushing for years. As an added bonus, these same Democrats believed that turning this agenda into public policy would benefit them for decades to come. For many Democrats, it seemed like a perfect opportunity to both achieve their programmatic goals and expand their electoral coalition through the public policy process. If they could help the right set of constituents they could increase the size of their coalition and remain the majority for years to come.

All these conditions created a context that justified, and to some, compelled a greater role for the federal government. President Kennedy made numerous proposals to address social problems, and he made some progress on a liberal agenda. Congress accepted his proposals to somewhat increase the minimum wage, expand support for public housing, increase programs to retrain workers displaced by new technology, and require equal pay for women in jobs similar to men. However, the Conservative Coalition was still significant and consistently able to block the liberal legislation mentioned earlier involving the minimum wage, civil rights, housing, unions, and education aid.[30] The Democratic Party held the presidency and Congress, but it was struggling to set a clear policy direction because the party was a mix of Southern conservatives and Northern moderates and liberals. The New Deal coalition born in the 1930s was still contending with its diversity.

The events of 1963 and 1964 provided an unexpected juncture for the party to change its direction. President Kennedy was assassinated in November 1963, and Lyndon B. Johnson succeeded him as president. The parties, at least as signified by their presidential candidates, took very different policy directions as 1964 unfolded. For Democrats, the issue was what directions President Johnson would pursue. He was a former member of the House and later Senate Majority Leader from Texas, and Kennedy had selected him as a running mate primarily to help him carry Texas specifically and help in the South more generally. In his years in Congress, Johnson behaved for the most part as a standard Southern Democrat, meaning that he regularly opposed civil rights legislation. He was certainly no liberal.

Yet Johnson was also the consummate politician, and by the late 1950s, he was becoming increasingly convinced that the Democratic Party's

---

[30] John D. Morris, "First Kennedy Congress Responds Coolly to the Call of the New Frontier," *New York Times,* September 28, 1961, p. 32.

future success lay less with Southern conservatives and more with liberals outside of the South, including blacks.[31] At the same time, civil rights marches were occurring with greater frequency and being met with more violence in the South and elsewhere. This violence was being presented regularly on the evening news, painting an ugly view of America. Upon assuming the presidency, Johnson immediately chose to lead the party in an unmistakably liberal direction. Historian William Leuchtenburg characterized Johnson's evolution thusly: By 1963, "Johnson had long since ceased to condone racism, and he was determined to be a change-maker" on civil rights.[32] Johnson immediately endorsed strong civil rights legislation he felt that the Democratic Party and the nation needed to respond to issues of poverty and racial inequality. He felt strongly that the South needed to accept equal rights and citizenship for blacks. He pushed the House and Senate to pass the legislation, and despite considerable resistance in the Senate, he was eventually able to secure passage and signed the legislation in July 1964.

Johnson acted boldly on other issues besides race. In his first State of the Union address in January 1964, he proposed a War on Poverty program. He and his staff had significant ambitions, accompanied by an increasingly prosperous society, to address problems of poverty. He then submitted legislation known as the Economic Opportunity Act, which created programs such as VISTA (Volunteers in Service to America) that was aimed at assisting the poor at the local level; Job Corps, to train those out of work; Head Start, to provide enrichment programs for low-income children; the Legal Services program, to provide legal assistance to the poor; and the Community Action Program, to create local agencies to enable the poor to become self-sufficient. As a whole, they embodied a liberal and aggressive program to try to reduce poverty.

In May 1964 in a speech at the University of Michigan, he proposed his Great Society agenda. Johnson was convinced that the problems of society – disparities in education, opportunity, housing, racial equality, and access to health care – could be remedied by government programs. Equality of opportunity could be provided. Other needs – better transportation systems, public support for cultural pursuits, protection of the environment and of consumers – could also be legislated. Problems could be solved. It was a broad and ambitious vision of the role government

---

[31] Leuchtenburg, *The White House Looks South.*
[32] Ibid., 300.

could play in society.[33] In Lyndon Johnson (at least the 1964 version), the Democrats had given their presidential nomination to an aggressive, unabashed liberal. Republicans responded with equal clarity, nominating Arizona Senator Barry Goldwater as their candidate. Goldwater was a staunch fiscal conservative, and he was adamantly opposed to a strong centralized government except for national defense. That logic lead him to vote against enacting national civil rights laws, at a time of intense controversy about the issue, on the grounds that such matters should be left to the states.[34] Goldwater suffered one of the worst defeats ever experienced in a presidential contest. He won only 39 percent of the popular vote and only 52 out of a possible 538 electoral votes. Lyndon Johnson had staked out a liberal agenda during 1964, and his party was waiting to see how the country would react. For many, Johnson's overwhelming victory made the public's wishes clear. It was easy for Johnson to believe that he had promised a clear liberal agenda and the electorate had given him an overwhelming mandate to enact that agenda.[35]

As important as Johnson's landslide presidential victory was for the Democrats' liberal wing, equally important perhaps was what happened in the congressional elections in 1964. The timing of the election also helped Democrats. For years, state legislatures had refused to redraw their district boundaries, even as the population moved from rural to urban areas. Many urban districts had far more people than rural districts, resulting in underrepresentation of urban, more liberal interests and overrepresentation of rural, more conservative interests. In 1962, the Supreme Court in the case of *Baker v. Carr* ruled that districts were to represent people and not trees. The Court established the one-man, one-vote rule, saying districts had to have roughly even populations. That set off a round of state redistricting efforts, which began a reduction of rural districts and an increase in urban districts.[36] The presidential contest between Goldwater and Johnson coincided with the creation of more

---

[33] Sidney M. Milkis, "Lyndon Johnson, the Great Society, and the Modern Presidency," in Sidney M. Milkis and Jerome M. Mileur (eds.), *The Great Society and the High Tide of Liberalism*, 1–49.

[34] Indeed, Goldwater's opposition rested purely on his views on the proper role of the federal government. Goldwater had been a member of the NAACP and the Urban League. He once stated, "I am half Jewish, and I know something about discrimination." See Jerry F. Hough, *Changing Party Coalitions: The Mystery of the Red State-Blue State Alignment* (New York: Agathon, 2006).

[35] Milkis, "Lyndon Johnson, the Great Society, and the Modern Presidency," 1–49.

[36] Julian E. Zelizer, *On Capitol Hill: The Struggle to Reform Congress and Its Consequences, 1948–2000* (Cambridge: Cambridge University Press, 2004), 74.

TABLE 6.3. Democratic success in House elections, 1954–1968

	Nation			Non-South			South		
Year	D	R	D%	D	R	D%	D	R	D%
1954	232	203	53.3	133	196	40.4	99	7	93.4
1956	234	201	53.8	135	194	41.0	99	7	93.4
1958	283	153	64.9	184	146	55.8	99	7	93.4
1960	263	174	60.2	164	167	49.6	99	7	93.4
1962	259	176	59.5	164	165	49.6	95	11	89.6
1964	295	140	67.8	205	124	62.3	90	16	84.9
1966	246	187	56.8	163	164	49.9	83	23	78.3
1968	243	192	55.9	163	166	49.5	80	26	75.5

Source: Jerrold G. Rusk, *A Statistical History of the American Electorate* (Washington, DC: CQ Press, 2001), 260.

urban districts in many states. The result of the 1964 elections was that Democrats ran up the largest majorities (a 155-seat edge in the House and a 36-seat advantage in the Senate) they had had in Congress since the 1930s.

The conclusion that 1964 provided a liberal mandate was supported by where these new members came from and the political views they brought with them. As Table 6.3 indicates, Democrats were able to win 62.3 percent of seats outside the South, a level not achieved since 1936. In addition, the greatest increase in success for Democrats came in the areas they were pursuing and thought they had to have to build a larger majority. The party had been trying for some time to expand its electoral base in Northern urban districts. As Figure 6.2 indicates, the party had made some gains in the 1930s in the more urban Northeastern districts, but they then dropped down to winning only about 50 percent of seats in those districts in the 1940s and 1950s. In the 1960 and 1964 elections, House Democrats achieved much greater success in the most urban districts and even won 50 percent of seats in the moderately urban districts.

These new House members were also more liberal. There were 96 new members in the House that assembled in 1965. Seventy-four of them were Democrats and they were more liberal than the returning party members. Within the Democratic Party, among those elected prior to 1964, 63.4 percent had liberal voting records in 1965–1966.[37] Among

---

[37] We use DW-NOMINATE scores to group members. Those with voting records of less than −.2 are grouped as liberals, those with records of −.2 to.2 as moderates, and those with records of more than .2 as conservatives. These cut points are arbitrary, because

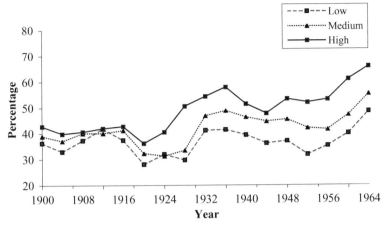

FIGURE 6.2. Democratic House percentages by density of districts, Northeast, 1900–1964

those elected in 1964, 79.7 percent had liberal voting records in 1965–1966. If we use their subsequent voting records, the House Democratic Party had acquired a much larger contingent of liberals because of the 1964 elections. The same change in the composition of the party occurred in the Senate, with more liberals elected.[38]

A LEGISLATIVE OUTPOURING

The presumed logic of elections is that politicians propose agendas and the electorate renders a reaction. After the 1964 election, the judgment was that the electorate supported a significant expansion of programs and Johnson and the Congress acted on that assessment. There was a remarkable outpouring of legislation, all increasing the federal government's role in trying to shape society.[39] The list here provides a sample of such legislation. The federal government was becoming active in trying to

---

there is no agreement about what constitutes a true liberal or conservative, but establishing some points allows us to track shifts in voting records over time.

[38] Carmines and Stimson, *Issue Evolution*.

[39] The volume of initiatives was significant and only some are presented here. For more detail, see Robert D. Divine (ed.), *The Johnson Years, Volume One: Foreign Policy, the Great Society, and the White House* (Lawrence: University Press of Kansas, 1981); Marshall Kaplan and Peggy L. Cuciti (eds.), *The Great Society and its Legacy: Twenty Years of U.S. Social Policy* (Durham, NC: Duke University Press, 1986); James L. Sundquist, *Politics and Policy: The Eisenhower, Kennedy, and Johnson Years* (Washington, DC: Brookings Institution Press, 1968); Irwin Unger, *The Best of Intentions: The Triumphs and Failures of the Great Society under Kennedy, Johnson, and Nixon* (New York: Doubleday, 1996).

affect local and higher education, health care, consumer safety, and the arts.

Great Society Legislation: A Sampling

- Elementary and Secondary Education Act of 1965: For the first time, the federal government provided funds to local schools. Traditionally, local schools had local control and relied on state-local funding.
- Higher Education Act of 1965: Increased federal money given to universities, and created scholarships and low-interest loans for students.
- Voting Rights Act of 1965: Provided for a federal role in assuring the rights of minorities to register and vote. Eliminated many locally administered tests to reduce registration.
- Social Security Act of 1965: Provided coverage of health care costs for senior citizens (Medicare), funded by the federal government and a new tax on wages.
- Social Security Act of 1965: Provided coverage of health care for low-income individuals without insurance (Medicaid). The federal government provided grants to states, which could design their own programs and receive reimbursement for a percentage of costs.
- National Foundation on the Arts and Humanities Act: Created nationally funded organizations to promote the arts and the humanities.
- Cigarette Labeling Act of 1965: For the first time, the federal government was requiring cigarette packages to carry warning labels about the dangers of smoking.
- Motor Vehicle Air Pollution Control Act (1965): For the first time, the federal government set standards about how much pollution cars could emit.

This burst of legislative enactments did not stop in 1965. In the next several years, legislation was enacted to protect consumers from chemicals, to eliminate racial discrimination in access to housing, to provide for a national public broadcasting corporation, to provide funding for mass transit systems, to regulate the safety requirements cars must meet, to provide for all sorts of consumer protection requirements, and to protect the environment. Liberals had acquired control of Congress, believed they had a mandate, and were finally in a position to push the Conservative Coalition aside. They seized the opportunity and enacted a volume of liberal legislation not seen since the 1930s. Party control and the interpretation of election results by the majority party mattered a great deal following 1964.

SETBACKS FOR THE LIBERAL DEMOCRATS

The Democratic Party's liberal wing had plenty of reasons to believe they were well situated. They controlled the White House and both chambers of Congress. After years of being blocked by conservatives, they were finally able to take action. Liberal legislation flew through Congress and was signed by the president at a pace not seen since the New Deal. However, as Democratic liberals were busy enacting laws and basking in the glow of their success, unexpected problems began to arise. These problems would eventually come to dominate the public dialogue and ultimately undermine the liberal Democrats. In 1965, Watts, an inner-city black neighborhood in Los Angeles, erupted into a lengthy riot over accusations of police brutality in the treatment of blacks. The riot made many Americans uneasy and undermined the implicit claim made by liberals that blacks just wanted equal treatment in society and to take advantage of new opportunities. Some liberals vaguely justified the outburst and argued that years of frustration had lead to such riots. Moderates worried that images of violent minorities undermined sympathy for the civil rights cause, and conservatives complained about a lack of law and order. Then in 1966, another major riot broke out in the Hough section of Cleveland over racial tensions. Others followed in major cities across the United States in what came to be known as the *Long Hot Summers*.

Many Americans became increasingly unsupportive of liberal social policies as they viewed scenes of costly violence and destruction on their television screens.[40] Democrats had hoped to claim credit for advancing the cause of minorities and the poor but were finding themselves faced with how to respond to threatening violence in cities. Their ambivalence concerned many Americans, and especially angered conservatives.

The Great Society programs established by liberals to respond to social problems were also generating criticism. The Community Action Program (CAP), funded directly by federal dollars, was providing jobs for activists who attacked city hall and angered established urban politicians. In some cases, stories of corruption and uncontrolled spending emerged. Legal

---

[40] Dennis E. Gale, *Understanding Urban Unrest: From Reverend King to Rodney King* (Thousand Oaks, CA: Sage Publications, 1996). For an official investigation of these riots, see National Advisory Commission on Civil Disorders, *Report of the National Advisory Commission on Civil Disorders* (New York: Bantam Books, 1968).

Aid, intended to provide low-income people with help against landlords and creditors, was being used to file suits against government, further angering local officials.[41] Welfare rolls were expanding rapidly and the perception, inaccurate as it was, was that minorities were choosing welfare over working.[42]

Furthermore, the justification for many of these programs was being undermined by social trends. Liberals had proposed numerous social programs as a way to help ameliorate problems of inequality of condition and opportunity. The presumption was that if blacks were given equal rights, programs to create opportunity, and support – expanded access to welfare, housing, and food stamps – then there should fewer angry people. That logic was particularly important in the early 1960s when the government was confronted with numerous civil rights protests. Legislation was seen as the way to calm down dissenters, while also closely tying them to the Democratic Party.[43] The problem facing liberals was that violent crime and urban riots were steadily increasing. The argument that programs that addressed peoples' needs would reduce anger and improve social and economic conditions was not being supported by events. Critics were arguing for the importance of respect for law and order.

The 1966 elections provided a sharp rebuke of the Democrats' liberal wing. The party lost a net of forty-nine seats in the House (see Table 6.2) and they lost eighteen of thirty-three Senate elections, lowering their advantage from 68–32 to 64–36. Johnson had lost much of his ability to get whatever he wanted from the Congress. It was also where Republican gains occurred that made Democrats wonder about their future. The party had always had a solid base in the South and their fortunes varied according to how they did outside the South. After the passage of the Civil Rights Act of 1964 in July, Johnson told his young press secretary Bill Moyers, "We have lost the South for a generation."[44] As Table 6.4 shows, the greatest opposition to the legislation had come from the South. In the South, the House vote among Democrats was eighty-six against and eight for the bill. The Republican Party was shifting to a more

---

[41] Daniel P. Moynihan, *Maximum Feasible Misunderstanding: Community Action in the War on Poverty* (New York: Free Press, 1970).

[42] Martin Gilens, *Why Americans Hate Welfare: Race, Media, and the Politics of Anti-Poverty Policy* (Chicago: University of Chicago Press, 1999).

[43] Perlstein, *Before the Storm*, 206–7; Frances Fox Piven and Richard A. Cloward, *Regulating the Poor: The Functions of Public Welfare* (New York: Pantheon, 1971).

[44] Robert Dallek, *Flawed Giant: Lyndon Johnson and His Times, 1961–1973* (New York: Oxford, 1998), 120.

TABLE 6.4. House regional and party divisions, 1964 Civil Rights Act

Region	Democrat		Republican	
	No	Yes	No	Yes
North	6	121	3	81
South	86	8	15	0
Other	10	54	8	27
Total	102	283	26	108

Source: Vote taken from *1964 CQ Almanac*, pp. 636–7.

conservative position on issues of race and federal intervention in state affairs,[45] and from 1960 to 1966, the number of Republicans in the South had gone from seven to twenty-three (see Table 6.3). Democrats had reason to worry about losing their solid base.

As if the tensions within the Democratic Party over race were not enough, the Vietnam War was becoming more and more controversial and a greater source of division within the party. The war had presented a difficult dilemma for President Johnson. Most Americans saw the United States as locked in a struggle to contain the spread of communism in the world. Russia was communist and seen as a serious threat. China had gone communist in 1949, expanding the presumed reach of communism. The 1950s had been a decade of public preoccupation with fear of communists. During that decade Americans were urged to build bomb shelters in case the Soviets launched a missile attack on the nation. There was continual concern about communist infiltration of American society. In 1961, the United States, worried about the spread of communism to Cuba when Fidel Castro took over in a 1959 revolution, launched an unsuccessful attack to change the regime. In 1962, surveillance planes discovered plans for Soviet missiles to be located in Cuba. This led to a showdown that took the United States to the brink of nuclear war with the Soviet Union before the issue was resolved.[46]

In the early 1960s, there was concern that communists were trying to expand into Southeast Asia. Given the enormous fear of communism in America, Johnson was afraid to be seen as the president who would allow

[45] Carmines and Stimson, *Issue Evolution.*
[46] Don Murton and David A. Welch, *The Cuban Missile Crisis: A Concise History* (New York: Oxford University Press, 2007); Norman Polmar and John D. Gresham, *DEFCON-2: Standing on the Brink of Nuclear War During the Cuban Missile Crisis* (New York: John Wiley & Sons, 2006).

an expansion of communism into this region of the world. His critics dismissed the threat that communism in Vietnam could affect America and argued that prosecution of the war was a serious mistake.[47] Much to his dismay, Johnson was finding that his liberal supporters were becoming his most vocal critics about the Vietnam War. Even Martin Luther King, Jr., who had confined his efforts to civil rights issues, saw the war as hurting these efforts and began to speak out against the war. Street protests against the war were steadily increasing.

The events of 1968 badly rattled the party. In January, the Viet Cong launched the *Tet Offensive*, an attack all across South Vietnam. The Johnson administration had been assuring everyone that Vietnam was under control. Although there were disputes about the success of the Viet Cong offensive, its boldness and breadth shattered the story the administration was presenting. In March, President Johnson stunned his party by announcing that he would not run for reelection.

Then things got worse when George Wallace, a former governor of Alabama, announced a bid for the presidency, threatening to take all the votes of Southern Democrats in a presidential election. Wallace campaigned on a platform of states' rights and opposition to federal bureaucrats intruding too much into the lives of Americans. The message was that national enactment of civil rights legislation had disrupted the Southern way of life for whites, and Wallace was going to serve as a spokesperson for resentment about this issue. Polls indicated that Wallace was doing well in Southern states and would probably take those electoral votes away from a Democratic candidate.

Then the Democratic National Convention was held in Chicago. All the problems and divisions of the party were exposed on national television. Youth protested in the streets about the Vietnam War, and Mayor Richard J. Daley of Chicago ordered the police to attack and remove them. The subsequent violence against protestors was beamed across the country.[48] Inside the convention hall, things were not much better. Some Southern states sent all white delegations to the convention and competing groups sent racially mixed delegations. Each competed for recognition as the official delegation. The fights tore the party apart. Hubert Humphrey, the current vice president and presumed successor to

---

[47] See, as an example of liberal criticisms, Arthur M. Schlesinger, Jr., *The Bitter Heritage: Vietnam and American Democracy* (Boston: Houghton Mifflin, 1966).

[48] Frank Kusch, *Battleground Chicago: The Police and the 1968 Democratic National Convention* (Westport, CT: Praeger, 2004); Daniel Walker, *Rights in Conflict: Chicago's 7 Brutal Days* (New York: Grosset and Dunlap, 1968).

Johnson, was struggling with how to mollify antiwar groups. Although he had a long history of being a liberal on many domestic issues, he was finding his image overwhelmed by Vietnam. Liberals were also angered because their two favored presidential candidates – Robert Kennedy and Eugene McCarthy – had been denied the nomination unfairly, the former by an assassin's bullet and the latter by the smoke-filled-room machinations of Democratic Party bosses. The convention conflicts made it difficult for the party to patch up its differences, and Humphrey's race was a struggle as he sought to separate himself from the shadow of Lyndon Johnson. Humphrey began the fall campaign with an extremely divided party, burdened by Vietnam, riots in American cities, and with Wallace taking some of the states that he needed. Although it was a close race in November, Republican candidate Richard Nixon won the presidency.[49]

In January 1965 Democrats were positive that the country was moving their way, ready for a liberal agenda. Johnson had won a landslide victory and carried numerous liberals into Congress along with him. All the signs were that they had a mandate to change the course of government policy and that they would be reaffirmed by the electorate. By November 1968, Republican Richard Nixon was the victor. A politician previously assumed to be finished as a presidential candidate (because of losses in a 1960 run for president and a 1962 run for governor of California) was in power. Democrats were left to try to assess what had happened to them. How had their fortunes and vision of a liberal society focused on equality of opportunity evaporated so quickly?[50] This assessment would be a long and tormented process.

[49] Theodore H. White, *The Making of the President, 1968* (New York: Atheneum Press, 1969).

[50] For a good discussion of this dynamic, see G. Calvin Mackenzie and Robert Weisbrot, *The Liberal Hour: Washington and the Politics of Change in the 1960s* (New York: Penguin Press, 2008).

7 Republicans: Reasserting Conservative Principles and Seeking a Majority

The 1968 election shook the Democrats' confidence in their liberal policy agenda. It began a lengthy period of grappling with charges that the party had moved too far left in its efforts to advance an activist government agenda. For Republicans, the 1968 elections provided a vague sense, amid considerable political chaos, that a more conservative message could be presented to the public. However, it would take some time for that possibility to fully emerge. In reality, 1968 was just one of several fitful efforts by conservatives to push the GOP in a more conservative direction, efforts that moderates consistently opposed. The origins of conservative efforts began much earlier than the late 1960s and took a considerable amount of time to come to fruition.

The story of how conservatives made a comeback in American politics is a long one. It is a story of belief, persistence, organization, failure, and setback, overcoming doubts, making renewed efforts, and eventually realizing gains among voters that conservatives had to attract to achieve electoral success. It is a process in which conservatives were often dismissed and moderates argued that a conservative appeal would not work. It took weaving together a coalition that many doubted could be assembled. It is, moreover, a perfect example of the model of gradual realignment as a party searches for a majority.

AN INTELLECTUAL REBUTTAL TO A GREATER ROLE FOR GOVERNMENT

The electoral success of Franklin Roosevelt and the New Deal appeared to indicate that a majority of Americans had come to accept a greater role for government. That interpretation was supported by many academics. By the late 1940s and 1950s, a group of historians and social theorists were arguing that a consensus prevailed in American politics and fundamental conflicts over the proper scope and role of the federal government were on the decline, and would soon disappear from the public debate.[1] There appeared to be little opposition to an expanded role for the national government. As Lionel Trilling wrote in 1950, "In the United States at this time liberalism is not only the dominant but even the sole intellectual tradition. For it is the plain fact that there are no conservative or reactionary ideas in general circulation."[2] Democrats had held the presidency for twenty consecutive years, and it seemed difficult to argue with the notion that most Americans saw government as a positive force in their lives. In 1960, Daniel Bell published *The End of Ideology*, which seemed to announce that passionate debates about the relative roles of government and individuals were going to decline.[3] Bell proposed that the American public was going to focus more on problem solving and less on competing visions of how the world should work.

Despite the apparent conquest by liberalism, there were those making the argument that an expanded role for government would eventually harm American society. A group of intellectuals, some of whom had fled the Nazis in Europe, saw dangers in a growing national government.[4] At the heart of their argument was concern about the oppressive effect of a big and controlling central government. A number of specific works played large roles in fueling the growth of the conservative movement. Perhaps no thinker had a bigger impact than Friedrich Hayek, who argued in *The Road to Serfdom* (1944) that the crucial attributes of a free society were individual freedom and the free market. He believed that individualism was central to making society prosper. The free market provided the right context for individuals to use their talents to pursue their goals,

[1] The argument that American politics operated within a broad consensus was made by historians such as Richard Hofstader, *The American Political Tradition and the Men Who Made It* (New York: Alfred A. Knopf, 1948). For a review of this school of thought, see John Higham, "The Cult of the 'American Consensus': Homogenizing Our History," *Commentary* 27 (1959): 94–5. This was followed by Louis Hartz, *The Liberal Tradition in America* (New York: Harcourt Brace, 1955).
[2] Lionel Trilling, *The Liberal Imagination* (New York: Harcourt Brace Jovanovich, 1950). William Rusher opens the preamble to his personal account of the rise of conservatives with what one suspects is a mocking restatement of Trilling's quote. William A. Rusher, *The Rise of the Right* (New York: William Morrow and Company, Inc., 1984), 11.
[3] Daniel Bell, *The End of Ideology* (New York: Free Press, 1962).
[4] Donald Critchlow, *The Conservative Ascendancy* (Cambridge, MA: Harvard University Press, 2007), 6–40, provides an excellent review of these authors. For the most thorough examination of the intellectual development of conservatism during this time, see George H. Nash, *The Conservative Intellectual Movement in America* (New York: Basic Books, 1976).

and the pursuit of these goals by individuals would yield a more prosperous society with greater freedom.[5] Ayn Rand, in *The Fountainhead*
(1943) and *Atlas Shrugged* (1957), created mythic figures who struggled
against conformist societies and governments. Russell Kirk's *The Conservative Mind* (1953) extolled the virtues of conservatism and warned that
only a return to conservative principles could save a declining society.
In 1962, Milton Friedman, a prominent University of Chicago economist,
published *Capitalism and Freedom*, promoting the virtues and freedom that
accompany free markets and capitalism. Conservatives embraced these
and other authors presenting the same themes and urged others to read
them. Their goal was to reestablish the conservative idea that individualism was a positive force in society and a large intrusive government would
be detrimental to innovation and ultimately to freedom in American
society.

There were numerous efforts to establish popular magazines to present
these conservative views to a larger audience. William F. Buckley, frustrated with the lack of an outlet for conservative views, founded perhaps the most famous and influential of these outlets when he established *National Review* in 1955. Buckley saw his magazine as crucial in
opposing communism and the ideas embodied in the New Deal, and in
exposing what he saw as the flaws of liberalism and the essential truths of
conservatism.[6] There were also activists trying to create organizations to
mobilize conservatives. Some, such as The John Birch Society founded by
Robert Welch in 1958, were preoccupied with communism. Others, such
as the Young Americans for Freedom established in 1960, were worried
about the encroachment of government on individual freedom.

There were also numerous efforts to get business leaders, troubled
by more and more regulations on business, actively involved in opposing government. These efforts eventually proved quite fruitful as some
prominent businessmen and their families such as Joseph Coors, Richard
Mellon Scaife, Fred Koch, and many more ultimately contributed tens of
millions of dollars to establish and fund conservative think tanks, support the work of conservative intellectuals, found and maintain conservative interest groups, and set up numerous vehicles for the dissemina-
tion of conservative thought. All of these efforts were ultimately aimed at

---

[5] Excellent overviews are contained in Jerry Z. Muller (ed.), *Conservatism* (Princeton:
Princeton University Press, 1997); and Eric Foner, *The Story of American Freedom* (New
York, W.W. Norton, 1998).

[6] Rusher, *The Rise of the Right*.

building a case against a large, activist American government and arguing in favor of the long-term benefits of individualism and reliance on free markets. Put simply, the goal of these conservative intellectuals, authors, activists, and financial donors was to challenge and eventually shatter the consensus in favor of big government that appeared to have been established in the wake of the New Deal and the end of World War II.[7]

POLITICAL LIMITATIONS

Even as intellectual activity and organizational efforts increased, conservatives within the Republican Party still faced many obstacles to success. Part of the difficulty they faced was reducing the power of the Eastern, more moderate wing of the party, and convincing others that a conservative message could attract voters. For years, the Northeastern moderates and even a few liberals had controlled the Republican Party.[8] This faction of the party (and thus the party as a whole) had a long history of being more supportive of civil rights than Southern Democrats.[9] Party leaders from the Northeast were skeptical that the party could ever win many elections in the South, and thought the party had to focus on increasing its support outside the South. After all, such a model had once produced a remarkable run of success for the GOP.

In 1952, the moderate wing of the party was so concerned about looking too conservative that they engineered a deal to deny the presidential nomination to the favorite of conservatives, Senator Robert Taft of Ohio. The moderates recruited Dwight Eisenhower, the general who had successfully managed World War II efforts, to be the party's candidate. He was not an opponent of the New Deal and presented a more moderate face for the party. In the 1952 elections, Eisenhower won 56 percent of the vote outside the South and 48 percent in the South.[10] In 1956, he

---

[7] For good summaries of these interconnected efforts, see Chip Berlet and Matthew S. Lyons, *Right-Wing Populism in America: Too Close for Comfort* (New York: Guilford Press, 2000); Niels Bjerre-Poulsen, *Right Face: Organizing the American Conservative Movement, 1945–1965* (Copenhagen: Museum Tusulanum Press, 2002); John Micklethwait and Adrian Wooldridge, *The Right Nation: Conservative Power in America* (New York: Penguin Press, 2004); Nash, *The Conservative Intellectual Movement in America*; Rick Perlstein, *Before the Storm* (New York: Hill and Wang, 2001); Rusher, *The Rise of the Right*.

[8] Nicol C. Rae, *The Decline and Fall of the Liberal Republicans from 1952 to the Present* (New York: Oxford University Press, 1989), 46.

[9] Edward G. Carmines and James A. Stimson, *Issue Evolution: Race and the Transformation of American Politics* (Princeton, NJ: Princeton University Press, 1989).

[10] Rusk, *A Statistical History of the American Electorate*, 140.

did even better, winning 59 percent outside the South and 49 percent in the South. In the 1958 congressional elections, many Republican conservatives lost and were replaced by liberals, providing further evidence that attracting voters with a conservative message would be very difficult. The Northeastern wing was convinced that nominating a moderate was the only way the party could appeal to a majority of Americans. As noted earlier, Democrats had a significant advantage in party identification across the nation in the early 1950s, and there was little evidence in election results that a conservative message would attract voters. On its face, there did not appear to be much in support of an argument that a conservative message would result in success at the ballot box and control of government.

Furthermore, there were those who argued that Republicans of a conservative stripe were still able to achieve their goals through the Conservative Coalition, formed in the late 1930s and comprised of Southern Democrats and conservative Northern Republicans. This coalition was regularly able to create a majority to shape legislation and defeat much of the agenda of liberals.[11] If the South was going to remain Democratic, some Republicans argued that the best approach was to work with Southern Democrats who would support conservative goals.

Finally, and perhaps most important, there were also problems with presuming that Americans were dissatisfied with the state of society. As noted earlier, family incomes were increasing, the economy was growing, and economic inequality was declining. Conservatives may have been angry about the general acceptance of the New Deal, but there did not appear to be widespread opposition to this greater role for government.

As the 1950s came to a close, the Republican Party found itself in difficult circumstances. The Northeast dominated the party and that wing of the party was convinced that to win the presidency Republicans had to win their traditional base in the Northeast and some Midwest states. To moderates, Dwight Eisenhower's presidential victories in 1952 and 1956 validated the belief that moderation was the route to winning. Conservatives were very troubled with the direction of American politics, and in

---

[11] John Robert Moore, "The Conservative Coalition in the United States Senate, 1942–45," *Journal of Southern History* 33 (August 1967): 369–76; James T. Patterson. "A Conservative Coalition Forms in Congress, 1933–1939," *The Journal of American History* 52 (March 1966): 757–72; James T. Patterson, *Congressional Conservatism and the New Deal: The Growth of the Conservative Coalition in Congress, 1933–1939* (Lexington: University of Kentucky Press, 1967).

their view, Northeast Republicans were too willing to reach accommodation with the Democrats. Eisenhower's governance, in the eyes of many conservatives, validated their anxieties. He was too willing to accept a significant role for government. The GOP was a minority party with two factions that were becoming increasingly unhappy with one another. If the analysis thus far in this book tells us anything, it is that ultimately something would have to give and one side would win out.

A RENEWED CONSERVATIVE COMMITMENT

Although many saw a consensus prevailing in American politics in favor of an activist federal government in pursuit of a liberal agenda, conservatives were still opposed to the growth of government and were building organizations to support conservative causes and candidates. Small groups of conservatives were forming around the country and connecting with each other.[12] They were angry about tax levels, about more government regulations and the federal government telling them where their children must go to school, about how guilty they should feel about segregation, and about the lack of focus on communism. Their goal was to find a candidate to make their concerns part of the public debate. To many, Senator Barry Goldwater of Arizona (first elected in 1952) was a promising possibility.[13] He was willing to speak out about limiting the federal government's intrusion into American lives. He extolled the virtues of individualism and business as the route to growth and freedom. He came from the West, which resented the extensive control the federal government had over land in that region.[14]

The 1960 presidential election frustrated conservatives. Some conservatives in the West sought to nominate Goldwater, but he was reluctant to enter the race, and in reality the battle for the Republican nomination was between Vice President Richard Nixon and New York Governor Nelson Rockefeller. Rockefeller, coming from a relatively liberal Northeast state, had become governor by being an advocate for an activist government. Nixon saw his main challenge as having to fend off Rockefeller,

---

[12] Lisa McGirr, *Suburban Warriors: The Origins of the New American Right* (Princeton, NJ: Princeton University Press, 2002).

[13] Perlstein, *Before the Storm.*

[14] Richard Conniff, "Federal Lands," *National Geographic* 185 (February 1994): 2–39. The federal government owned or regulated from 29 to 85 percent of lands in the western states by the 1990s, creating continual tension between western individualists and federal guidelines.

and he focused on reaching an accommodation with him. Conservatives did not like either of these men, and they largely lost out in the maneuvering that went on as the party selected its presidential standard bearer. Even more discouraging for Republicans of all stripes was that Nixon lost the 1960 election and Republicans were completely out of power.

THE GOLDWATER CAMPAIGN AND INTERPRETING ELECTION RESULTS

Conservatives, however, continued unabated in their belief that the future of the Republican Party lay in an embrace of their ideology. In 1962, William Rusher, then publisher of the *National Review*, argued that the future of the party would come from success in the South, and that Barry Goldwater, with his opposition to government intrusion, could bring about that success.[15] The argument for a Southern strategy had emerged.[16] Goldwater, then head of the National Republican Senatorial Committee (intended to assist GOP Senate candidates), was regularly visiting the South during that time to make speeches and raise money, and he was receiving warm receptions. Clifford White, a talented and committed conservative, was organizing conservatives across the country to nominate Goldwater (unbeknownst to Goldwater himself) in what became known as the "Draft Goldwater" movement.[17] The Eastern, more moderate wing of the party, on the other hand, remained convinced they had to present a moderate presidential candidate to have any chance at victory.[18] Conservatives, however, were better organized, having spent several years recruiting supporters to fill state and national convention slots. They prevailed and Barry Goldwater was nominated in 1964. Conservatives finally had their spokesman.

And what a spokesman Goldwater was. *The Conscience of a Conservative* (1960) – Goldwater's famous statement of political belief[19] – expounded

---

[15] William Rusher, "Crossroads for the GOP," *National Review* (February 12, 1963): 109–12.

[16] As we have noted a number of times, the moderate wing of the GOP found such arguments almost absurd. Yet voices within the GOP advocating a Southern strategy grew more numerous over time, and by the early 1970s, some academics were writing of the merit of such arguments. See E. M. Schreiber, "'Where the Ducks Are': Southern Strategy Versus Fourth Party System," *Public Opinion Quarterly* 35 (Summer 1971): 157–67.

[17] Rusher, *The Rise of the Right*.

[18] Perlstein, *Before the Storm*, 158–80.

[19] Goldwater was assisted in writing this work by prominent conservative activist L. Brent Bozell, Jr. Bozell was also very close to William F. Buckley.

on the rectitude of conservatism, the propriety of free markets, and the essential nature of individual and states' rights to the preservation of freedom. It railed against high levels of federal taxing and spending, cursed the New Deal welfare state, and warned of the dangers of federal involvement in education. Perhaps most forcefully, Goldwater argued vehemently that the Soviet Union was the ultimate threat to the United States, and that the nation must defeat the Soviets by any means necessary, including the use of nuclear weapons if needed. The campaign of Barry Goldwater presented Americans with a clear statement of conservative principles.

Unfortunately, 1964 did not turn out as planned. President Kennedy was generating considerable hostility for his positions on civil rights and efforts to defuse relations with Russia. It is possible that he would have entered the 1964 election in a weakened state. However, his assassination in November 1963 generated enormous sympathy for his goals, and former Vice President and now President Lyndon Johnson was able to position himself as the man to implement Kennedy's legacy. It became harder to generate zealous attacks against Lyndon Johnson. The Johnson campaign was also able to portray Goldwater as an extremist. Goldwater's convention acceptance speech, with the title of "Extremism in the Defense of Liberty is no Vice," helped the Democratic campaign nurture that image. During the campaign, they presented the infamous "Daisy" television commercial that showed a small child in a field, plucking daises, and then an atomic bomb going off in the background. The ad only aired once, but it successfully raised the question of whether Americans wanted to trust Goldwater with the power to start a war. The answer, for most, was an overwhelming no.

The results of the 1964 election were seen by most as a serious setback for conservatives, and even today it is difficult to see them any other way. Lyndon Johnson received 61.1 percent of the popular vote, the highest received by any presidential candidate since a meaningful two-party system was established in 1828. House Democratic candidates received 57.4 percent of the national vote, the highest in the post–Civil War existence of the party. Perhaps most important was that Republicans received only 43.9 percent outside the South, losing their majority outside the South. Conservatives, after years of struggle, had gotten a conservative nominated as a presidential candidate and he had brought a tremendous defeat upon the party. The judgment of commentators was that conservatives had presented arguments and they had been firmly rejected. James Reston of *The New York Times* wrote, "He has wrecked his party for a long

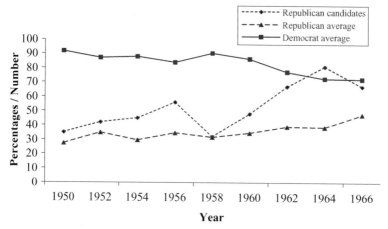

FIGURE 7.1. Partisan change in Southern House elections, 1950–1966

time to come." A *New Yorker* columnist wrote, "The election has finished the Goldwater school of political reaction."[20]

While most analyses saw a serious setback for the conservative cause, some conservatives saw a reason for optimism. William Rusher of *National Review* had argued that the party could succeed in the South, and Goldwater did win five Southern states – Alabama, Georgia, Louisiana, Mississippi, and South Carolina.[21] In 1961, Goldwater had famously stated that if the Republicans wanted to gain votes, they needed "to go hunting where the ducks are," and Goldwater and many of his conservative supporters saw plenty of ducks in the South. Although some considered the assessment of 1964 as grasping, it was the first time the party received more electoral votes in the South (37) than outside the South (15). The party had its lowest percentage of seats (32.2) in the House since 1932 (21.0). Nonetheless, the party continued to make some progress in the South, increasing its number of House seats from eleven to sixteen. In 1950, the party had 35 candidates for the 114 seats in that region. As Figure 7.1 indicates, those thirty-five averaged 27.3 percent of the vote. In 1964, they had eighty-one candidates who averaged 38.6 percent. The party was making inroads. There was some hope, but conservative Republicans needed to find a way to build on that small measure of success.

---

[20] Perlstein, *Before the Storm*, ix.

[21] For a discussion of the importance of this, see Bernard Cosman, *Five States for Goldwater: Continuity and Change in Southern Presidential Voting Patterns http://polarizedamerica. com/dwnomin.htm* (University of Alabama Press, 1966); David Lublin, *The Republican South: Democratization and Partisan Change* (Princeton, NJ: Princeton University Press, 2004).

A RESURGENCE?

Nineteen sixty-five and early 1966 represented a difficult period for Republicans. Lyndon Johnson was sure he had a mandate for a liberal agenda, and Democrats had an overwhelming majority in Congress. Democrats enacted bill after bill expanding the role of government, and Republicans could do little to slow things down. However, then events began working against the Johnson administration and the Democrats. Crime was on the rise, welfare rolls were increasing, and urban rioting was spreading across the nation. Republicans had an opening, but the conservatives needed some evidence that they could reassert a conservative message and that it would result in success at the ballot box.

The 1966 election results provided that evidence. Nationally, Republicans picked up a net of forty-seven seats in the House and won eighteen of thirty-four contests in the Senate. Republicans regained the majority outside the South. Changes in the South were particularly important. In that region, the party picked up another seven seats in the House, moving from sixteen to twenty-three. Their number of House candidates in the South was down from eighty-one in 1964 to sixty-four in 1966 (see Figure 7.1), but the average percentage of the vote won for those running was now up to 47.3, and the average percentage won by Democratic candidates was steadily sliding. About one-third of the GOP's Southern House candidates were now winning. Republicans still had a long way to go in the South, but the results were encouraging.

The 1966 election also fundamentally altered the situation of Republican House incumbents. Since the 1932 landslide for Democrats, Republican incumbents had been struggling to achieve the same level of electoral success that Democrats enjoyed. From 1946 through 1964, 70.9 percent of Democrats had *safe seats*, defined as seats won with 60 percent or more of the vote. During that time, 43.6 percent of Republicans achieved vote percentages of that level or more. In the 1966 elections, 89.2 percent of Republican incumbents in the House were safe, while the success of Democratic incumbents declined.[22] For the first time in decades, Republican incumbents were achieving the electoral success of Democrats.

The challenge for Republicans was to build on this success in the South. Their efforts in that region were both helped and hurt by Alabama Governor George Wallace. George Wallace's 1968 independent presidential candidacy served as a test of conservative themes in the South but it was

[22] Jeffrey M. Stonecash, *Reassessing the Incumbency Effect* (New York: Cambridge University Press, 2009).

also a threat to take electoral votes from Republicans. Wallace had built his career in Alabama by opposing integration and the meddling intrusion of the federal government. In 1963, he stood in the doorway of the University of Alabama to oppose the entrance of black students, arguing that the issue was whether it was possible to stop the "march of centralized government that is going to destroy the rights and freedom and liberty of the people of this country."[23] Although Wallace was often seen as a racist opposing integration, it was also clear that his popularity was based on his stand against a powerful national government intruding into the lives of the working and middle class. He was a symbol of resistance to integration, but he was also becoming a populist figure who was tilting against a strong national government and expressing support for local autonomy.[24]

It was an emerging portrayal of government as the oppressor of the average man; the same argument conservative intellectuals had been making for years now presented by a champion of the Southern, white working class. For years, liberals had made the argument that society was dominated by big business and economic elites, and that government was the vehicle to contain that influence and provide some responsiveness to the average man. Consumer protection laws had been enacted to provide some leverage for individuals against large corporations. Now conservatives were presenting themselves as jousting against overbearing federal officials who were trying to tell people how to live. It was an argument liberals did not think others would accept as plausible, but one that Wallace's supporters embraced.

He combined that stance with anger about a lack of respect for traditional values and behavior. He appealed to a strong conviction among many Americans that economic or racial injustice did not justify crime, and sometimes vaguely and sometimes not-so-vaguely connected crime and welfare abuse to blacks. As one supporter, an ex-Marine, put it to a black member of the audience at a rally for Wallace in Wisconsin:

> I live on Walnut Street and three weeks ago tonight a friend of mine was assaulted by three of your countrymen or whatever you call them. They beat up old ladies eighty-three years old, rape our womenfolk. They mug people. They won't work. They are on relief. How long can we tolerate this?[25]

[23] Dan T. Carter, *The Politics of Rage* (New York: Simon & Schuster, 1995), 137.
[24] Carter, *The Politics of Rage*, 207–9; Dan T. Carter, *From George Wallace to New Gingrich: Race in the Conservative Counterrevolution, 1963–1994* (Baton Rouge: Louisiana State University Press, 1996); Michael Kazin, *The Populist Persuasion* (New York: Basic Books, 1995), 221–42.
[25] Perlstein, *Before the Storm*, 321.

A growing number of Americans were becoming concerned and angry about crime, welfare, illegitimate births, and a decline in morals. To conservatives, traditional values were being threatened and no one seemed to care. Liberals were seen as just apologists for all these behaviors, and deniers of the crucial role of individual responsibility as the norm that keeps society working. To conservatives, these were universal norms of behavior that everyone should have to adhere to.

To conservatives, it was not just that irresponsible behavior was being tolerated or even justified, but liberal elites were scorning those adhering to traditional norms of behavior as old-fashioned and intolerant. George Wallace's approach was to try to create a cultural populist anger about elites abusing the "little man." Populism had a long history, tracing back to at least the 1800s, of the average man mobilizing to act against economic abuses – low wages, poor working conditions, and control of loan interest rates – by economic elites.[26] Wallace's goal was to capitalize on the anger about elites who he saw as telling the average man that he was racist and parochial for opposing integration, busing, and intrusion by federal officials.[27] The new form of populism involved rejecting elites who were trying to tell hardworking people what to think and how to behave.

The challenge for Republicans was how to appeal to those angry about these matters and opposed to government intrusion without looking like they were racist and in favor of segregation. The party was changing its stance on civil rights, trying to find a path between equal rights and not having government tell people who they had to live with. By the late 1960s, the GOP was moving away from supporting civil rights legislation because it thought the new laws had gone too far in allowing government intrusion into communities and the rights of homeowners.[28] The key for conservatives was to determine the right mix.

THE SOUTHERN STRATEGY

The 1968 election reflected all the complexities facing the Republican (or GOP) party. Richard Nixon had again emerged as a primary candidate for the party's nomination. His political maneuverings that year indicated the changes the party was struggling with. Nixon was convinced that the party could make significant gains in the South with a conservative

[26] Lawrence Goodwyn, *The Populist Moment: A Short History of the Agrarian Revolt in America* (New York: Oxford University Press, 1978).
[27] Kazin, *The Populist Persuasion*, 221–44.
[28] Carmines and Stimson, *Issue Evolution*, 64.

message, but he also had to fend off another effort by the relatively liberal New York Governor Nelson Rockefeller to gain the nomination.[29] The presence of George Wallace as a presidential candidate also complicated his strategy. Nixon had to be conservative enough to compete with and take votes from Wallace in the South, but careful not to alienate too many Northern moderates or he would lose some of those states in the November general election. He needed to oppose national intrusion and support traditional values without sounding racist.[30]

This presidential election also indicated the differences between the priorities and logic of the presidential and congressional wings of the parties. Presidential candidates seek to find an electoral coalition that will win the presidency. They have to win majorities (or pluralities in 1968 with Wallace present) within enough states to win the Electoral College. The Republican congressional party was largely based outside the South. After the 1966 elections, Republicans had 187 seats in the House and 36 in the Senate. In the House, 119 (59 percent) were in the North and only 26 (14 percent) were in the South. In the Senate, four were from the South. The number of seats was growing. However, amid the turmoil of 1968 many members of Congress were worried that tilting too far to the right might hurt some incumbents outside the South.[31]

For Nixon, the choice was clear. The South was growing along with the Sunbelt – the string of states stretching from the South to California – and there were more electoral votes in those areas.[32] The South was changing as was the Sunbelt. The South had been the poorest region of the nation for decades and was now growing in population and its income was catching up with the rest of the nation.[33] Perhaps most important, much of the growth in the South and Sunbelt was driven by jobs and the expansion of suburbs, filled with relatively prosperous whites who felt that they had earned their newfound success.[34] Nixon called these

---

[29] Rae, *Decline and Fall of Liberal Republicans from 1952 to the Present.*

[30] Carter, *The Politics of Rage*, 324–70; Kevin P. Phillips, *The Emerging Republican Majority* (New Rochelle, NY: Arlington House, 1969).

[31] Rae, *Decline and Fall of Liberal Republicans from 1952 to the Present.*

[32] Phillips, *The Emerging Republican Majority*; and, Rick Perlstein, *Nixonland: The Rise of a President and the Fracturing of America*, New York: Scribner, 2008), 341–42.

[33] Earl Black and Merle Black, *Politics and Society in the South* (Cambridge, MA: Harvard University Press, 1987).

[34] For the growth of suburbs, see Dennis R. Judd and Todd Swanstrom, *City Politics: The Political Economy of Urban America*, sixth edition (New York: Pearson/Longman), Chs. 8 and 10. For the views that dominated in many suburbs, see Lisa McGirr, *Suburban Warriors: The Origins of the New American Right* (Princeton, NJ: Princeton University Press, 2002).

voters the *Silent Majority* and built a campaign on the idea that most Americans were troubled by turmoil and changing social mores, but were less inclined to speak up.[35] He thought that much of this silent majority was in the South.

Nixon, having lost the presidency in 1960 and the California governorship in 1962, was determined to win. To do that, he had to exploit a trend that began in 1948, and expand on Goldwater's success in winning Southern votes. Until 1948, the South had been solidly Democratic (with the exception of 1928) in both presidential and House voting. This was part of a national pattern where districts that went strongly Democratic for the House went strongly Democratic for presidential candidates. Likewise, districts that went strongly Republican did so for both races. The result was a strong and consistent relationship between presidential and congressional voting results.

As noted in Chapter 5, parts of the South abandoned the Democratic Party in 1948 and voted for third-party candidate Strom Thurmond in the presidential contest because of Harry Truman's actions regarding civil rights. Figure 7.2 indicates how dramatic that change was. It tracks the correlation or association between presidential–House Democratic results across House districts since 1900. The association declined dramatically in 1948. The Southern vote in 1948, however, did not go for a Republican. It went to Dixiecrat Strom Thurmond instead, and the question was whether a transition to Republicans would occur in future elections or if the South would return to the Democrats without a third-party candidate like Thurmond in the race.

Dwight Eisenhower, running as the Republican presidential candidate in 1952 and 1956, capitalized on the unease felt about Democratic presidential candidate Adlai Stevenson of Illinois, and did fairly well in the South (48.0 percent in 1952 and 48.9 percent in 1956). Eisenhower did better than prior candidates, and he was able to lower the association between Democratic presidential and House votes to a level less than that which had prevailed from 1900 to 1944. His success also resulted in an increase in the number of *split-outcomes*, or House districts in which the party winning the House contest and the presidential vote differed. Eisenhower won enough House districts in the South in 1952 and 1956 to increase the percentage of split-outcomes to 19 percent in 1952 and 29 percent in 1956. The latter was the highest percentage for the years

---

[35] Matthew D. Lassiter, *The Silent Majority: Suburban Politics in the Sunbelt South* (Princeton, NJ: Princeton University Press, 2007).

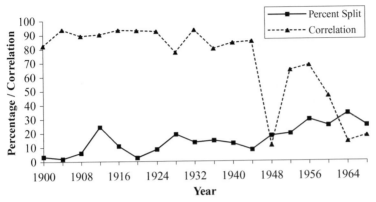

FIGURE 7.2. Correlation of House–president results and percent of split-outcomes, 1900–1972. *Note:* Percentages are expressed as ranging from 0 to 100, while correlations are rescaled to range from 0 to 100 rather than 0 to 1. *Source:* Data compiled by Stonecash; see Appendix B. A *district* is defined as having a split outcome when the party winning the House contest is different from that winning the presidential vote within the district. Those districts, from 1900 to 1948, in which the presidential vote is not known, are not included. The missing scores involve counties with multiple districts within the county (Cook in Illinois, New York City, Suffolk [Boston] in Massachusetts, etc.). Data on these outcomes have never been collected and disaggregated for these counties.

1900–56. Each such outcome suggested that a Republican House candidate might do well in that district in the future. The evidence indicated gains could be made in areas that Democrats had previously controlled without much of a problem.

The 1960 and 1964 results provided further evidence and hope for Republicans. Nixon, despite losing in 1960, averaged 44 percent in Southern House districts. Goldwater was able to average 48.7 percent in Southern House districts and create an even higher percentage of split-outcomes, 33.8.[36] Nixon thought that if he could do well in the South and hold on to some of the states outside the South, he could win in 1968. His calculations, however, were enormously complicated by the presence of George Wallace, who won five Southern states.[37] Nixon had

---

[36] Data results compiled by authors. While some of Nixon's success in 1960 could be chalked up to Kennedy's Catholicism, which was unpopular in the South, no such claim could be made regarding Goldwater's showing in 1964.

[37] Wallace won Alabama, Arkansas, Georgia, Louisiana, and Mississippi. He also received one electoral vote from a faithless Nixon elector in North Carolina.

to carefully gauge his appeal, stressing that he would support the law on bussing students to achieve racial balance, but make it clear that he would do only what he had to do and was not supportive of the idea.[38]

Nixon won in a close election, and continued the GOP pattern started by Eisenhower of doing relatively well in the South in presidential elections. The presence of Wallace made it difficult to compare percentages, but for the first time, a Republican presidential candidate averaged a higher percentage (34.2) in Southern House districts than the Democratic candidate (31.7). More important, if the total of Wallace and Nixon votes is taken as reflective of the conservative vote, then 68.3 percent of the Southern vote could possibly be attracted with a conservative message. If Wallace had not been present, the Republicans might presume that they could achieve a majority in the South. Outside of the South, Nixon ran relatively even in House districts (45.1 to 46.8 percent for Hubert Humphrey the Democrat). If a Republican could win the South and hold half of the areas outside the South, it would be difficult for a Democrat presidential candidate to win. Nixon did not carry a Republican majority with him in the House or Senate, but if Republicans could eventually win in districts and states where Nixon won, the party could expand its base.

NIXON'S AMBIVALENCE, WATERGATE, AND A PARTY SETBACK

In 1969, Republicans seemed poised to make significant strides as a more conservative party. Nixon had done well in the South and the party gained five House seats nationally; three of those were in the South. John Tower, a conservative Texas Republican, ran for the Senate and won, becoming the first Republican senator from the South *since the 1870s*. The Republican House members elected in 1966 and thereafter were more conservative than existing members.[39] Nixon had chosen Spiro Agnew, the conservative Maryland governor, as his vice-presidential candidate. Agnew played the role of being a harsh critic of liberals and protestors, calling them "nattering nabobs of negativism" and "effete impudent snobs," which pleased conservatives to no end.

---

[38] Perlstein, *Nixonland: The Rise of a President and the Fracturing of America*, 282–5.

[39] A higher DW-NOMINATE score indicates a more conservative voting record. In 1968, the continuing House Republicans had scores of .26, while those entering the House after 1968 had scores of .32. The shift was small but sent a signal to the party that more conservative members could be elected.

Despite this potential, Nixon was uneasy about being seen as too conservative. He made his opposition to bussing clear and his Attorney General John Mitchell took a tough stance in favor of law and order. However, he also proposed the negative income tax, which would have provided income to all those working but who still fell below a certain income level. He also established the Environmental Protection Agency, recognizing environmental problems that many conservatives did not see as serious enough to justify government intrusion. Both acts by Nixon appealed to liberals and angered conservatives. His maneuvering for reelection in 1972 was helped enormously by other unexpected events. In May 1972, George Wallace was shot multiple times by an assassin seeking publicity. Wallace was unable to run in 1972, reducing the risk of lost Southern votes. The Democratic Party nominated George McGovern, who was quickly labeled as one of the most liberal candidates to ever run. Nixon was able to win easily in 1972, carrying more House Republicans with him to get the party closer to a majority. Republicans won even more House seats in the South, increasing their number to thirty-four up from twenty-seven. As Figure 7.2 indicates, with McGovern doing so badly (particularly in the South), the percentage of split-outcome seats increased to an all-time high of 43.7. Most of these were again districts where a Republican presidential candidate won and a Democratic House incumbent was able to continue winning. Republicans were certain that as Democrats retired, in the future they could win many of these seats.

Within two decades a dramatic transformation of the party's success in presidential elections had occurred. Dwight Eisnehower did fairly well in the South and won some states, but he still did better in the traditional base of the party, the Northeast. Barry Goldwater was the first to reverse the pattern of where the party did well, winning some states in the South and losing in the Northeast. Nixon, after struggling to cope with the candidacy of George Wallace in 1968, was able in 1972 to do better overall while replicating Goldwater's pattern of doing relatively better in the South. After decades of relatively greater success in the Northeast the party was now doing relatively better in the South.[40]

The hopes of the party that this success would continue, however, were abruptly thwarted by the Watergate scandal. Despite polls indicating that

---

[40] Mark D. Brewer and Jeffrey M. Stonecash, "Changing the Political Dialogue and Political Alignments: George Wallace and his 1968 Presidential Campaign," presented at the 2009 Midwest Political Science Association Meetings, Chicago, Illinois, April, 2009.

Nixon would win the 1972 presidential campaign easily, the Nixon campaign worried that Democrats had some strategy to unseat their candidate. The campaign hired several men to break into the Democratic headquarters in the Watergate building to search their files. The break-in was then discovered. The problem for Nixon was that he knew of the break-in and eventually participated in efforts to cover up the campaign's connection to the break-in. The cover-up became the issue and Nixon's staff tried to stifle the investigation. The White House's role in a cover-up then became the focus of congressional inquiries. During the hearings, one staff member revealed that conversations in the Oval Office were taped. The confrontation over those recordings – Congress wanted them and Nixon did not want to surrender them – eventually ended up before the Supreme Court, which ruled that Nixon had to provide the tapes. After a tense confrontation over the issue of whether Nixon would comply, Nixon resigned in August 1974, becoming the only president in the nation's history to resign from office.

The effect on the Republican Party was devastating. The public had acquired a very negative image of the GOP, and in the November 1974 elections many Republicans were swept from office. Democrats picked up 48 seats in the House and 4 in the Senate, giving them majorities of 291–144 in the House and 60–38 in the Senate. Much of the progress the party had made in recent years was reversed. The party even suffered setbacks in the South, losing seven seats in the House from what they had held in 1972.

The damage from Watergate did not end with the 1974 elections. Gerald Ford, Nixon's vice president became president and decided that the only way to put Nixon and Watergate behind the nation and avoid a lengthy and acrimonious trial was to pardon Nixon. He did so, saying, "Our long national nightmare was over." Although many praised Ford for moving on and resolving the issue, his poll ratings dropped and his chances for reelection were hurt.

In addition, the growing influence of the conservative movement created problems for Ford within his own party. During the 1960 and 1968 nomination processes, Nixon had to fend off Nelson Rockefeller, the liberal Republican governor of New York. The Eastern, more moderate, wing was still very significant within the party. Ford himself was aligned with this wing of the party, as was shown by his selection of Rockefeller as his vice president. The conservative wing was never enamored of Ford, and by 1976, they were challenging Ford for the nomination, pushing

Ronald Reagan as their candidate. Reagan, a former actor who had converted from being a Democrat to a Republican in 1962 at least in part because of his liking of Barry Goldwater, was a rising star in the party. He was elected governor of California in 1966 and espoused simple and clear conservative messages – crime and protest should be contained, there should be less government, and too many people were on welfare – and he soon became a serious competitor to Ford in the nomination process. Reagan had sought the nomination in 1968 but lost out to Nixon. In 1976, Reagan won several primaries and came close to taking the nomination away from Ford. It was unusual for a sitting (but of course unelected) president to be so seriously challenged, and the situation was indicative of the rising clout of conservatives within the party. Although Ford survived the primaries, he did not survive the general election, losing to the Democratic nominee, Georgia Governor Jimmy Carter.

By 1977, the GOP appeared to be in significant disarray. The sweeping win of Nixon in 1972 had been squandered. Republicans had lost the White House, and they had lost seats in the House and the Senate. In the House, the Democratic majority following the 1964 elections was 295–140. In the 1972 elections, the Democratic majority was reduced by fifty-three seats to 242–192, the closest the party had been to a majority since the 1956 elections. Following 1974, the Democratic majority was back to 291–144 and in 1976, it was 292–143. In the Senate, even with only one-third of its seats up for election in 1974 and 1976, Democrats were back to a 61–38 advantage after 1976. What had looked like a sustained Republican recovery in 1972 after the 1964 elections was now a return to minority status, with a long way to go to get close to a majority.

There was also an ongoing and contentious debate within the party about what direction to take. The Eastern wing was worried about its declining influence and the rising influence of conservatives and the South. Their concern was that a conservative message would not be well received by voters. After all, the nation had yet to elect a clearly conservative president since the advent of the New Deal. To moderates, the base of the party was still in the North, and the attempt to present a conservative presidential candidate in 1964 had failed and hurt the entire party. Conservatives, however, saw the world very differently. The party was continuing to gain seats in the South, and it was apparent to conservatives that a backlash against liberal policies and apologies for increases in crime and welfare policies was developing. Conservatives wanted to exploit that growing conservative sentiment.

There were also events occurring in society that convinced conservatives that they had to increase their efforts to restore proper morals and find a party to adopt the accompanying policies. Homosexuality had long been kept quiet, but beginning with the Stonewall riots of 1969, things began to change conspicuously. That riot involved a police raid of a gay bar in New York City. Patrons resisted the police and challenged the notion that gays should have to hide their status. Their actions were followed shortly by the formation of the gay rights movement, seeking nondiscrimination in employment and housing. Conservatives believed homosexuality was a sickness and should not be accepted.[41]

In 1973, the U.S. Supreme Court issued its *Roe v. Wade* ruling, declaring that women had a right to abortion. Just as with homosexual relations, another practice that had long existed but was not acknowledged or discussed publicly, was pushed out in the open, and in the case of abortion, made legal. To conservatives, social decline and the abandonment of traditional morals were clearly evident. School prayer had been abolished, abortion was now legal, and gays were coming out into the public. In 1970, the Internal Revenue Service (IRS) announced that it would no longer grant tax-exempt status to private schools that practiced racial discrimination in accepting students. In the late 1970s, President Jimmy Carter went further and considered removing tax exemption from religious schools, which were regarded as nonprofit, on the grounds that the tax exemption was creating indirect government support for religion. The exemption was was not eliminated, but conservatives were angered. Carter further angered conservatives in 1980 when his White House Conference on Families expressed support for many different appropriate models of the family, abortion rights, and the Equal Rights Amendment (ERA), among other liberal positions.[42] Divorce, crime, and welfare reliance were increasing and government was either tolerating deviant behavior or taking away support for traditional norms.[43] Although Republicans were struggling electorally, conservatives were growing increasingly angry and trying to find a political outlet for their frustrations.

---

[41] The American Psychiatric Association classified homosexuality as a disease until 1973.

[42] Leo P. Ribuffo, "Family Policy Past as Prologue: Jimmy Carter, the White House Conference on Families, and the Mobilization of the New Christian Right," *Review of Policy Research* 23 (March 2006): 311–37.

[43] For an overview of the development of these social changes, see Mark D. Brewer and Jeffrey M. Stonecash, *Split: Class and Cultural Divides in American Politics* (Washington, DC: CQ Press, 2007).

REAGAN, CONSERVATIVE IDEAS, DEMOGRAPHIC CHANGE, AND BUILDING A COALITION

The Republicans' 1980 presidential selection process again pitted an Eastern moderate, George H. W. Bush, against a conservative, Ronald Reagan. Bush presented a serious challenge to Reagan, but lost and agreed to become the vice-presidential candidate instead. In the campaign Reagan staked out a clear conservative set of positions. He stated his support for a strong national defense, tax cuts, and turning many programs back to the states. His statement of support for states' rights was seen by many as an indication of his support for efforts to resist desegregation, though he denied that. Reagan favored returning prayer to public schools, opposed the Equal Rights Amendment establishing equality for women, and supported a constitutional amendment to ban abortion.

Reagan's campaign was helped a great deal by the national economy and problems with Iran. The economy was not doing well, with unemployment, inflation, and interest rates rising to very high levels. Presidents are generally held accountable (or get credit) for the national economy, even if they are not responsible, and Carter's ratings among Americans were hurt by these conditions. Furthermore, Carter looked impotent because of events unfolding in Iran. Religious militants had taken over the U.S. Embassy in Iran and were holding U.S. personnel hostage. Carter had sent a secret rescue mission that ran into numerous problems, resulting in failure and the death of several soldiers. The image of the United States unable to retrieve its personnel provided a basis for Reagan to criticize Carter for having allowed the United States to have become weaker in the world. Reagan was able to win by ten percentage points.

Reagan's victory was also because of his ability to project a personal style and set of policy ideas that were well received by the public. One of the most important aspects of Reagan's presidency was his demeanor as a spokesperson for conservative views. Many conservatives who had preceded Reagan often expressed hostility to existing situations. Senator Joe McCarthy and the House Un-American Activities Committee (HUAC) had often come across as fearful of communism, aggressive, and angry in their pursuit of their cause. Barry Goldwater was widely portrayed as a shoot-from-the-hip conservative who did not always present a reasoned critique of liberalism. Richard Nixon had always been hard to trust.

However, Reagan presented a very different face for conservatism. He was positive, optimistic, had a sunny view of life, was quick with a quip, and believed in the power of individualism and free markets. He presented the idealistic side of conservatives: the belief that anyone could make it in America, and that cultivating the principle of individual responsibility was essential. Rather than angrily attack, he was more inclined to use humor to get his point across, saying, "Government is not the answer, government is the problem," or "The most terrifying words in the English language are: I'm from the government and I'm here to help."[44] He also said he wanted everyone to have a chance to get rich. His message was that individuals and families were most important, that government got in the way, and its role in American society should be reduced. After years of conservatives who attacked liberals, Reagan presented himself as a commonsense optimist who chided liberals for denying simple truths about the nature of individuals and government.[45] He made the case for conservative ideas more than the case against liberals. This proved to be crucial to Reagan's – and eventually the GOP's – success.

Reagan did this most effectively in making the argument that lower taxes and less government would be good for the economy. In prior decades, conservatives had opposed taxes and government on the grounds that they diminished individual freedom. With incomes rising steadily from the 1940s through the 1960s, this argument had little impact. With incomes stagnant, inequality beginning to increase, and the security of corporate employment declining beginning in the 1970s, voters were experiencing greater economic anxiety and searching for answers on how to improve the economy. Reagan provided a plausible argument that taxes and regulation were stifling work effort and the inclination to innovate and create new businesses. His argument was a simple one: Cutting taxes and regulations would reverse these patterns and improve the economy. Democrats had little in the way of answer and Republicans enjoyed a steady advantage in voters' sense of which party could best handle the economy.[46]

---

[44] Reagan offered the first of these quotes in his First Inaugural Address (January 20, 1981) and offered the second in his opening remarks at a presidential news conference on August 12, 1986.

[45] For an overview of Reagan, see Garry Wills, *Reagan's America* (New York: Penguin Books, 1988). For a good discussion of Reagan as the appealing optimist, see James T. Patterson, *Restless Giant: The United States from Watergate to Bush v. Gore* (New York: Oxford University Press, 2003), Ch. 5.

[46] Mark A. Smith, *Right Talk* (Princeton, NJ: Princeton University Press, 2007), 178–93.

As president, Reagan acted on his beliefs. He sought to reduce federal regulations on business. He sought less demanding environmental protection laws so businesses had to comply with fewer regulations, which he argued would increase economic growth. He proposed and was able to achieve significant tax cuts early in his administration. He proposed significant increases in defense expenditures to build up the military to create a strong national defense system. He sought real budget cuts in social programs.[47]

In the process of pursuing these goals, Reagan and other conservative Republicans attempted to broaden the party's electoral base. The party aspired to attract five groups to the party: Southerners, fiscal conservatives, suburbanites, white males, and cultural conservatives (evangelical Protestants and Roman Catholics in particular).[48] There was overlap among the groups, which often made appeals easier. Many conservative Southern white males, for example, were troubled about the demise of traditional values. Reagan's appeal to these groups was relatively straightforward. He emphasized states' rights, local autonomy, and the importance of individualism and restraining the growth of government. He was unequivocal in his opposition to crime and growing welfare rolls. He became known for his anecdotes about "welfare queens," who he said drew multiple checks and lived well off of welfare. He spoke out against the steady increase in illegitimate births, called for the return of prayer to public schools, and perhaps most important, indicated in no uncertain terms that he opposed abortion.[49]

Reagan was building, in a decidedly less angry style, on the arguments of Barry Goldwater and George Wallace about the betrayal of individualism, the importance of sound moral values, and cultural populism. His argument was that many people were working hard, living by the rules, and paying taxes, but they were being betrayed by a system that provided benefits to those who did not want to work. Cultural elites were dismissing fundamental values of individual responsibility and labeling

[47] John L. Palmer and Isabel V. Sawhill, *The Reagan Record* (Cambridge, MA: Ballinger Publishing, 1984).

[48] Andrew E. Busch, *Reagan's Victory: The Presidential Election of 1980 and the Rise of the Right* (Lawrence: University Press of Kansas, 2005); Geoffrey Layman, *The Great Divide: Religious and Cultural Conflict in American Party Politics* (New York: Columbia University Press, 2001); David C. Leege, Kenneth D. Wald, Brian S. Krueger, and Paul D. Mueller, *The Politics of Cultural Differences: Social Change and Voter Mobilization Strategies in the Post-New Deal Period* (Princeton, NJ: Princeton University Press, 2002).

[49] For a review of the trends that troubled conservatives, see Brewer and Stonecash, *Split*.

those who articulated those concerns as intolerant or worse. The presumption was that he was building a base of "Reagan Democrats," working and middle-class Democrats in the North who had had enough of paying taxes to support handouts for the lazy and those having babies out-of-wedlock – and who now were crossing over to vote for a Republican president. They had listened to "bleeding heart" liberals apologize for crime and the destruction of public housing.[50] They wanted a president who validated their emphasis on individual discipline and responsibility.[51] An emphasis on reduced federal government powers would appeal to the South and certain interests in the West, and an emphasis on individualism and personal responsibility should appeal to conservatives across the country.

As Republicans surveyed the American landscape, they saw tremendous possibilities for appealing to those embracing this individualistic view of society. Many middle- and working-class whites had moved to the suburbs. As they interpreted their lives, it was hard work that had yielded them the benefits of suburban life, yet they were paying taxes to support those in central cities who did not work hard. The percentage of Americans living in suburbs had steadily increased following World War II.[52] By 1990, more people were living in suburbs than in rural areas or in central cities, and they represented a bloc Republicans thought they could cultivate.[53] The movement to the suburbs was producing a sorting out economically[54] and socially, with those of similar views clustering together. That clustering created greater homogeneity within suburbs and reinforced the tendency for people to adopt similar political identities.[55] Republicans were sure that a message of individualism, less government, and lower taxes would appeal to suburban voters.

The tricky part of coalition creation was how to appeal to social conservatives, many of whom were deeply influenced by their religious beliefs

[50] See Thomas B. Edsall and Mary Edsall, *Chain Reaction: The Impact of Race, Rights, and Taxes on American Politics* (New York: W.W. Norton, 1991).
[51] Stanley B. Greenberg, *Middle Class Dreams: Politics and Power of the New American Majority* (New Haven, CT: Yale University Press, 1996).
[52] Judd and Swanstrom, *City Politics.*
[53] Alison Mitchell, "Two Parties Seek to Exploit a Relentless Suburban Boom," *New York Times,* May 4, 1999, p. A1.
[54] Kenneth T. Jackson, *Crabgrass Frontier: The Suburbanization of the United States* (New York: Oxford University Press, 1985); Edward J. Blakely and Mary Gail Snyder, *Fortress America: Gated Communities in the United States* (Washington, DC: Brookings Institution Press, 1997).
[55] Bill Bishop, *The Big Sort: Why Clustering of Like-Minded America is Tearing Us Apart* (New York: Houghton Mifflin, 2008).

and behaviors. These were the voters troubled about what they saw as an increasingly decadent, immoral society.[56] Abortion was now legal, sex was on television more often, pornography was widespread, and illegitimate births were increasing. School prayer had been banned and Christian schools were under scrutiny from the IRS. Conservative religious leaders, increasingly appalled by what they saw as rampant moral decay, wanted government to either enforce morality or at least not make immorality legal. They wanted laws or even a constitutional amendment banning abortion. They wanted rulings that would limit what could be on television and available to the public. They wanted prayer back in schools. They wanted what they saw as the proper role of religion in American life restored. They wanted welfare rules changed so that women with multiple children would not get additional support.[57]

The dilemma, at least to some, was whether it was possible to combine a pro-business, reduced government role with a greater role for government in supporting moral behavior. To many conservatives the two together seemed feasible. Capitalism was valuable to promote freedom and economic growth, but people need to practice virtue within this system and government must do its best to encourage proper behaviour. But to others, bringing the two into a coalition seemed implausible.[58] One wanted less government involvement, while another wanted more. Yet the focus of their efforts was in different spheres – business versus private life – so there was hope that the combination might work.

Aside from the philosophical problems, there were also practical issues of whether the votes of cultural conservatives could be attracted. Many of those deeply troubled about cultural issues were Southern, born-again, evangelical Protestants who believed in salvation only through accepting Jesus Christ as their personal savior and the Bible as the authoritative word of God. For many evangelicals of the time, their religion inclined them to focus on the hereafter, not worldly political involvement, and they had a history (at least since the Scopes Trial in the 1920s) of limited political involvement. The larger society was corrupt and sinful, and thus should be avoided. There were signs that this withdrawal from

---

[56] James Davison Hunter, *Culture War: The Struggle to Define America* (New York: Basic Books, 1991).

[57] Hunter, *Culture Wars*; Matthew C. Moen, *The Christian Right and Congress* (Tuscaloosa: University of Alabama Press, 1989); Robert Wuthnow, *The Restructuring of American Religion: Society and Faith since World War II* (Princeton, NJ: Princeton University Press, 1988).

[58] E. J. Dionne, *They Only Look Dead* (New York: Touchstone, 1997).

politics was changing as they became concerned about moral decline, but the future was uncertain.[59] They spoke a different language and saw the world differently. Could Republican politicians learn their language? In addition, many of the evangelicals who did participate in electoral politics had been Southern Democrats for decades and they might not be willing to change. Finally, most of the Republican base was still outside the South. That base was more concerned about old-time fiscal restraint by government and individual discipline. They were religious, but in a different and much less intense way. There was a danger that appeals to religious conservatives might alienate the GOP traditional base.

Beginning in the mid-1970s, a number of conservative Republican operatives began addressing this situation in earnest. Leaders of the conservative element within the Republican Party such as Howard Phillips, Richard Viguerie, and Paul Weyrich began working in earnest with evangelical leaders such as Jerry Falwell, Timothy LaHaye, and Pat Robertson to bring evangelicals into the Republican Party while trying not to alienate the party's traditional base of support among fiscal conservatives.[60]

Reagan was crucial to pulling such a marriage off. The challenge for Reagan was to send a message of understanding to cultural conservatives without alienating the traditional base. One example of how Reagan did this was by working statements of concern about abortion into some of his speeches. In the late 1970s and early 1980s, there was no difference in the partisan preferences of those who were pro-choice and pro-life. Reagan's goal was to gradually attract more of those opposed to abortion. He could not move too fast out of concern that he might alienate those pro-choice or at least somewhat ambivalent about the whole debate. He also sought to send a clear message of support for Christian conservatives by having the IRS announce in 1982 that it would no longer withhold tax-exempt status for schools that might be deemed to be practicing racial discrimination. That move was overturned in a 1983 court decision involving Bob Jones University, but the policy move plus his statements about

[59] Christian Smith, with Michael Emerson, Sally Gallagher, Paul Kennedy, and David Sikkink, *American Evangelicalism: Embattled and Thriving* (Chicago: University of Chicago Press, 1998).

[60] Layman, *The Great Divide*; Moen, *The Christian Right and Congress*; Duane M. Oldfield, *The Right and the Righteous: The Christian Right Confronts the Republican Party* (Lanham, MD: Rowman & Littlefield, 1996); Kenneth D. Wald and Allison Calhoun-Brown, *Religion and Politics in the United States*, fifth edition (Lanham, MD: Rowman & Littlefield, 2007), Ch. 8.

abortion did help differentiate Reagan and the Republicans from the Democrats. At the same time Reagan was sending these types of messages to religious conservatives, he was also relentlessly pounding away on the dangers of big government and the virtues of individualism and free markets.

Reagan's goal was to push the party and its image to a more conservative position across the board. He wanted less government and lower taxes. He wanted fewer regulations of business. He wanted more emphasis on traditional values. He wanted more Republican success in the South, while trying to hang on to fiscal conservatives outside the South. Although there were times during his presidency when he compromised with Democrats, he did push the image of the GOP in a more conservative direction.[61] In many ways, the wedding of religious conservatives to fiscal conservatives and small government advocates during the Reagan years is one of the most impressive and important developments of twentieth-century American politics.[62]

The 1988 presidential election created some doubt about how enduring this image change was going to be, at least as influenced by presidents. George H. W. Bush, Reagan's vice president, ran and won as the party nominee. He was much more representative of the Eastern and more moderate wing of the party, and less comfortable with the strong conservative positions of Reagan. He announced that he would have a "kinder and gentler" administration and was less than enthusiastic in his support for the goals of cultural conservatives. Although he ran for office pledging "No new taxes," he did agree to a tax increase in 1991 as part of a budget compromise with Democrats. In the 1992 race, with third-party candidate H. Ross Perot in the race, he lost to Bill Clinton.

While the conservative image of the party projected by George H. W. Bush may have been somewhat muddled during the late 1980s, the congressional parties were pushing ahead with their own agendas. The party continued to make progress in the South, replacing retiring Democrats with conservative Republicans.[63] The new Republican representatives and senators were more conservative than existing members, and they

---

[61] Robert M. Collins, *Transforming America: Politics and Culture in the Reagan Years* (New York: Columbia University Press, 2007); Sidney M. Milkis, *The President and the Parties: The Transformation of the American Party System since the New Deal* (New York: Oxford University Press, 1993).

[62] For a discussion of this delicate coupling, see Thomas B. Edsall, *Building Red America: The New Conservative Coalition and the Drive for Permanent Power* (New York: Basic Books, 2006).

[63] Black and Black, *Politics and Society in the South.*

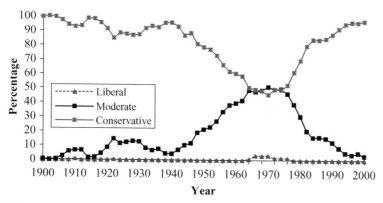

FIGURE 7.3. Presence of liberals, moderates, and conservatives in the House Republican Party, 1900–2000. *Source:* DW-Nominate scores taken from the Web page of Keith Poole, http://polarizedamerica.com/dwnomin.htm

were changing the overall voting record of the party.[64] Figure 7.3 tracks the relative presence of moderates and conservatives within the party over time. Republican conservatives were arriving from suburbs in the South and they were adamant in their opposition to government programs like welfare. They wanted lower taxes and were more supportive of the cultural conservatives.

Perhaps most important, the newer conservative members were impatient with the large number of moderates that had become significant within the party. That was particularly evident in the House. Republicans had been in the minority since the 1954 elections, and they seemed to be stuck in a permanent minority. Newer members, such as Newt Gingrich of Georgia, Tom Delay of Texas, and Dick Armey of Texas (all elected during the late 1970s and early 1980s from Southern suburban districts), wanted to pursue a more aggressive conservative agenda. They felt the Republican Party was mired in the minority because it was too accommodating with the Democrats. They were frustrated with their leaders who in their opinion were too accepting of minority status and content to get the scraps that the Democrats occasionally threw them.[65] They blamed

[64] In the 1970s, the average Democratic House member had a score of −.29 (a lower score is more liberal) and the average Republican was .27 (a more conservative score). In the 1980s, the average Democrat was at −.31 and the average Republican was at .34. Those Republicans who entered before 1982 were at .32 while those entering in the 1980s were at .36.

[65] Daniel J. Balz and Ronald Brownstein, *Storming the Gates: Protest Politics and the Republican Revival* (Boston: Little, Brown, and Company, 1996).

much of this on the presence of too many moderates within the Republican Party.

The increasing predominance of conservatives among House Republicans led to the desire to present the party as a clear conservative alternative to the public. Members like Gingrich felt that the Republican leadership was too accommodating and the party "...had to have somebody who was willing to fight." Gingrich thought that compromise "...totally blurred all the issues between the parties. We want to delineate for the country what the real choices are."[66] Gingrich acted on those concerns in 1983, creating the Conservative Opportunity Society, a group of members wishing to focus on individualism and reducing the role of government social programs.

They also wanted to get more Republican members to vote with the party on conservative positions. They wanted to build support for conservative positions to bend policy in that way and then project that image to the electorate to attract conservative support. To create greater party unity, Gingrich and his supporters seized on rule changes that had been made in the 1970s intended to displace conservative Southern Democrat committee chairs. Frustrated by the inability to pass liberal legislation, Democrats had eliminated the strict seniority rule for appointing chairs. This created the potential for the party to appoint chairs based on loyalty to the party.[67] Democrats had not been willing to fully use those powers, but Gingrich began to put pressure on Republican members to think in terms of acting cohesively to create a conservative alternative. As conservatives gradually replaced moderates within the party, this argument was met with more acceptance. In a series of moves in the late 1980s and early 1990s, Gingrich and his supporters challenged and replaced much of the party leadership with conservatives.[68] Republicans remained in the minority in the House, but more and more Republicans voted with their party, creating greater unity during the 1980s.

That unity became important during the presidency of George H. W. Bush. In an effort to balance the budget, Bush agreed to a deal with Democratic leaders in Congress, who held the majority in both houses,

---

[66] Ronald Brownstein, *The Second Civil War: How Extreme Partisanship Has Paralyzed Washington and Polarized America* (New York: Penguin Press, 2007), 138, 143.

[67] David Rohde, *Parties and Leaders in the Post-Reform House* (Chicago: University of Chicago Press, 1991); and Nelson Polsby, *How Congress Evolves: Social Bases of Institutional Change* (New York: Oxford University Press, 2004).

[68] Brownstein, *The Second Civil War*, p. 145.

to increase taxes. House Republicans refused to go along with any tax increases, allowing the congressional party to present itself as conservative and opposed to tax increases. Gingrich did not want to muddle the party image in any way, and forced Bush to accept the tax increases with a minimum of GOP support in Congress.

Gingrich, faced with a Democratic president after 1992, had even more opportunity to define the congressional Republicans as a whole. During 1993 and 1994, he had his party firmly oppose Clinton's efforts to establish some sort of national health care system, arguing that it gave bureaucrats too much control, took away individual choice, and created too much government intrusion into the private sector. Clinton also proposed and secured passage of a plan to reduce the federal budget deficit by raising taxes on the most affluent. Gingrich mobilized his party to oppose the package, arguing that his party had to stand against tax increases and for tax cuts. Then in the 1994 congressional campaign, Gingrich – now the Minority Leader in the House – proposed a "Contract with America," endorsed publicly by Republican House candidates on the steps of the Capitol. Congressional parties had not previously presented platforms or policy commitments to the American public. Gingrich was trying to define the image of the party.

The "Contract with America" did two things. First, it required that Congress live under the same laws that everyone else did. Congress would be audited, expenditures would be cut, committee meetings would be open, and tax increases would require a three-fifths majority. They also promised to bring to a vote within the first one hundred days ten bills summarized in the bulleted list presented next. It was a bold move, disparaged by many, but it certainly fit well with Gingrich's goal to define the Republican Party as a conservative alternative. The bills in the Contract explicitly expressed conservative sentiments. Raising taxes should be very difficult and the federal budget should be balanced. Crime laws should be tougher to protect the law-abiding. Welfare should be limited, and immoral behavior (such as having more babies while on welfare) should not be rewarded. American troops should be under American control only, not that of the United Nations. Frivolous lawsuits that badger business should be limited. In short, individuals should be more responsible, government support should be limited, and the private sector should be given more respect. The ideals that had first emerged in the 1950s with fledging conservative efforts within the GOP were being put front and center as the position of the House Republicans. Although cultural issues got little attention, Gingrich's goal of creating a clear conservative alternative on economic issues was being tested.

There was considerable dispute about the relevance of the Contract to 1994 election outcomes.[69] The Contract was not widely known among all Americans, but it was known among many likely voters and more affluent voters. They moved significantly to support Republicans.[70] Some argue that the Contract had little impact and the primary factors driving voting in 1994 were matters like the complicated and bureaucratic national health care plan,[71] or Clinton's proposal to allow homosexuals in the military, or his support for NAFTA (North American Free Trade Agreement) because it would cost Americans jobs.[72]

THE REPUBLICAN CONTRACT WITH AMERICA[73]

1. A balanced budget/tax limitation amendment and a legislative line-item veto.
2. An anticrime package including stronger truth-in-sentencing, "good faith" exclusionary rule exemptions, effective death penalty provisions, and more spending on prisons and law enforcement.
3. Discourage illegitimacy and teen pregnancy by prohibiting welfare to minor mothers and denying increased Aid to Families with Dependent Children payments for additional children while on welfare, cut spending for welfare programs, and enact a tough two-years-and-out provision with work requirements to promote individual responsibility.

---

[69] David W. Brady, John F. Cogan, Brian J. Gaines, and Douglas Rivers, "The Perils of Presidential Support: How the Republicans Took the House in the 1994 Midterm Elections," *Political Behavior* 18 (December 1996), 345–67.

[70] See Jeffrey M. Stonecash and Mack D. Mariani, "Republican Gains in the House in the 1994 Elections: Class Polarization in American Politics," *Political Science Quarterly* 115 (Spring 2000): 93–113, for a summary of the evidence about what shaped the 1994 elections.

[71] Theda Skocpol, *Boomerang: Health Care Reform and the Turn against Government* (New York: W.W. Norton, 1997).

[72] NAFTA was legislation designed to lower trade barriers among America, Canada, and Mexico. Its proponents argued that it would be beneficial to all countries. American factories could move to Mexico and benefit from cheaper labor, allowing goods to be sold in America to be produced at lower costs. Mexicans, making more money, would be able to buy more American-made goods. Presumably both countries would benefit. Others argued that the primary effect would be the loss of American jobs and higher profits for American companies.

[73] The full text is available at: http://www.house.gov/house/Contract/CONTRACT.html.

4. Child support enforcement, tax incentives for adoption, strengthening rights of parents in their children's education, stronger child pornography laws, and an elderly dependent care tax credit to reinforce the central role of families in American society.

5. A $500 per child tax credit, begin repeal of the marriage tax penalty, and creation of American Dream Savings Accounts to provide middle-class tax relief.

6. No U.S. troops under UN command and restoration of the essential parts of our national security funding to strengthen our national defense and maintain our credibility around the world.

7. Raise the Social Security earnings limit, which currently forces seniors out of the work force, repeal the 1993 tax hikes on Social Security benefits, and provide tax incentives for private long-term care insurance to let older Americans keep more of what they have earned over the years.

8. Small business incentives, capital gains cut and indexation, neutral cost recovery, risk assessment/cost-benefit analysis, strengthening the Regulatory Flexibility Act, and unfunded mandate reform to create jobs and raise worker wages.

9. "Loser pays" laws [on lawsuits to discourage frivolous suits], reasonable limits on punitive damages, and reform of product liability laws to stem the endless tide of litigation.

10. A first-ever vote on term limits to replace career politicians with citizen legislators.

Although the impact of the "Contract with America" can be debated, what happened in the 1994 elections was very clear. After forty years of being in the minority in the House, Republicans took over the majority and also achieved a majority in the Senate. In the House, they picked up a net of forty-two seats, and a total of seventy-three new Republicans (some replacing existing Republicans) came into office. As a group, they were strongly committed to Gingrich's conservative vision. In the Senate, the party gained eight seats and held a 52–48 majority.[74] The transition had been a long one, but after decades of work, Republicans achieved a majority in Congress and it was conservatives who had engineered the

---

[74] This majority was eventually expanded to 54–46 as two Democratic senators – Richard Shelby of Alabama and Ben Nighthorse Campbell of Colorado – switched their party identification to Republican after the 1994 elections.

transition. The perception was that the contract's statement of conservative principles had been crucial to the Republican takeover.

The Republicans used that control to propose cuts in taxes and budgets and to confront President Clinton. They regularly presented him with tax cuts that provided large benefits to those with higher incomes, arguing that entrepreneurs needed to be encouraged and not penalized. They consistently sought to curtail the availability of welfare, arguing that it promoted indolence and immoral behavior by supporting women who had babies out of wedlock. How these confrontations evolved will be discussed shortly. The important matter is that conservatives were now in charge of the party, and they were using that power to achieve their agenda and send a message to voters about what they represented as a policy alternative.

POLITICAL TRANSFORMATION

The goal of the conservative wing of the Republican Party was to gradually attract conservatives within the electorate and ultimately transform the composition of the party. The change over time was significant in obvious and less obvious ways.[75] In Congress, the Republican leadership

---

[75] The concern here is with what transpired politically. As an aside, it should be noted that the recognition and analysis of this realignment was delayed among many academics because of their reliance on a framework that interpreted the changes that began in the 1960s as a movement away from parties. Beginning in the 1960s, academics noticed increases in the percentages of voters who were identifying themselves as independents, splitting their vote for president and House and Senate candidates between parties (Verba and Nie, 1972). There was also an increase in split-outcomes and a decline in the association between House and presidential outcomes in House districts. These trends were interpreted as the beginning of dealignment, driven by candidates who wanted to create an electoral base built on personal attachment rather than partisan loyalties (Mayhew, 1974a). The presumption was that congressional incumbents, largely in the House, were able to pull voters away from party voting and get them to identify with the individual member of Congress, creating a personal, candidate-centered politics (Wattenberg, 1991; Jacobson, 2001). That framework guided much of academic research and diverted attention from a gradual partisan realignment that was leading to a resurgence of identification with parties and a decline in split-ticket voting (Bartels, 2000). For discussions of these different frameworks and their consequences for how academics conduct research, see Stonecash, Brewer, and Mariani (2003) and Stonecash (2006). It was also the case that the argument of Walter Dean Burnham (1970) that change came about primarily through major, dramatic realignments in which crisis drove voters away from one party to another prompted many academics to focus on the search for a "critical" realignment rather than "secular" or more gradual changes. Although these frameworks did divert attention for some time, works using a secular realignment approach began to appear in the 1980s (Black and Black, 1987) and 1990s and later (Abramowitz and Saunders, 1994, 1998; Jacobson, 2003; Polsby, 2004) and there are now numerous studies focusing on the secular realignment that created the current political conditions.

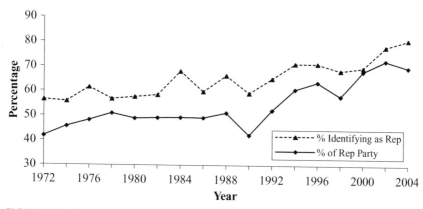

FIGURE 7.4. Percentage of conservatives identifying with Republican Party and percentage of party derived from conservatives, 1976–2004

had changed from Northern to Southern. After Republicans took over in 1995, Gingrich was elected Speaker and Texans such as Tom DeLay and Dick Armey acquired prominent positions. In 1996, Bob Dole, the Senate Majority Leader (Kansas), resigned to run as the Republican presidential candidate. He was replaced by Trent Lott, a Republican from Mississippi. A party that once derived almost all of its seats from outside the South was now led by Southerners.

The more significant change involved who the party was attracting. The goal of conservatives as far back as the 1950s had been to get the Republican Party to project a more conservative message and attract conservatives, men, Southerners, and those with strong moral and religious commitments to the party. Ronald Reagan's statements and the policy positions of the congressional parties had been intended to present such an image and attract those groups.

As Figure 7.4 indicates, these efforts were gradually bringing more of those who identified themselves as conservative to identify with the Republican Party. In the 1970s, 50–60 percent of conservatives identified with the party. By the 1990s, approximately 70 percent did so, and in the 2000s it was more than 80 percent. Furthermore, conservatives were coming to comprise a larger share of the party. By the 1990s, 60 percent of all those identifying with the party said they were conservative. The Republican Party was increasing the homogeneity of its electoral base and was able to speak with more of a unified and consistent voice on issues to a more conservative base. Essentially the same pattern prevailed for those with strong religious attachments. Beginning in the 1970s, those

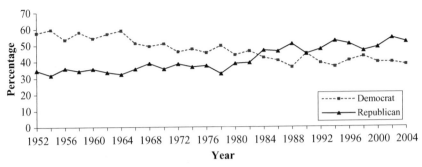

FIGURE 7.5. Party identification (with leaners) for white men, 1952–2004

who attended church regularly or placed great faith in the Bible moved to be more supportive of the Republican Party.[76]

Another goal since the 1970s and perhaps earlier, was to attract white men, whose economic gains were beginning to slow and were frustrated by the continual suggestion that they were intolerant and racist.[77] Just as with the conservatives, the party steadily increased the percentage of white men it attracted. As Republicans emphasized individualism, white men were gradually shifting from identifying as Democrats to Republican. Figure 7.5 indicates just how this transition occurred. From 1952 to 1964, white men were about twenty percentage points more Democratic. Following the burst of liberal legislation in 1964–6, that advantage narrowed and for the next twenty years, the difference varied from six to fifteen percentage points. Then in 1984, Republicans gained an advantage and by 1994 they had a sixteen-point advantage. They have kept that advantage since 1994. Over the last forty years, a twenty-point deficit among men was transformed into a roughly fifteen-point advantage.[78]

[76] Geoffrey Layman, *The Great Divide: Religious and Cultural Conflict in American Party Politics* (New York: Columbia University Press, 2001); Laura R. Olson and John C. Green, "The Worship Attendance Gap," in Laura R. Olson and John C. Green (eds.), *Beyond Red State, Blue State: Electoral Gaps in the Twenty-First Century American Electorate* (Upper Saddle River, NJ: Pearson, 2009), 40–52.

[77] Thomas B. Edsall and Mary B. Edsall, *Chain Reaction* (New York: W.W. Norton, 1991).

[78] In contrast, women were consistently twenty percentage points more Democratic from 1952 to 1982, with no change in this difference in 1966 when men changed. From 1984 to 1988, women were evenly divided between the parties, but then from 1900 to 1998 they were ten to twelve points more Democratic. This difference between men and women in party identification led to considerable analysis of the gender gap (Kira Sanbonmatsu, *Democrats/Republicans and the Politics of Women's Place* [Ann Arbor: University of Michigan Press, 2002]); see also Karen M. Kaufman, "The Gender Gap," in Olson and Green (eds.), *Beyond Red State, Blue State: Electoral Gaps in the Twenty-First Century American Electorate*, 92–108. For awhile the focus was on why women were voting more Democratic, but in recent years the focus has been on why men are voting more Republican (Kuhn, 2007).

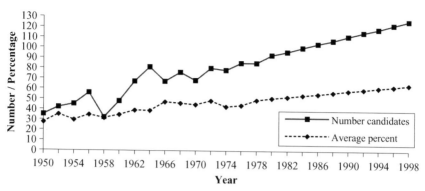

FIGURE 7.6. Republican success in the South: Number of House candidates and average percentage of vote, 1950–1998

This greater success among conservatives, individuals for whom religion was highly salient, and men was helping the party make steady inroads with white Southerners, another group the party was trying to attract. As Figure 7.6 indicates, the party was making steady progress in the number of candidates they presented in House elections (from 35 in 1950 to 126 in 1998), and the percentage of the vote received by those running was steadily increasing. In 1950, Republicans had won 2 of 105 seats. In 1994, the party finally won a majority of seats, sixty-three to sixty-two. In 1996 and 1998, they won seventy-one, compared to fifty-four for Democrats. The same transition was occurring in the Senate. In 1950, the party held none of the twenty-two seats, but after the 1996 elections, Republicans held fourteen of the twenty-two seats.

The success in the South was gradually helping the party's national appeal. For decades, Republicans had been severely hindered nationally by their disadvantage in the South. Reversing that regional disadvantage helped the party's national situation, as shown in Figure 7.7. From 1952 to 1982, approximately 35 percent of the public identified with the Republican Party. In 1984, after President Reagan had helped create a more conservative image for the party, that percentage increased to forty. In 1994, with the congressional party adding to the clarity of the image of the party, it increased further to 43 percent, narrowing the Democratic advantage. There were reasons for Republicans to believe that their political support was trending upward.

These gains were not coming without a political cost, however. Creating a clear party image was helpful in attracting conservatives to the party, but it also served to alienate others as the party image became more conservative across a broader range of issues. The stronghold of the party for

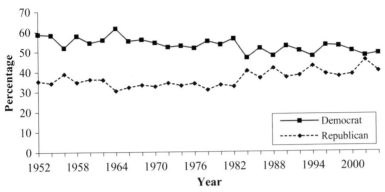

FIGURE 7.7. Percentage of voters identifying as Democrat or Republican, including leaners, NES Data, 1952–2004

over 100 years had been the Northeast. That region of the country has always had many conservatives supportive of fiscal restraint and limited government. It does not, however, have as high of a percentage of evangelical Protestants and social conservatives as the rest of the country.[79] The movement of the Republican Party into the South increased the reliance of the party on evangelical Protestants. It also increased the emphasis of the party on policies to use government to intrude into private lives and influence individual behavior. Social conservatives wanted prayer restored to schools, abortion limited, homosexual rights restricted, and welfare cut back, especially for recipients who did not exhibit the traditional family arrangement. Many of these positions alienated those concerned with only fiscal and governmental restraint. While the preferences of Southerners in the party's agenda became more influential, the party was losing support in the Northeast (Figure 7.8).

From 1952 to 1994, the percentage of the nation identifying as Democratic decreased from 58.7 to 47.4 percent. In the Northeast, it increased from 48.7 to 54.8 percent. Democrats increased their average percent of the presidential vote and increased the percentage of House and Senate seats they won within the region. While the Republican Party was gaining in the South, it was losing in the moderate and more liberal Northeast.

---

[79] Howard L. Reiter, "Counter-Realignment: Electoral Trends in the Northeast, 1900–2004," presented at the 2007 Social Science History Association Meetings, Chicago, Illinois, November 15–18, 2007. He defines the Northeast as Maine, New Hampshire, Vermont, Massachusetts, Rhode Island, Connecticut, New York, New Jersey, Pennsylvania, and Delaware.

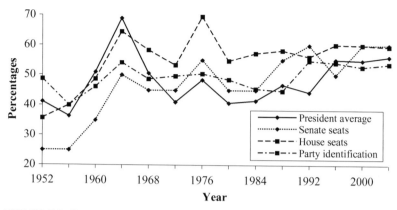

FIGURE 7.8. Democratic gains in the Northeast, 1952–2004

These losses slowed the ability of Republicans to seize the majority. The pursuit of new constituents can prompt the loss of an older base.[80]

The process of Republicans securing a different constituency was lengthy, but it ultimately began a fundamental reshaping of the electoral bases of the parties. What was once Democratic territory – the South – became dominated by the Republicans. What was once Republican territory – the Northeast – became dominated by Democrats. The process of change was gradual and created considerable confusion about the state of the two parties in American politics for several decades. Beginning in the 1950s, Eisenhower did better in Southern states than prior Republican candidates had. Democrats, many of them incumbents, kept winning House seats, reducing the relationship between House and presidential results, as shown in Figure 7.9. Goldwater in 1964 and Nixon in 1968 and 1972 made even greater inroads into the South, further reducing the presidential–House relationship. As they did so, the percentage of House districts with split-outcomes steadily increased.

As Republicans made progress in the South in the 1980s and 1990s in House and Senate elections, it brought electoral outcomes for president, House, and Senate contests into alignment. The same pattern occurred in the Northeast. As these two regions shifted party allegiances, the electoral bases of the parties became clearer and more homogeneous. The overall relationship between House and presidential election results came

[80] D. Sunshine Hillygus and Todd G. Shields, *The Persuadable Voter: Wedge Issues in Presidential Campaigns* (Princeton, NJ: Princeton University Press, 2008), 45.

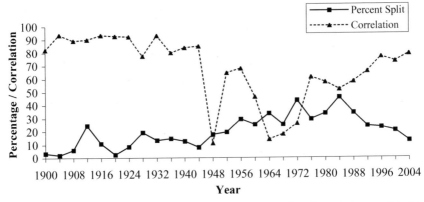

FIGURE 7.9. The association of House–president results: Correlation and split-outcomes, 1900–2004. *Note:* Percentages are expressed as ranging from 0 to 100, while correlations are rescaled from 0–1 to 0–100.

back together, but with each party having different geographical electoral bases.[81]

INTERPRETING AND ACTING ON THEIR ELECTORAL BASES

After decades without a majority in Congress, Republicans had transformed themselves by attracting a more conservative electoral base. Republicans in the House and Senate were being elected in districts or states where their presidential candidate did well. More and more Republicans trying to gauge the relative conservatism of their district could use presidential results as a guide and conclude that they were representing a conservative district.[82]

The logic the Republicans had pursued and the sweep of victories the party enjoyed in the 1994 elections set the stage in 1995 for a showdown on the direction of national public policy. Newt Gingrich was elected Speaker and set out to sharpen the contrast with President Bill Clinton. The House passed all but one of the ten items in the "Contract with

[81] Charles S. Bullock, III, Donna R. Hoffman, and Ronald Keith Gaddie, "Regional Variations in the Realignment of American Politics, 1944–2004," *Social Science Quarterly* 87 (September 2006): 494–518; James E. Campbell, "Party Systems and Realignments in the United States, 1868–2004," *Social Science History* 30 (Fall 2006): 359–86; Robert W. Speel, *Changing Patterns of Voting in the Northern United States: Electoral Realignment, 1952–1996* (University Park: Pennsylvania State University Press, 1998).

[82] William M. Leogrande and Alana S. Jeydel, "Using Presidential Election Returns to Measure Constituency Ideology: A Research Note," *American Politics Quarterly* 25 (January 1997): 3–18.

America" (the exception being term limits) within a short period of time. Gingrich proposed a significant tax cut and a budget with cuts in social programs. He was convinced that President Clinton would have to comply, given the strength of the Republican showing in the 1994 elections.[83] He was so convinced of the strength of their position that in the Fall of 1995, when Congress and the president could not agree on a budget, Gingrich refused to pass legislation providing temporary funds to keep the government running. He was certain the public would blame the president for shutting down the government. He misjudged public reaction, and Republicans were blamed for the shutdown. Gingrich was forced to pull back and compromise with Clinton, and the image of the congressional party as too zealous forced Republicans to compromise for awhile. The party continued to present bills containing large tax cuts, but Clinton regularly vetoed them. Republicans were establishing their party as focused on seeking lower taxes and less government, although they were not yet successful in actually cutting taxes.

They did succeed in changing welfare, however, marking a major change in American social policy. The welfare rules had always bothered Republicans. An individual could get on welfare and stay as long as the individual was deemed eligible. To conservatives, this provided an incentive for individuals to not work and rely on welfare. They had pushed for change before, but with a majority they could now present Clinton with a bill to end that arrangement. After a protracted battle with Clinton, who did think the promise of lifetime support was indefensible, an agreement was reached to change the system. No recipient could stay on welfare for more than two years at one time, and no one could receive support for more than five years over a lifetime. To further convey the change, the name of the program was changed from Aid to Families with Dependent Children (AFDC) to Temporary Assistance for Needy Families (TANF). They made their focus clear by calling the bill the Personal Responsibility and Work Opportunity Reconciliation Act of 1996. The legislation allowed Republicans to fulfill one of their long-standing promises to change a major social program.

The differences between the parties took on an even sharper edge when Bill Clinton was forced to admit to a sexual relationship with White House intern Monica Lewinsky. Clinton then had to deal with issues of whether he lied about that relationship, and House Republicans chose to impeach

---

[83] Balz and Brownstein, *Storming the Gates*; David Maraniss and Michael Weisskopf, *Tell Newt to Shut Up* (New York: Simon & Schuster, 1996).

him, even though public opinion was clearly against proceeding with impeachment. The party proceeded, however, because Republicans were strongly in favor of impeachment.[84] That led to a Senate trial, where Clinton was eventually acquitted. The battle sharpened differences between Democrats and Republicans and resulted in increased animosity between the two parties.

The Republican interpretation of the 1994 elections was that they had secured strong support from the public for a conservative agenda. They had presented an increasingly conservative agenda over the years and had received strong electoral support. However, much as with the Democrats following the 1964 election, they may have overestimated their degree of support. While voters regularly say that they want lower taxes and less government, they are consistently much less supportive of cutting specific programs.[85]

Although Republicans may have struggled with what to do with their new found majority in Congress, the plan of stressing conservative themes and remaking the party as a serious alternative to Democrats had succeeded. They had fundamentally shifted their electoral base geographically. Their greatest strength was in the fastest-growing areas of the country. More Americans saw themselves as conservatives than as liberals, and most of the conservatives were in the Republican Party. Identification with Republicans was increasing. Perhaps most important, they had shifted the national debate, making conservative ideas respectable and a major force in discussions of American public policy. The crucial issue was what Democrats would do to respond to these changes.

---

[84] Gary C. Jacobson, *A Divider, Not a Uniter* (New York: Pearson, 2007), 20.

[85] Benjamin I. Page and Robert Y. Shapiro, *The Rational Public: Fifty Years of Trends in Americans' Policy Preferences* (Chicago: University of Chicago Press, 1992); David O. Sears and Jack Citrin, *Tax Revolt: Something for Nothing in California* (Cambridge, MA: Harvard University Press, 1982). In addition, Erikson et al. find that some Americans who identify themselves as conservatives support liberal policies. This happens much less frequently among self-identified liberals. Robert S. Erikson, Michael MacKuen, and James A. Stimson, *The Macro Polity* (New York: Cambridge University Press, 2002).

8 The Struggle of Democrats to Interpret Change and Respond

In the mid-1960s, the Democratic Party had a sizeable majority in Congress and held the presidency, just as they had for most of the previous forty years. They enacted a wide array of legislation to address a variety of social problems and established new social welfare programs such as Medicaid and Medicare. Yet by 1969 Republican Richard Nixon, a presumably washed-up politician, was sitting in the Oval Office, and Democrats were being widely attacked as the party of social disorder and undeserving minorities, and the party that could not or would not support traditional American values. The 1968 presidential nominating process had torn the party apart, and many were uncertain about how the Democratic Party could possibly reconcile its conflicting factions.

As gloomy as things appeared in 1969, the reality is that it was only the beginning of their struggles. In 1972 with a new set of rules for nominating presidential candidates, the party selected South Dakota Senator George McGovern as its candidate. McGovern was quickly labeled as very liberal (Nixon went even further, regularly calling McGovern a radical) and he suffered a crushing defeat in 1972, taking many congressional Democrats with him. The implosion of the Nixon presidency with Watergate gave the party a temporary reprieve in 1974, and the party significantly increased its majorities in both chambers of Congress in those elections. In 1976, the party nominated and elected Governor Jimmy Carter of Georgia as president, but he was not regarded as effective and by the end of his term, inflation was running at a very high rate, unemployment was high, and the economy was regarded as a mess. Republicans continued to make progress in winning congressional seats in the South, further eroding the Democrats' once solid base.

The Democrats felt the full force of these developments in the 1980 presidential election. Ronald Reagan, former Hollywood B-list actor and avowed conservative, defeated Carter for the presidency. Only sixteen years earlier the Democrats had crushed the Republicans when the party had nominated the conservative Barry Goldwater for president. However, in 1980 the results were much different. Democrats struggled to understand what Reagan's election meant for their party. Was the Republican victory in 1980 due to Reagan's charisma, Carter's lack of it, the poor state of the economy, or did Reagan's win represent some embracing of conservatism that Democrats had to deal with? After enacting a large tax cut, which many Democrats voted for, Reagan was reelected with a landslide in 1984. He had made his opposition to many government programs clear and was reelected. He was also doing very well in the South, winning many states and districts in that region. If Reagan was winning and then winning again in their once solid base, what was the party to do to counter his appeal? In 1988, the argument that Reagan was a fluke because of his style and charm ("The Great Communicator," as he was called) became harder to make when George H. W. Bush was elected president. He possessed little of Reagan's charm, but was still elected largely by making the case to voters that a vote for him would be a vote for an extension of the Reagan years. As the dust settled after the 1988 presidential election, even the most obtuse Democrat had to realize the party was facing some serious issues.

By the late 1980s and early 1990s the Democratic Party was engaged in a full-fledged debate about what was happening to them. From the mid-1960s through the early 1990s more people identified with the Democrats than with Republicans, and the party consistently held the House of Representatives by a comfortable margin and usually the Senate as well. Yet from 1968 to 1992 the party held the presidency in only four out of twenty-four years (1977–1980). There were clearly reasons for the party to worry about its position with voters. The last Democratic president that American remembered fondly was John Kennedy, and he last occupied the White House in 1963. Warm feelings toward the party because of Franklin Roosevelt were fading even further back into the mists of time.

Then in 1992, it appeared to Democrats that their fortunes might be improving. Bill Clinton, the Democratic governor of Arkansas, won the presidency and the party held healthy majorities in both the House and Senate. President Clinton set off on an ambitious plan to dramatically expand health care insurance in the nation, regarded by many liberals as perhaps the last piece of unfinished business from the New Deal and the Great Society. Clinton's proposal died without even coming up for a vote in Congress. Democratic hopes were then abruptly and badly damaged when Republicans swept into power following their victories in the 1994 congressional elections, reducing Clinton to having to assert that he was "still relevant." Democrats had further evidence that the party was in trouble and needed to consider why they were losing support among American voters. The Democratic Party of late 1994 and early 1995 seemed to be a mess, and there did not appear to be any quick and easy way to clean things up.

CONFLICTING ANALYSES OF THEIR PLIGHT

The difficulty for Democrats was that there was little agreement about what to do to restore the Democratic Party to majority status. The party needed to know who it was losing, what groups it could recover or attract to regain the majority, and what message or messages would be effective in reversing its fortunes. When they were in a similar situation, the Republicans had expanded their electoral base by attracting more conservatives and some moderates and were now winning more elections. Democrats were struggling to develop an equally coherent plan and were being deluged with very different interpretations of what happened and what they should do to respond. We summarize the two arguments first and then explore them in greater depth in the latter part of this chapter.

Some thought that the party had become too liberal and particularly too liberal on issues of race and social welfare. They argued that the party's stance on social issues was alienating middle- and working-class whites, reducing class political divisions, and making it harder to focus on issues of economic inequality and opportunity. The critics of the party argued that middle-class values were not being given enough respect. To critics, the party was so preoccupied with compensating for the injustices inflicted on minorities that many liberals were apologizing for, almost justifying, crime, illegitimate births, and social disorder as understandable, given the conditions some people faced. To critics the answer was for the party to adopt a moderate image on racial issues and the welfare state, and focus more on ensuring equality of opportunity and supporting the working class and the middle class.

Others thought that the party was not liberal enough. They argued that the party base was changing anyway as they lost conservative Southerners. They argued the party might as well accept the change and treat it as an opportunity to create more clarity of its image. If the party became even more liberal on welfare state issues, it might then be able to motivate the less affluent to vote more. Lower-income individuals tend to

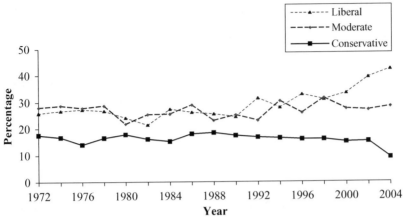

FIGURE 8.1. Composition of Democratic Party: Percentage of party liberal, moderate, or conservative, 1972–2004

vote at a lower rate, and if the party could build a stronger connection with them and motivate them to vote, they could use that greater participation to create a majority. They argued that inequality and immigration were increasing, providing a larger base of individuals who might be appealed to with a focus on class and inequality issues. They also thought that the country was changing and becoming more tolerant of different lifestyles and homosexuality. They thought that as these changes evolved, there would be less receptivity to Republican efforts to impose uniform moral codes, and thus the Democrats would ultimately benefit by becoming more liberal across the board.

The battle of which direction to follow was complicated by the composition of the party. In the 1950s, Republicans began with a conviction that a substantial percentage of voters were conservative, and that because of this, they could make their party more conservative and be successful. This was bolstered by evidence that a substantial percentage of the party was already conservative, and also that a relatively large chunk of the Democratic Party was also conservative and increasingly discontent. Democrats were not so fortunate. They faced the problem that there were fewer liberals than conservatives in the electorate. Surveys in the 1970s and 1980s indicated that only about 25 percent of the electorate identified as liberal, while 36 to 45 percent saw themselves as conservative. In addition, the party began any discussions of what to do with a much more diverse electoral base. As Figure 8.1 indicates, as the party began to grapple with what direction to follow in the 1970s, less than 30 percent of those identifying with the party also identified themselves as liberal.

Almost 20 percent were conservative and another 30 percent did not see themselves as having any ideological position (not shown). Almost 50 percent of Democratic identifiers in the 1970s and 1980s were unlikely to respond positively to liberal positions on issues. Democrats were not (and still are not) a party of liberal consensus.[1] And there did not appear to be a large untapped reservoir of liberals outside of the party either.

THE "TOO LIBERAL" ARGUMENT

The criticism that the party had become too liberal began to build in the late 1960s and early 1970s. Following the turmoil the party experienced at its 1968 national convention (about which southern delegations would be seated as the legitimate representatives of particular states), the party reformed its process of selecting delegates. To reformers, the problem was that party elites were stifling activists. The reforms reduced the influence of party leaders and made it easier for liberal activists with diverse concerns to influence the process of selecting a party candidate.[2] George McGovern, who had chaired the commission that designed the changes, took advantage of these new rules and became the party's presidential nominee.[3] He quickly was labeled as very liberal and the party was seen as too preoccupied with minority rights and liberal causes, resulting in a resounding defeat in the presidential election of 1972. Any urgency for the party to rethink its positions was temporarily set aside as the Watergate scandal resulted in more congressional seats in the 1974 election. Jimmy Carter, the governor of Georgia, won the presidency in 1976, and did well in the South, suggesting that maybe the party was in good shape. The 1980 win of Reagan forced a renewal of the debate of what direction the party should take. Reagan called Democrats hopelessly liberal and won. Reagan's landslide reelection in 1984 and George H. W. Bush's election in 1988 removed any doubt that the Democrats' defeat in 1980 had been a fluke, caused solely by the combination of a poor economy and an

---

[1] Nelson W. Polsby and William G. Mayer, "Ideological Cohesion in the American Party System," in Nelson W. Polsby and Raymond E. Wolfinger, *On Parties: Essays Honoring Austin Ranney* (Berkeley: Institute of Governmental Affairs Press, 1999); Paul M. Sniderman, Michael Tomz, and Robert Van Houweling, "Party Competition and Partisan Asymetries in Ideological Cohesion," presented at the 2008 Midwest Political Science Association Meetings, Chicago, IL, April.

[2] Nelson Polsby, *Consequences of Party Reform* (New York: Oxford University Press, 1983).

[3] McGovern was the first chair of the Commission on Party Structure and Delegate Selection (popularly known as the McGovern-Fraser Commission). The chairmanship was later assumed by Minnesota Congressman Donald Fraser.

incumbent president widely seen as weak and bumbling. The Democrats
were in trouble.

The 1980s were dominated by the debate about whether the party was
becoming too closely identified with liberal policies, such as quotas and
affirmative action, designed to help blacks.[4] Critics of the party argued
that the party had become "too concerned about fringe issues" such as
abortion, civil liberties, feminism, gay rights, civil rights, and affirmative
action rather than bread-and-butter economic issues. The party could not
reconcile the concerns of its divergent constituencies.[5] To these critics, the
party's stances on social issues had alienated its old core constituency: the
white, working-class Italians, Irish, Polish, and other ethnics who were
the base of the party during the New Deal era.[6] The conclusion was that
the party had to move away from strong support for liberal positions on
social and racial issues and focus more on economic issues relevant to the
white working- and lower-middle class.[7]

The crucial argument being made to Democrats was that working-class
whites were deserting the party because of a bundle of social issues. Academics had conducted studies of tolerance by education level and concluded that those with less education were least tolerant of free speech
and civil liberties.[8] The emerging conclusion was that the intolerance of
the working class was leading them to be more concerned and hostile
about party positions involving race, feminism, gay rights, and abortion
than about issues of economic opportunity. They were moving away from
the Democratic Party because of the social issues, resulting in a decline in
class divisions.[9]

---

[4] Gordon MacInnes, *Wrong, for All the Right Reasons: How White Liberals Have Been Undone by Race* (New York: New York University Press, 1996), 73–88.

[5] Robert J. Samuelson, "A Schizophrenic Party," *The National Journal* (August 23, 1980): 1408.

[6] Ronald Radosh, *Divided They Fell: The Demise of the Democratic Party, 1964–1996* (New York: Free Press, 1996).

[7] Thomas B. Edsall and Mary D. Edsall, *Chain Reaction: The Impact of Race, Rights, and Taxes on American Politics* (New York: W.W. Norton, 1991).

[8] Herbert McClosky, "Consensus and Ideology in American Politics," *American Political Science Review* 58 (June 1964): 361–82; James W. Prothro and Charles W. Griggs, "Funda-mental Principles of Democracy: Bases of Agreement and Disagreement," *Journal of Politics* 22 (February 1960): 276–94; Samuel Stouffer, *Communism, Conformity, and Civil Liberties* (New York: Doubleday, 1955). For more recent research supporting this finding, see Ewa A. Golebiowska, "Individual Value Priorities, Education, and Political Tolerance," *Political Behavior* 17 (March 1995): 23–48; W. Paul Vogt, *Tolerance and Education: Learning to Live with Diversity and Difference* (Thousand Oaks, CA: Sage Publications, 1997).

[9] Seymour Martin Lipset, *Political Man*, expanded edition (Baltimore: Johns Hopkins University Press, 1981), 87.

Perhaps the most explosive issue was that of race. The presumption was that race was the "transforming issue" of American politics.[10] It involved a whole host of issues, such as busing, open housing, access to public and private facilities, voting rights, affirmative action, concerns about crime, and welfare. The argument of liberals was that America had done a huge immoral injustice to blacks, and policies needed to be enacted to expand opportunity and provide more support for minorities who were struggling largely because of past actions by the white majority. The difficulty for liberals in making this argument was that many whites did not see themselves as having created segregation and the problems of minorities. Their reaction was that minorities should have the same opportunities as they did, but not additional assistance.[11] Working-class whites felt that they had worked hard, played by the rules, and struggled to succeed, and now they were being blamed for something they did not create.[12] They were also angry about the array of benefits they felt minorities were receiving undeservedly, such as welfare.[13]

The votes in the South for Barry Goldwater in 1964 and nationwide for George Wallace in 1968 were taken as an early sign that race issues were prying whites away from the Democratic Party. Wallace's campaign was particularly important here. He expressed hostility to the national government and its liberal experts and their social engineering and won significant votes.[14] Some argued that Wallace's appeal to working-class whites may have been about much more than race: it may have really been about being told what to do by government officials.[15] The dominant interpretation, however, was that race reactions were involved and that explained why many whites began leaving the party in the 1960s and continued to do so in the 1970s and 1980s.[16]

---

[10] Edward G. Carmines and James A. Stimson, *Issue Evolution: How Race Transformed American Politics* (Princeton, NJ: Princeton University Press, 1989), 14.

[11] Jonathon Rieder, "The Rise of the 'Silent Majority'," in Steve Fraser and Gary Gerstle (eds.), *The Rise and Fall of the New Deal Order* (Princeton, NJ: Princeton University Press, 1989), 248–58.

[12] David Paul Kuhn, *The Neglected Voter: White Men and the Democratic Dilemma* (New York: Palgrave Macmillan, 2007).

[13] Martin Gilens, *Why Americans Hate Welfare: Race, Media, and the Politics of Anti-Poverty Policy* (Chicago: University of Chicago Press, 1999).

[14] Dan T. Carter, *The Politics of Rage: George Wallace, the Origins of the New Conservatism, and the Transformation of American Politics* (New York: Simon & Schuster, 1995); Edsall and Edsall, *Chain Reaction*.

[15] Michael Kazin, *The Populist Persuasion* (New York: Basic Books, 1995).

[16] Earl Black and Merle Black, *The Vital South* (Cambridge, MA: Harvard University Press, 1992); Peter Brown, *Minority Party: Why Democrats Face Defeat in 1992 and Beyond* (Washington, DC: Regenry Gateway, 1991); Edward G. Carmines and Geoffrey C. Layman,

To others, race issues were just part of a change in the issues most important to voters. *Values* – expressions of how people should live – were becoming more important than class. Class divisions were declining in relevance because economic growth was raising the general level of affluence in society, and more people were enjoying a middle-class lifestyle. There were fewer "working class" citizens to appeal to.[17] Concerns with materialism were declining; people were more concerned about the quality of life.[18] As economic issues became less relevant, concerns about race, crime, abortion, divorce, and juvenile delinquency issues were becoming more important to voters.[19]

The critics of the Democratic Party argued that the elites dominating the party had missed the shift in electoral concerns.[20] The elites of the party had ignored or dismissed these concerns, and were alienating the working class with their rejection of traditional values and their embrace of various minority groups. The party was attracting well-educated and affluent elites who were less sympathetic to the concerns of presumably less tolerant working-class whites. The result was a political inversion, with the party improving its fortunes among the more affluent and losing support among the working class.[21]

"Issue Evolution in Postwar American Politics: Old Certainties and Fresh Tensions" in Byron E. Shafer (ed.), *Present Discontents: American Politics in the Very Late Twentieth Century* (Chatham, NJ: Chatham House Publishers, 1997), 89–134; Steven M. Gillon, "The Trail of the Democrats: Search for a New Majority," in Peter B. Kovler (ed.), *Democrats and the American Idea* (Washington, DC: Center for the National Policy Press, 1992), 288–9; Arthur Sanders, *Victory* (Armonk, NY: M. E. Sharpe, 1992).

[17] Daniel Bell, *The Coming of Post-Industrial Society* (New York: Basic Books, 1973); Seymour Martin Lipset, *Political Man*; Robert A. Nisbet, "The Decline and Fall of Social Class," *The Pacific Sociological Review* 2 (Spring 1959): 11–17; Harold L. Wilensky, "Class, Class Consciousness, and American Workers," in William Haber (ed.), *Labor in a Changing America* (New York: Basic Books, 1966), 12–28.

[18] Samuel P. Huntington, "Postindustrial Politics: How Benign Will it Be?" *Comparative Politics* 6 (January 1974): 163–91; Ronald Inglehart, *Silent Revolution* (Princeton, NJ: Princeton University Press, 1977); Ronald Inglehart, *Culture Shift in Advanced Industrial Society* (Princeton, NJ: Princeton University Press, 1990).

[19] David C. Leege, Kenneth D. Wald, Brian S. Krueger, and Paul D. Mueller, *The Politics of Cultural Differences: Social Change and Voter Mobilization Strategies in the Post-New Deal Period* (Princeton, NJ: Princeton University Press, 2002); Nicol C. Rae, "Class and Culture: American Political Cleavages in the Twentieth Century," *Western Political Quarterly* 45 (September 1992): 629–50; John K. White, *The Values Divide: American Politics and Culture in Transition* (New York: Chatham House Publishers, 2003. For more recent evidence of the impact of values, see Marc J. Hetherington and Jonathan Weiler. Authoritarianism and Polarization in American Politics, N.Y.: Cambridge University Press, 2009.

[20] Ben J. Wattenberg, *Values Matter Most* (New York: Regnery, 1996), 19–26.

[21] Everett Carll Ladd, Jr., "Liberalism Turned Upside Down: The Inversion of the New Deal Order," *Political Science Quarterly* 91 (Winter 1976–7): 577–600; Everett Carll Ladd, Jr., and Charles D. Hadley, *Transformations of the American Party System* (New York: W.W. Norton,

There were reasons to doubt the conclusions of these studies, as will be discussed shortly. In any case, Democrats were presented with a flood of arguments that the party had made a mistake in not appreciating the importance of values to ordinary Americans. They were told that Republicans were using value issues to attract the white working class. The conclusion was that class divisions were declining as the working class began to vote Republican and the Democratic Party's most reliable base defected. The conclusion that class divisions were declining became a regular conclusion in academic analyses[22] and in popular commentary.[23]

The argument of the moderates within the party was clear. The Democratic Party, rightly or wrongly, had become too closely identified with minorities of various stripes. The argument was that liberals, troubled by guilt about past injustices and the condition of minorities, had become apologists for increases in welfare rolls and crime. Welfare and crime were seen by many people, again rightly or wrongly, as so-called minority issues. The party found itself apologizing for men who were deserting their wives, for illegitimate births, for crime, and for lengthy stays on welfare, all because it was presumed that these behaviors were the product of society.[24] In doing so, they had ceased to honor the importance of individual responsibility. Moderates argued that the party had to stress its support for opportunity while signaling its unwillingness to support a welfare system that allowed people to stay on welfare for an open-ended number of years. The party had to stress its commitment to law and order to refute the criticism of Republicans that Democrats were bleeding-heart liberals who empathized more with criminals than victims, more with welfare recipients than those who saw themselves as working hard everyday to make ends meet and care for themselves and their families.[25]

1975); Everett Carll Ladd, Jr., Charles D. Hadley, and Lauriston King, "A New Political Realignment?" *The Public Interest* 23 (Spring 1971): 46–63.

[22] Numerous studies made that argument. For examples, see Paul R. Abramson, John H. Aldrich, and David W. Rohde, *Change and Continuity in the 1992 Elections* (Washington, DC: CQ Press, 1995); Robert A. Alford, *Party and Society: The Anglo-American Democracies* (Westport, CT: Greenwood Press, 1963); Norvall D. Glenn, "Class and Party Support in the United States: Recent and Emerging Trends," *Public Opinion Quarterly* 37 (Spring 1972): 31–47; David G. Lawrence, "The Collapse of the Democratic Majority: Economics and Vote Choice Since 1952," *Western Political Quarterly* 44 (December 1991): 797–820; David G. Lawrence, *The Collapse of the Democratic Presidential Majority* (Boulder, CO: Westview Press, 1997).

[23] Everett Carll Ladd, Jr., "Is Election '84 Really a Class Struggle?" *Public Opinion* (April/May 1984): 41–51; Neal R. Pierce and Jerry Hagstrom, "The Voters Send Carter a Message: Time for a Change – to Reagan," *The National Journal* (November 8, 1980): 1876–8.

[24] Thomas Byrne Edsall and Mary D. Edsall, *Chain Reaction*.

[25] James Barnes, "The Democrats' 'Vision Thing,'" *The American Enterprise* (March/April, 1990); Dom Bonafede, "For the Democratic Party, It's a Time for Rebuilding and Seeking

Into this uncertainty and unease stepped Bill Clinton and the Democratic Leadership Council (DLC). The DLC was founded by Democratic operative Al From in 1985 in the wake of Ronald Reagan's landslide reelection. The DLC was (and is) the most prominent voice making the argument that Democrats are too liberal. Its members – initially overwhelmingly Democratic public officials – set out to return the party to its past emphasis on the concerns of the white working and middle class. The DLC wanted a liberalism that looked more like that offered by FDR and John Kennedy and less like that expounded by George McGovern and 1984 Democratic presidential nominee Walter Mondale. The party had to emphasize personal responsibility and the concerns of the average American had to be emphasized for the party to have electoral success and put less emphasis on the concerns of minorities. When Bill Clinton – a former DLC chairman – won the 1992 presidential election while running as a so-called new Democrat, the DLC believed that their views had been vindicated.[26]

It was these arguments that became the basis for accepting welfare reform in 1996. Republicans were in control of Congress and were making an issue of the need to end an open-ended commitment to welfare. President Clinton had always opposed the existing rules. He regularly promised to "end welfare as we know it" on the campaign trail during the 1992 campaign, and reiterated this promise in his first State of the Union address in 1993. After much negotiation, Clinton and the Gingrich-led Republicans in Congress finally agreed to legislation that fundamentally changed the welfare system. As noted earlier, the new legislation imposed two limits: No individual could be on welfare for more than twenty-four consecutive months, and over a lifetime no individual could receive support for more than five years. The official name of the final

New Ideas," *National Journal* (February 21, 1981): 317–20; William Galston, "The Future of the Democratic Party," *The Brookings Review* (Winter 1985): 16–24; William Galston and Elaine C. Kamarck, "The Politics of Evasion: Democrats and the Presidency" (Washington, DC: The Progressive Policy Institute, September, 1989); Stanley B. Greenberg, *Middle Class Dreams: Politics and Power of the New American Majority* (New York: Times Books, 1996); Robert Kuttner, *The Life of the Party: Democratic Prospects in 1988 and Beyond* (New York: Penguin Books, 1987); Mark J. Penn, "The New Democratic Electorate," *The New Democrat* (January/February 1998): 6–9; Ronald Radosh, *Divided They Fell: The Demise of the Democratic Party, 1964–1996* (New York: Free Press, 1996); William Schneider, "An Insider's View of the Election," *Atlantic Monthly* (July 1988): 29–57.

26 Kenneth S. Baer, *Reinventing Democrats: The Politics of Liberalism from Reagan to Clinton* (Lawrence: University Press of Kansas, 2000); Jon F. Hale, "The Making of the New Democrats," *Political Science Quarterly* 110 (Summer 1995): 207–32; Everett Carll Ladd, Jr., "1996 Vote: The 'No Majority' Realignment Continues," *Political Science Quarterly* 112 (Spring 1997): 1–28.

legislation – The Personal Responsibility and Work Opportunity Act – in many ways says it all. Republicans in Congress voted for the legislation and almost half of Democrats supported it, arguing that open-ended support was politically indefensible and that the party had to change its identity as the party of welfare.[27]

The moderates' argument that the party needed to change its image has continued. Commentators continue to argue that the party has lost touch with the working class or the middle class, and the party is too dominated by cultural elites who sometimes vaguely and sometimes explicitly treat the working class condescendingly.[28] The persistence of this concern emerged again during the 2008 presidential primary contest. During an April fundraiser in San Francisco, Democratic nominee Barack Obama was taped saying:

> "You go into these small towns in Pennsylvania and, like a lot of small towns in the Midwest, the jobs have been gone now for 25 years and nothing's replaced them," he said. "And it's not surprising, then, they get bitter, they cling to guns or religion or antipathy to people who aren't like them or anti-immigrant sentiment or anti-trade sentiment as a way to explain their frustrations," he added.[29]

These remarks were immediately taken as once again reflecting the elite notion that the commitments of blue-collar workers to guns and religion were not sincere, but were somehow just the product of economic frustrations that they could not address. The implication was that their values and attachments were perhaps superficial and would perhaps evaporate if only their economic problems could be solved. The remarks lead to a barrage of criticisms that he as a Democratic candidate, educated at Harvard Law School, was out of touch and did not understand that blue-collar workers had sincere value commitments and they resented the failure to respect those values.

---

[27] For an in-depth examination of the 1996 Welfare Reform, see Ron Haskins, *Work Over Welfare: The Inside Story of the 1996 Welfare Reform Law* (Washington, DC: Brookings Institution Press, 2006).

[28] Thomas Frank, *What's the Matter with Kansas? How Conservatives Won the Heart of America* (New York: Metropolitan Books, 2004); Kuhn, *The Neglected Voter: White Men and the Democratic Dilemma*; Ruy A. Teixeira and Joel Rogers, *America's Forgotten Majority: Why the White Working Class Still Matters* (New York: Basic Books, 2000). The party went so far as to hire a consultant to travel the country prior to the 2000 elections to conduct seminars about how to use the language of "values" in their political discussions. See Alison Mitchell, "Democrats Again Face Voter Doubt Over Values," *New York Times*, August 20, 1996, p. A18.

[29] http://news.bbc.co.uk/2/hi/americas/7344532.stm.

The outburst of criticism and attempts to explain away the comments that followed indicated just how sensitive party members were about the issue. The party was worried that well-educated and affluent elites were conveying a condescending view of working-class whites and their culture, and those opinions were driving away their core constituency.

THE NOT-LIBERAL-ENOUGH ARGUMENT

While moderates were arguing the party was too liberal, liberals were arguing that voices like the DLC were interpreting change incorrectly, and that the real problem was that the party was failing to capitalize on changing economic and social conditions to build a new majority. Economically, inequality in the distribution of income and wealth was steadily increasing, and the percentages of the public without health insurance and pensions were increasing. Those in lower income brackets were being hurt the most by these changes. Socially, immigration was increasing and bringing in new voters. Tolerance for homosexuals and single mothers was increasing. In short, the composition and attitudes of society were changing. There were more who were not faring well economically. There were more who were new to American society and might appreciate a focus on equality of opportunity. There was more acceptance of difference in a variety of areas." The essence of the argument of this group was that there was a growing electorate likely to be receptive to messages of equality of opportunity and treatment and of government playing a role in this. The challenge for the party was to do a better job establishing a clear image of responding to these concerns.

As the optimists saw it, conditions were developing in a way for the party to be successful with a liberal-moderate stance. The party had been constrained in the past by its conservative wing and they had finally shed them. Class political divisions were not declining but growing, indicating that the party could focus on frustrations about wages and benefits in a changing economy. Furthermore, with the enfranchisement of Blacks and the flood of Latino immigrants, there was an emerging base that the party could attract. In order to capitalize on this opportunity, the party had to be clear in its unequivocal support of the disadvantaged, economically and socially. Moving toward the center might win an election or two, but it would squander an opportunity to build a coalition that would ensure long-term success.[30]

---

[30] John B. Judis and Ruy Teixeira, *The Emerging Democratic Majority* (New York: Scribner, 2002).

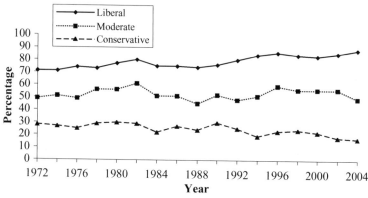

FIGURE 8.2. Democratic Party identification by self-identified ideology, non-South, 1972–2004

For this argument to be accepted there were several hurdles to be cleared. First was the issue of how to interpret the changes of the last thirty years. Whereas critics saw a party losing its core base, others saw a series of shifts that were to be expected and probably welcomed if the party was going to establish a clear image. The Democratic Party had always had a diverse base, which had limited its party unity in Congress from the 1930s through the 1970s. As the Republicans gradually attracted conservatives, fewer conservatives identified themselves as Democrats, both outside and within the South. Figure 8.2 indicates, for all those outside the South, the percentages of self-identified liberals, moderates, and conservatives who have identified as Democrats over time. By 2004, 88 percent of liberals and 49 percent of moderates were identifying as Democrats. The loss for the party was among conservatives, among whom identification as Democratic declined from 28 to 17 percent. The loss of conservatives and gains among liberals was part of the gradual shift in the geography of the party's base. Democrats had lost their dominance in the South, but they had steadily gained in the Northeast and now dominated that region.[31]

The same pattern had played out in the South, but with a much bigger change among conservatives. In 1972 (Figure 8.3), 50 percent of conservatives in the South identified with the Democratic Party. By 2004, only

---

[31] Howard L. Reiter, "Counter-Realignment: Electoral Trends in the Northeast, 1900–2004," presented at the 2007 Social Science History Association Meetings, Chicago, IL, November 15–18, 2007; Robert W. Speel, *Changing Patterns of Voting in the Northern United States: Electoral Realignment, 1952–1996* (University Park, PA: Pennsylvania State University Press, 1998); Alan Ware, *The Democratic Party Heads North, 1877–1962* (New York: Cambridge University Press, 2006).

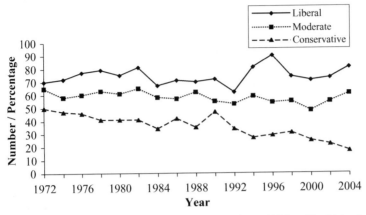

FIGURE 8.3. Democratic Party identification by self-identified ideology, South, 1972–2004

17 percent did, just as was the case outside the South. The Democratic Party had lost (or shed, in the eyes of liberals) conservatives in the South. Political alignments in the South and the rest of the country were now very similar.[32]

Although many were discouraged that the party was losing supporters, liberals were arguing that the retention of Southern conservatives had been improbable and the result of the historical antipathy of the region to the Republican Party following the Civil War. It was logical and inevitable that conservatives would move to the Republican Party, and bemoaning the change was futile.[33] To many it was beneficial for the party to shed conservatives so they could develop a more consistent image.

Despite the barrage of analyses arguing that Democrats were alienating the white working class, the evidence was not supportive of that conclusion. Table 8.1 indicates the percentage of those in the bottom third and top third of the income distribution who have voted for or identified with Democrats since 1952. Two matters are important. First, support for Democrats among those in the bottom third has been, with some fluctuations, at about the same level over six decades. Second, the difference in support between the top and bottom third has increased. Class divisions, at least as measured this way, have not declined but grown. The conclusion could easily be that Democrats are not losing the working class.

---

[32] Byron E. Shafer and Richard Johnston, *The End of Southern Exceptionalism: Class, Race, and Partisan Change in the Postwar South* (Cambridge, MA: Harvard University Press, 2006).

[33] Thomas F. Schaller, *Whistling Past Dixie: How Democrats Can Win Without the South* (New York: Simon & Schuster, 2006).

TABLE 8.1. Democratic support by income: Percent voting for and identifying with Democrats, by decade, 1950s–2000s (whites only)[34]

Decade	Presidential voting			House election voting			Party identification		
Income	Low	High	Diff	Low	High	Diff	Low	High	Diff
1950s	42	38	4	56	48	8	51	43	8
1960s	49	47	2	56	52	4	50	41	9
1970s	42	33	9	61	49	12	53	45	8
1980s	43	29	14	60	47	13	52	40	12
1990s	53	37	16	59	41	18	53	39	14
2000s	53	41	12	53	43	12	50	42	8
Change	11	3	8	−3	−5	4	−1	−1	0

The party certainly could be troubled that they are not attracting a higher level of support among the bottom third, but the evidence does not indicate that they are losing this part of the electorate.[35]

Furthermore, there were clear reasons for liberals to believe that the party could present itself as the advocate for those struggling in American society, and voters would see a party concerned about their problems.[36] Economic changes were creating greater inequality and were leaving many without health insurance and pensions. Access to college was becoming more difficult. Surely these issues were becoming more important to voters. With immigration changing the composition of American society, there were also more nonwhites who might be sympathetic to issues of inequality, and who might provide more voters to expand the base of the party.

[34] Numbers are the percent indicating they either voted for Democrats in the presidential (vcf0705) and House elections (vcf0707), or identified with the Democratic Party (vcf0303). The percentages for each year within a decade are averaged. The data are taken from the National Election Studies files for 1948–2004. To derive the groupings of low and high (bottom and top third) of income groupings, the groupings of family income for each year were recoded so that those in the 0–33 percentile were in the bottom third, and those in the 66–100 percentile were coded as top third. Only whites are included because for the last several decades their behavior has been the primary concern.

[35] Jeffrey M. Stonecash, *Class and Party in American Politics* (Boulder, CO: Westview Press, 2000).

[36] Thomas Ferguson and Joel Rogers, "The Myth of America's Turn to the Right," *Atlantic Monthly* (May 1986): 43–53; Robert Kuttner, *The Life of the Party: Democratic Prospects in 1988 and Beyond* (New York: Penguin Books, 1987); Harold Meyerson, "Wither the Democrats?" *The American Prospect* 22 (March–April, 1996): 79–88; S. M. Miller and Karen Marie Ferroggiaro, "Class Dismissed?" *The American Prospect* 21 (Spring 1995): 100–4.

TABLE 8.2. Pre-tax average household income by income groups (2004 dollars), 1979–2004

Income quintile	1979	2004	% change 1979–2004	Dollar change 1979–2004
Lowest fifth	15,100	15,400	2.0	$300
Second fifth	32,700	36,300	11.0	$3,600
Middle fifth	49,000	56,200	14.7	$7,200
Fourth fifth	66,300	81,700	23.2	$15,400
Top fifth	127,100	207,200	63.0	$80,100
Top 10%	165,600	297,800	79.8	$132,200
Top 5%	225,400	443,400	96.7	$218,000
Top 1%	498,200	1,259,700	152.9	$761,500

Source: Congressional Budget Office, *Effective Federal Tax Rates, 1979 to 2004*, Table 4C, December 2006. Data from http://www.cbo.gov/publications/bysubject.cfm?cat=33. All figures are adjusted for inflation, or the dollars are expressed in constant dollars, or the ability to purchase equivalent amounts in the two years.

After World War II until the early 1970s, inequality in the distribution of income had steadily declined. All levels of income had experienced income increases, with those at the bottom increasing the most, resulting in diminished differences by 1970.[37] After 1970, that trend reversed and inequality began to steadily increase.[38] The differences were increasing because those at the top were making much more and those in the bottom half were experiencing little gain. Table 8.2 indicates how incomes have changed over the past twenty-five years. Those in the bottom fifth in 1979 are compared with those in the bottom fifth in 2004. Over twenty-five years, those in the bottom fifth realized a gain of 2 percent in income, while those in the top fifth had a 63 percent gain.

The liberals in the party saw a society in which over the last several decades the working class had to be experiencing growing economic frustration. More wives were working, but even with an additional income earner, median family incomes were increasing only modestly.[39] The wages of men (especially those of men with only a high school degree)

---

[37] Sheldon Danziger and Peter Gottschalk, *America Unequal* (Cambridge, MA: Harvard University Press, 1995).

[38] Aviva Aron-Dine, "New Data Show Income Concentration Rose Again in 2006," Center on Budget and Policy Priorities, March 27, 2008, http://www.cbpp.org/3-27-08tax2.htm.

[39] Pew Research Center, "Annual Growth Rate of Real Income Across the Family Income Distribution: 1947 to 1973 versus 1973 to 2005," http://pewsocialtrends.org/charts/?chartid=532&topicid=5.

were gradually declining.[40] Union membership was declining, and more workers were not receiving health insurance as a part of their job. More were working without a pension program that provided a certain level of benefits after a set number of years. Fewer workers stayed with the same employer for long periods, and more were expected to set aside money from their income to provide for their retirement. Workers were operating in a world of greater uncertainty while corporate executives were allocating themselves higher salaries.[41]

To liberals there was a clear case to make that there was a constituency that needed government programs to help improve their situation. There was a clear sense that this very large constituency – from the most poor to the middle class struggling with health insurance, retirement, and college costs – could be appealed to with a higher minimum wage, universal health insurance, protection of Social Security, and higher federal grants for college.[42]

There is also the issue of the changing composition of American society. Since the 1960s, there had been a steady growth in immigration, with most of it involving Latinos. They tend to identify with and vote Democratic, although many are not yet naturalized and registered to vote.[43] To some, this is a less affluent population, facing issues of economic adjustment and opportunity, and already leaning toward the Democratic Party. Their presence is changing the composition of the electorate and could provide an expanded electoral base for the party.

Table 8.3 indicates how much the composition of the society has changed. After each census, reports provide a profile of each House district, indicating the percentage that is nonwhite. Each district can then be classified as to the percentage of the population that is nonwhite, as indicated by respondents to the census survey. These districts, with some exceptions, are set following each decennial census and continue for a decade. In the 1960s, 22.1 percent of House districts consisted of 20 percent or more of nonwhites. After the 2000 U.S. Census, 50.8 percent are in that category. The situation of having 20 percent or more of nonwhites

---

[40] Jeff Madrick and Nikolaos Papanikolaou, "The Stagnation of Male Wages," Schwartz Center for Economic Analysis, The New School, n.d., http://www.newschool.edu/cepa/publications/policynotes/Stagnation%20of%20Male%20Wages.pdf.

[41] Jacob S. Hacker, *The Great Risk Shift: The Assault on American Jobs, Families, Health Care, Retirement, and How You Can Fight Back* (New York: Oxford University Press, 2006).

[42] Paul Krugman, *The Conscience of a Liberal* (New York: W.W. Norton, 2007).

[43] Paul Taylor and Richard C. Fry, "Hispanics and the 2008 Election: A Swing Voter," The Pew Hispanic Center, December 6, 2007. http://pewhispanic.org/reports/report.php?ReportID=83.

TABLE 8.3. Distribution of House districts by the percentage nonwhite, 1960s–2000s

The nation	Decade of apportionment and % distribution				
% Nonwhite	1960s	1970s	1980s	1990s	2000 data
0–9	64.8	61.6	44.8	40.6	22.5
10–19	13.1	18.5	24.9	24.6	26.7
20 plus	22.1	19.9	30.3	34.9	50.8

is important, because it indicates a significant base for any Democratic candidate. Although there are reasons to be cautious (many of these non-whites may be too young to vote, may not currently be eligible to vote, or are not registered to vote), there is a sense among many Democrats that there is a potential base for the future.

Together, these trends suggest to some that a liberal economic message will succeed. Democrats are not losing the white working class. Inequality is increasing, people are losing benefits, and there is a greater immigration population to appeal to. To these advocates, the problem is that the party has not staked out a clear position as a party seeking to help these workers.[44]

Finally, there are those within the Democratic Party who believe that Republicans have overreached on social issues. They argue that American society is becoming more accepting of diverse ways of living, and that as the party has become more conservative on social issues, it has alienated those who are more accepting. They argue that many people are uneasy about how Republicans alluded to race in the 1988 presidential elections with an ad focusing on a released black felon, Willie Horton. Over time, Republicans have aligned themselves with some religious leaders who regard homosexuality as a sickness, even as society itself has become more accepting.[45] In 2005, the party took a strong legislative stance against the courts allowing the removal of a feeding tube for a woman who had been in that state for several years. Many party members apparently thought the public would support their position, but public opinion was clearly opposed to their position.[46] The party's position on abortion has also hurt them among some groups. Those with higher education and income tend to be more supportive of abortion

[44] Michael Kazin, "The Worker's Party?" *New York Times*, October 19, 1995, p. A25.
[45] Brewer and Stonecash, *Split*, 169.
[46] http://www.gallup.com/poll/15310/Public-Supports-Removal-Feeding-Tube-Terri-Schiavo.aspx.

rights, and they have moved more Democratic in presidential voting in recent years, apparently out of uneasiness with the Republican Party's position on the issue.[47] The argument is that the pursuit of the fiscal conservatives plus social conservatives that Republicans have pursued has resulted in a party image that many voters are becoming uneasy with. The Democratic Party can capitalize on that uneasiness by presenting itself as the party of tolerance.

THE PERSISTING DEMOCRATIC DEBATE

The debate continues within the Democratic Party: Should it be more moderate or more liberal? Critics argue that it became too liberal beginning in the late 1960s and lost the presidency in 1980, 1984, and 1988 as a result. To the moderates, the success of Bill Clinton in 1992 and 1996 was because he was explicitly less liberal and attracted those in the middle. They argue that his political problems in 1994 and 1995 were because he forgot that lesson. His first move as president was a proposal to allow gays to serve openly in the military. He then focused on establishing a national health care plan (seen as a liberal initiative) rather than changing the welfare system. His venture into changing the health care system failed miserably, and contributed to the Republican takeover of Congress in 1994. To some within the Democratic Party, it is clear that the only way the party can win elections and control government is by projecting an image of moderation and then governing accordingly.

The views of moderates were again important in the latter years of the George W. Bush presidency, which will be discussed in more detail next. To moderates the gains in congressional seats made in 2006 and 2008, giving them a majority, should be interpreted with caution. They note that voting in 2006 was largely driven by disapproval of George W. Bush and opposition to the Iraq War, and not necessarily by support for liberal Democratic initiatives.[48] They note that of Democratic House members elected in 2006, fifty-eight were in districts that George Bush won in 2004, while only nine Republicans were in districts won by Democrat John Kerry. Following the 2008 elections, seventy-seven Democrats were in districts won by Bush in 2004. If the vote in a district is taken as an

---

[47] Jeffrey M. Stonecash, "Income Gaps," in Laura R. Olson and John C. Green (eds.), *Beyond Red State, Blue State: Electoral Gaps in the Twenty-First Century American Electorate* (Upper Saddle River: Pearson, 2009), 65–8.

[48] Gary C. Jacobson, "The War, the President, and the 2006 Midterm Elections," presented at the 2007 Midwest Political Science Association Meetings, Chicago, IL, April 2007.

indication of the underlying disposition of a district, then these Democrats have to be careful about compiling a liberal voting record.[49]

The more liberal wing of the party believes that the electorate is more liberal than is often concluded,[50] and that future demographic trends will result in an electoral base more receptive to liberal policies. They argue that although most Americans say they want less government and lower taxes, when asked about cutting specific programs, voters are in practice much more liberal and want to preserve programs.[51] They also argue that with inequality increasing and fewer employers providing health insurance and pension programs that promise specific benefits at retirement, there are more voters who will be receptive to their message. They believe the Democrats can present themselves as more tolerant of diverse social behaviors and less inclined to intrude into people's lives. The most passionate liberals argue that if the party does not stand for these voters, it really has no reason to exist.

The 2008 Democratic primary reflected the cautious moderate versus the more liberal divisions within the party. Barack Obama and Hillary Clinton did not differ significantly on domestic policy, although Obama had a record of more consistent opposition to the Iraq War. The contest was also complicated by the simultaneous possibility of two firsts in American politics: a female and a black nominee for president. A central issue was whether nominating a black candidate would be seen as too liberal by whites and would harm the party's prospects. Hillary Clinton (embodying a possible breakthrough herself as a female party nominee) could not argue against making a new type of nominee, but she did argue that a black candidate would be seen as too liberal and would not attract the votes of the "white working class" vote, and that she could do better at attracting that vote in the general election.[52]

In making her case, she was raising the issue that Democrats were still struggling with. Obama represented the wing that wanted a clear liberal stance, particularly on the Iraq War. Yet for years the party had been hearing statements such as: "No Democrat except Lyndon Johnson in 1964 has won a majority of the white middle class vote since

[49] Carle Hulse, "Gaining Seats, Democrats Find Their House Ideologically Divided," *New York Times*, May 18, 2008, p. A25.

[50] Robert S. Erikson, Michael B. MacKuen, and James A. Stimson, *The Macro Polity* (New York: Cambridge University Press, 2002).

[51] Benjamin I. Page and Robert Y. Shapiro, *The Rational Public: Fifty Years of Trends in Americans' Policy Preferences* (Chicago: University of Chicago Press, 1992).

[52] John Harwood, "A Fault Line that Haunts the Democrats, *New York Times*, May 4, 2008, Week in Review, p. 1.

Truman's squeaker";[53] or, following the 1994 elections: "Working-class voters...deserted the Democrats in droves."[54] It is also true that no Democratic presidential candidate has ever won without at least some success in the South. Hillary Clinton persisted through the long primary season by persistently raising the issue of Barack Obama's electability: Was a liberal candidate who appealed to the liberal wing of the party electable? Even after Obama's primary and then general election victory – in which he won three former Confederate states (Florida, North Carolina, and Virginia) – this is a question that the party is still struggling with.

[53] Blair Clark, "Can We Put New Life in the Party?," *The Nation* (November 2, 1985): 443.

[54] Ruy A. Teixeira and Joel Rogers, "Volatile Voters: Declining Living Standards and Non-College Educated Whites." Working Paper No. 116, August 8, 1996. Economic Policy Institute, 13–14; Teixeira and Rodgers, *The Forgotten Majority*, 83.

9 George Bush and Further Polarization

While Democrats continued to search for direction, Republicans had their own struggles. By January 2001, political trends and events appeared to have put them in their best situation in decades. Then, following the 2006 and 2008 elections, the party was clearly in trouble. Republicans had to decide if voters did not like their party and its policies or if anti-Republican sentiment was simply a reflection of the thoroughly unpopular presidency of George W. Bush. If it was the latter, then the party could wait for the memory of Bush to fade away. If it was the former, then Republicans had some serious reassessment to do. Determining which of these explanations was more likely was not an easy task.

The George W. Bush presidency represented the first unified Republican control of the presidency and Congress since 1953.[1] The primary question was what the GOP would do with its power. Republican success had been gradually increasing in recent decades, and the early 2000s was the party's best chance to implement the policies they supported. With the attraction of more conservatives to the Republican Party and the loss of Northeast moderates, the party now had less internal diversity and its best opportunity to enact a conservative agenda.

There was little doubt that Congress was primed for such an agenda. Conservative Republicans had a stranglehold on the majority in the

---

[1] The first session of the 83rd Congress (1953–1955) was a tumultuous time in the U.S. Senate. Nine members died (including one suicide) and one resigned. The Republicans maintained control throughout, despite have less seats than the Democrats at various points during that Congress. During the two terms of George W. Bush, the Republicans controlled Congress in its entirety for the 108th and 109th Congresses (2003–2007). The GOP controlled the House during the 107th Congress, but party control of the Senate changed hands three times during the 107th. Republican control of both chambers came to an end with the 100th Congress (2007–2009) as the Democrats assumed control of both the House and Senate.

House, and although conservative prospects were not as bright in the Senate, Republican leadership in that body was also clearly conservative and they had high hopes of finishing what Ronald Reagan had started twenty years earlier. The crucial issue was what type of agenda George W. Bush would pursue as president. He had run as a compassionate conservative, a position whose policy implications were not clear.[2] He had also proposed what would eventually become known as the No Child Left Behind Act, which would put greater pressure on schools where student test scores were not good to improve those scores. The policy sounded like a moderate effort to make schools pay more attention to students in less affluent districts. It also represented a relatively large federal intervention in education policy, something that many conservatives had long resisted. Bush had won a closely contested race with Democrat Al Gore and then was helped by the Supreme Court decision in December 2000 that a recount of votes in Florida could not proceed. Given the closeness of the race and anger that swirled around the protracted battle over the Florida votes, many thought that George W. Bush would pursue a moderate course as president.[3]

He chose not to follow that path. Bush's first proposal as president was a very large cut in the personal income tax. His argument was that high taxes were restricting individual spending and rewards for entrepreneurial activity within the economy. In making the proposals, he was aligning himself with an array of conservatives who were antitax and wanted to restrict the flow of personal income tax revenue to the federal government.[4] Many believed that the proposal, in which the bulk of the dollar benefits went to the more affluent,[5] was simply an opening gambit

---

[2] Bush's thinking here was strongly influenced by the work of conservative academic Marvin Olasky. See Marvin Olasky, *The Tragedy of American Compassion* (Washington, DC: Regnery Publishing, 1992); Marvin Olasky, *Compassionate Conservatism: What It Is, What It Does, and How It Can Transform America* (New York: The Free Press, 2000).

[3] Gary C. Jacobson, *A Divider, Not a Uniter: George W. Bush and the American People* (New York: Pearson/Longman, 2007).

[4] Two of the most prominent such groups are the Club for Growth (http://www.clubforgrowth.org/) and Americans for Tax Reform (http://www.atr.org/). Each group has been very active in promoting a lower tax agenda and making sure those they regard as the creators of new jobs pay lower rates than has been the case in the past. Grover Norquist, president of Americans for Tax Reform, has stated numerous times that his ultimate goal is to shrink the federal government "down to the size where we can drown it in the bathtub." In advocating for tax reductions as a way to shrink government, Norquist and others like him are following the same strategy used by Ronald Reagan. Tax cuts mean less government revenue, and less revenue means less government.

[5] The Bush administration emphasized the average tax cut per person and also noted that the percentage reductions were similar across income levels.

and that compromise would follow. Bush, however, had no interest in negotiating. He declined to compromise and insisted on his proposal being passed. Republicans in Congress overrode strong Democratic opposition and with almost unanimous support within the party enacted Bush's tax cut.

He followed that with another decision that indicated he was not going to adopt a moderate stance. In March 2001, he announced he was withdrawing the United States from an international treaty negotiated in Kyoto, Japan, during the late 1990s. The treaty was to get nations to agree to take steps to reduce greenhouse gas emissions, which contribute to global warming. The treaty was not well received in Congress because of concerns about harmful effects on the U.S. economy and because China, a major and rapidly growing polluter, was not required to take similar steps to reduce its emissions. Although there were reasons to be skeptical about the treaty, his decision to withdraw shaped the president's image as unmistakably conservative.

Within a short time in office, he had adopted two clear stances that labeled him as a strong conservative. He put forward other conservative positions and pushed Congress to adopt his preferred policies while communicating that moderation and compromise were not going to prevail. Bush's approach to governing prompted considerable speculation about whether his conservative stance was likely to continue and what was driving it. After all, as governor of Texas, Bush had developed a reputation as a bipartisan operator who was willing to compromise. Some saw his positioning as just reflecting his personality and perhaps not the direction of the party.[6] However, there was also evidence that the party could feel confident about pursuing a clear conservative direction. Republicans gained control of the House in 1994 with a conservative set of proposals. Meanwhile, more and more of their seats were in districts won by Republican presidential candidates. The constituencies of the president and Republican House members were increasingly the same, making concerted party action easier. In the 2000 election, George Bush won 227 of the 435 House districts, a majority of all districts. If Republicans in Congress could count on a relatively strong partisan vote in their districts like Bush received, then working with him and supporting his proposals would be good for them and good for the president. Furthermore, more and more Republican members of Congress held the same conservative

---

[6] Robert Draper, *Dead Certain: The Presidency of George W. Bush* (New York: Free Press, 2007); Jacob Weisberg, *The Bush Tragedy* (New York: Random House, 2008).

policy views as Bush,[7] so voting to support his policy goals was desirable. The party was steadily attracting higher percentages of voters who identified themselves as conservative[8] and there were more conservatives in the country than liberals. The party leadership had been advocating moving in a conservative direction since at least 1980, and their electoral fortunes had improved. Conservatism seemed to be paying off for the Republicans on Election Day.

Perhaps most important, the president's chief political advisor Karl Rove had apparently concluded that the Republicans' ability to further expand their electoral base was limited, so the emphasis had to be on greater support among their conservative base. His conclusion, after careful review of the 2000 results, was that Bush was unlikely to get more than 51 percent of the vote in a reelection bid. Rove saw voters as so polarized that the prospects of persuading certain groups to vote Republican were unlikely. He concluded that the best chance for Bush to win in 2004 was to energize and mobilize conservatives.[9] For example, Rove concluded that Bush could get four million more evangelical Protestant votes in 2004 than he did in 2000 if a direct appeal was made to this group. The party then made a massive effort to turn these voters out on Election Day in 2004.[10] This strategy of squeezing every last conservative vote out of the American electorate led to a greater focus on pushing for conservative policies, and for making sure that emphasis was known to voters. This focus was seen as valuable for reinforcing the party's base. It also fit with Bush's desire to be seen as a bold and decisive leader who pursued clear policy directions. He made it clear to Democrats that there would be little negotiation about his agenda. The result was that for the first nine months of 2001, the Republican Party set off on a clear conservative direction. The basis for further sorting and polarizing of the electorate was set.

Then the September 11, 2001, attacks on the United States by Osama bin Laden and Al-Qaeda occurred, and for a while party divisions were

---

[7] Robert S. Erikson and Gerald C. Wright, "Voters, Candidates, and Issues in Congressional Elections," in Lawrence C. Dodd and Bruce Oppenheimer (eds.), *Congress Reconsidered*, seventh edition (Washington, DC: Congressional Quarterly Press, 2001), 67–96.

[8] Jacobson, *A Divider, Not a Uniter*; Jeffrey M. Stonecash, "The Rise of the Right: More Conservatives or More Concentrated Conservatism?" in John C. Green and Daniel J. Coffey (eds.), *The State of the Parties*, fifth edition (Lanham, MD: Rowman & Littlefield, 2006), 317–30.

[9] Ronald Brownstein, *The Second Civil War: How Extreme Partisanship Has Paralyzed Washington and Polarized America* (New York: Penguin Press, 2007), 287–8.

[10] Alan Cooperman and Thomas B. Edsall, "Evangelicals Say They Led Charge for GOP," *Washington Post*, November 8, 2004, p. A01.

suspended. The shock of the attacks created a strong sense of "us versus them," and the parties subdued their differences for a number of months. There was talk that the pressures to unify were so strong that the parties might set aside their differences and focus on external threats. There was a clear "rally around the flag" phenomenon in the country, and support for George Bush as the leader of the nation increased.

EXTERNAL THREATS AND THE NEOCONSERVATIVES

The spirit of bipartisanship did not last long. The attack brought to the surface differences between the parties that had been developing for some time among party elites but had not been brought into the open and made part of the electoral dialogue. The central issue quickly became how the United States should respond to external threats and what measures had to be taken domestically. Republicans argued for an aggressive policy of confronting threats, even if the action was unilateral. President Bush asserted what became known as the *Bush Doctrine*, the prerogative of the United States to engage in preemptive military actions if it believed that a foreign nation or outside groups was planning to harm the United States or its interests.[11] Democrats were more inclined to favor forming international alliances to try to contain threats and preferred diplomacy to the use of military force.

For much of the twentieth century, Republicans had been the party that wanted to focus on domestic matters while Democrats seemed more willing to involve the United States in international affairs. Indeed, Republicans were often accused of being *isolationists*, or inclined to keep the country out of foreign entanglements. This began to change with Ronald Reagan.[12] In the pre-Reagan era, when there was a perceived threat (such as with World War II, or the North Korean attack on South Korea), there was a relatively unified response to the issue. That translated into bipartisan public support for military action. Even the Vietnam War, which eventually divided the public, did not become a war in which Republicans and Democrats differed much in their support.[13] The collapse

---

[11] David Gray Adler, "George Bush, the War Power, and the Imperial Presidency," presented at the Annual Meeting of the American Political Science Association, Chicago, IL, 2004; Mary Buckley and Robert Singh, *The Bush Doctrine and the War on Terrorism: Global Reactions, Global Consequences* (New York: Routledge, 2004).

[12] Benjamin O. Fordham, "The Evolution of Republican and Democratic Positions on Cold War Military Spending: A Historical Puzzle," *Social Science History* 31 (Winter 2007): 603–36.

[13] Gary C. Jacobson, "The Public, the President, and the War in Iraq," presented at the 2005 Midwest Political Science Association Meetings, Chicago, IL, April 2005.

of the Soviet Union in the late 1980s raised the possibility that the demise of the *cold war* – the tense standoff between Russia and the United States over who would dominate – signaled the end of fundamental conflicts within the world. Not only might the world be safer, but many concluded that the lesson of Vietnam was that the United States should be very careful about pursuing efforts to intrude in the affairs of other countries. Some concluded that our ability to change other countries was limited and was likely to consume more resources and credibility than such efforts were worth.

Others, known as *neoconservatives*, largely within the Republican Party, had been developing another set of conclusions.[14] This less-than-unified group included many who had once been liberal but had concluded that liberalism had failed. They moved to a more conservative set of positions, so they were seen as "new" or neoconservatives. Their central reaction to the Vietnam War was that it had created a paralyzing sense of failure and a hesitancy to use military power to affect the world. Proponents of such a worldview – individuals like Vice President Richard Cheney, Paul Wolfowitz, Richard Perle, and Donald Rumsfeld, and a number of intellectuals who were anonymous to the public – thought that with an international world filled with threats to the United States and with the Soviet Union no longer a super power, America could direct its attention to these other threats. Some of them also thought that it was possible to promote democracy and free markets in other countries, which would ultimately reduce threats from totalitarian regimes and make America safer. In short, they made the case for a strong military presence and a very active role for the United States in changing the world.

To neoconservatives, the 9/11 attacks verified much of their world view. They saw the world as filled with nations led by dangerous dictators and terrorists who were threatened by the principles of freedom and wanted to damage the United States. Many of these prominent neoconservatives were within the Bush administration when 9/11 occurred, and they forcefully made their case that the response should be a strong and immediate military response. Their view that American democracy embodied a moral society that was being threatened by dangerous elements fit well with George W. Bush's view that there was good and evil in the world and that he was justified in attacking it.[15]

The combination of the neoconservatives' views, their prominent roles within the Bush administration, and Bush's own views played a major

[14] James Mann, *The Rise of the Vulcans: The History of Bush's War Cabinet* (New York: Viking Adult, 2004).
[15] David Domke, *God Willing* (London: Pluto Press, 2004).

role in shaping the administration's response to 9/11. The nation was searching for a way to respond to the first major attack on American soil since Pearl Harbor, and the neoconservatives provided an answer that reflected their views. The response also was very compatible with the GOP's evolving electoral base.

President Bush quickly moved to present the situation as a confrontation of good versus evil and the United States versus the terrorists. In late 2001, the United States invaded Afghanistan to remove the *Taliban*, an Islamic fundamentalist regime, from controlling the country. The argument was that the country was harboring Osama bin Laden. In his January 2002 State of Union address, Bush portrayed Iran, Iraq, and North Korea as embodying the "Axis of Evil," arguing that they were countries seeking to acquire nuclear weapons and pursue dangerous goals within the world community. In September 2002, he issued a formal statement of his strategic view (*National Security Strategy of the United States*), asserting that the United States had the right to preemptively attack other nations if we suspected they might threaten our security.[16]

In October 2001, Bush submitted the USA PATRIOT Act (Uniting and Strengthening America by Providing Appropriate Tools Required to Intercept and Obstruct Terrorism Act of 2001) to Congress and insisted on immediate passage, suggesting that opponents to the legislation were not concerned about protecting America. Some Democrats asked questions about whether the USA PATRIOT Act was being given careful enough consideration and whether it granted too much power to the president. Yet most Democrats were reluctant to go on the record as voting against efforts of the president to protect the country. In the House of Representatives, Republicans voted 211–3 in favor of the USA PATRIOT Act, and Democrats voted 145–62 for the bill. The opposition came largely from members from liberal districts that had not voted for George Bush in 2000.

By that fall, he was also making it clear that he saw Iraq and its leader Saddam Hussein as having dangerous weapons of mass destruction, and Hussein as being connected to international terrorism. Bush also made it clear he was considering invading that country. He continually presented the situation as a simple choice of democracy, freedom, and morality versus totalitarian amoral terrorists. Time and time again, Bush spurned nuance in favor of blunt language that made it clear to other nations that

---

[16] The document was published September 20, 2002. http://www.whitehouse.gov/nsc/nss.html.

they were in his view either "with us or against us" on issues of foreign policy – no ambiguities, no grey areas.

This way of seeing the conflict was compatible with Bush's world view and with the religious constituency the party had been attracting in the last two decades. There were many who saw the United States as a Christian nation with admirable and morally correct principles. Bush presented international terrorists as those who were totalitarian in their thought and who rejected the freedom of democratic societies. They were also seen as possessing a most decidedly un-Christian outlook. These views resonated with those with stronger attachments to religion.[17] To those who felt the United States had the morally correct position, Bush's stance was very appealing.

PARTISAN MOBILIZATION

In the months immediately following 9/11, President Bush's job approval ratings rose to levels never experienced by any president, reaching 90 percent in some polls in late 2001. A "rally around the flag" mood prevailed, with partisan differences set aside in the face of an external threat.[18] That unity did not last, however, in large part because of how George Bush and the Republican Party in Congress chose to deal with opponents. His primary approach to Congress and the Democrats was to insist that they go along. He also presented crucial policies as for the good of the country and suggested that anyone who did not accept his policies was not concerned about the safety of the country.

When he submitted the USA PATRIOT Act to Congress, he gave members very little time to read or revise the large and complicated bill. He insisted that it be enacted immediately or the security of the United States might be threatened. He submitted the bill in October 2001 and put considerable pressure on Congress to "protect America." He also submitted a resolution in September authorizing the use of force against Iraq. Many

---

[17] James L. Guth, John C. Green, Lyman A. Kellstedt, and Corwin E. Smidt, "Faith and Foreign Policy: A View From the Pews," *The Review of Faith and International Affairs* 3 (Fall 2003): 3–9.

[18] For the original discussions of the "rally round the flag" effect, see John E. Mueller, "Presidential Popularity from Truman to Johnson," *American Political Science Review* 64 (March 1970): 18–34; John E. Mueller, *War, Presidents, and Public Opinion* (New York: John Wiley and Sons, 1973). For the rally effect as it relates to George W. Bush and 9/11, see Marc J. Hetherington and Michael Nelson, "Anatomy of a Rally Effect: George W. Bush and the War on Terrorism," *PS: Political Science and Politics* 36 (January 2003): 37–42.

members resented the pressure prior to the 2002 elections, but felt compelled to vote for the bill because of Bush's portrayal of dissenters. Equally troubling was how Republicans dealt with Max Cleland, a senator from Georgia running for reelection in 2002. Cleland had served in Vietnam and lost several limbs in that war. He opposed the policies of George W. Bush. The Republican response was to run television ads against him during the 2002 campaign suggesting that he was sympathetic to Osama bin Laden.[19] Cleland was defeated. Democrats found it hard to believe that a disabled veteran could be successfully accused of being unpatriotic, and they were angered that Republicans would employ such tactics.

For awhile, actions such as those above helped the image of the Republican Party. For decades, more voters had identified with the Democratic Party than the Republican Party. The Republicans had acquired a brief advantage in party identification in 1995, but that had quickly eroded as the party pursued a conservative agenda to cut the budget. The forceful way that Bush and the Republicans had responded to 9/11 was seen positively, and by 2002, 43 percent identified as Republicans and 43 percent identified as Democrats.[20] President Bush and the Republicans were presenting themselves as engaged in a *War on Terror* to defend America, and public opinion polls indicated that Bush was seen as able to handle this better than the Democrats. It appeared that the Republican approach to foreign policy issues was seen positively, thus helping the party attract more voters.

Democrats were reluctant to strongly oppose George Bush post-9/11. The country was very supportive of the Bush administration and wanted action taken to counter any terrorist threats. President Bush had made it clear in 2002 that he would attack opponents in campaigns, and Democrats were worried about being seen as unconcerned about terrorism. Some Democratic members of Congress raised questions about the resolution authorizing the use of force against Iraq, but their numbers were not large. The reluctance of Democrats to strongly oppose the policies of George W. Bush was furthered by the events of 2003. The president and his staff engaged in a protracted presentation of the case for attacking Iraq in early 2003 and then launched an attack in March of that year. The military conquest was surprisingly quick, and by May of that year, George Bush was able to land on an aircraft carrier off the coast

---

[19] For a summary of these events, see Jacobson, *A Divider, Not a Uniter*, 69–94.

[20] The Pew Research Center for the People and the Press, "Trends in Political Values and Core Attitudes: 1987–2007: Political Landscape More Favorable to Democrats," March 22, 2007. Available at: http://people-press.org/reports/display.php3?ReportID=312.

of California in a carefully orchestrated event, and stride to the cameras to announce the end of military hostilities with a banner behind him that said "Mission Accomplished." By June 2003, George Bush and the Republican Congress had taken on terrorists in Afghanistan and Saddam Hussein in Iraq and won. A new Department of Homeland Security was officially established in January 2003. New laws were passed to grant the federal government more authority to track terrorists.

In mid-June of 2003, there seemed to be little that could go wrong for George Bush. In November 2004, he won a second term as president and announced that he had acquired "political capital" and that he intended to spend it. Rove's strategy of appealing to and then mobilizing the party's base to the fullest appeared to have worked.[21] Rove saw the last several years as evidence that the country was moving Republican and that the message of the Bush administration in particular and conservative Republicanism in general was being well received. Following the election, Rove explained that he saw the country as on the verge of a partisan realignment to the Republican Party, much like that which occurred in 1896.[22]

A REVERSAL OF FORTUNES

The scenario that Republicans were hoping for was soon to collapse; indeed, there were signs of trouble for the GOP even before Bush won his second term in 2004. As happens again and again in politics, events destroy the plans of politicians. In late 2003, events began unfolding in a way that altered the positive image that George W. Bush and the Republican Party had built up. The Republicans paid the price for bad news because they were the party that held the White House and the Congress, and they were perhaps hurt even more because the White House and congressional leaders had been largely dismissive of working with Democrats. George Bush had indicated he had little interest in compromising with Democrats on domestic issues or foreign policy. He indicated that he was going to portray his opponents as not sufficiently concerned about America at a time of national peril. His actions solidified his

---

[21] Brownstein, *The Second Civil War: How Extreme Partisanship Has Paralyzed Washington and Polarized America*, 288–9; Evan Thomas, Eleanor Clift, Jonathan Darman, Kevin Peraino, and Peter Goldman, *Election 2004: How Bush Won and What You Can Expect in the Future* (New York: Public Affairs, 2004).

[22] Joshua Green, "The Rove Presidency," *Atlantic Monthly* (November 2007). Available at: http://theatlantic.com/doc/; James Moore and Wayne Slater, *The Architect: Karl Rove and the Master Plan for Absolute Power* (New York: Crown Publishers, 2006).

support among conservatives and those with strong religious attachments, but they also drove away liberals and many moderates. The result was a more polarized electorate. These divisions were not just a product of George Bush, as divisions had been increasing for some time, but he pushed them along.[23]

Beginning in the late summer of 2003 and continuing steadily for the next several years, the news coming out of Iraq turned negative. President Bush had created the impression that hostilities would soon subside and that things would improve in that nation. Although the administration largely dismissed concerns that conflict was increasing in Iraq, the number of casualties of American soldiers began to increase, as did the occurrence of attacks on Iraqi citizens and bombings throughout the country. The war had been presented as something that might cost $60 billion, but the costs were rising steadily far beyond that amount.

The turn of events was made worse by the steady emergence of books criticizing the planning for a postwar Iraq and the execution of military operations after the toppling of Hussein.[24] The image of the successful execution of war with Iraq began to slip away as more reports indicated that the Secretary of Defense had dismissed the need to plan for what happened after the United States won a military conquest over Saddam Hussein. As costs and casualties began to rise, Bush's approval ratings began a steady decline. Although events were slipping away from the Republicans, President Bush did not change his partisan approach to criticism, and the divisions between the parties increased.

Although Bush won a second term and the GOP maintained control of Congress in 2004, events continued to harm Republican fortunes. In August 2005, Hurricane Katrina hit New Orleans, causing enormous damage. The city is below sea level and is protected by a series of levees that hold back the water. The hurricane destroyed the levees, flooding the city and wreaking havoc across the larger region. The Bush administration appeared to not appreciate the severity of the damage and delayed in responding to the disaster. Despite delayed efforts to respond, the

---

[23] Jacobson, *A Divider, Not a Uniter.*

[24] The number of books became considerable after a while. For examples, see Michael R. Gordon and Bernard E. Trainor, *Cobra II: The Inside Story of the Invasion and Occupation of Iraq* (New York: Pantheon, 2006); Michael Isikoff and David Corn, *Hubris: The Inside Story of Spin, Scandal, and the Selling of the War in Iraq* (New York: Crown, 2006); Scott McClellan, *What Happened: Inside the Bush White House and Washington's Culture of Deception* (New York: Public Affairs, 2008); George Packer, *Assassin's Gate: America in Iraq* (New York: Farrar, Straus and Giroux, 2005); Thomas E. Ricks, *Fiasco: The American Military Adventure in Iraq* (New York: Penguin Press, 2006).

administration gave the impression that it was either not well organized
to respond to national disasters or that what happened in New Orleans
was not of high importance to the administration. There were defenders
who argued that the federal government was responding and that much
of the problem involved the incompetence and politics of state government, but the event further damaged the image of the Bush administration. This plus the declining conditions in Iraq through 2005 and 2006
badly harmed the image of the Republican Party.

The damage was evident in the trends of job approval of George W.
Bush and identification with the Republican Party. About 50 percent
of the public approved of President Bush's job performance before 9/11.
After that, his approval ratings established a record at almost 90 percent, and the differences in ratings by party affiliation declined. As events
unfolded over the next several years, Democrats and then independents
gradually moved away from Bush, leaving him with positive job approval
ratings only among Republicans. Bush had become a very polarizing figure, drawing strong support within his own party, but he was steadily
alienating independents and Democrats.

Bush had polarized voters so much that information was being received
and accepted through a partisan lens. Two years after the invasion of Iraq,
and with no weapons of mass destruction found at that point, 80 percent
of Republicans believed that Iraq possessed such weapons. Only 33 percent of Democrats believed that.[25] The partisan filtering of information
was so strong that in 2005, when Bush tried to change Social Security
by taking money from current revenues to establish personal accounts
for individuals, Republicans believed he was trying to save the system
while Democrats and independents believed he was trying to dismantle
the system.[26]

Presidents are the most visible representative of their party, and the
fortunes of George W. Bush were affecting the support the Republican
Party had developed during the early 2000s. The party had pulled even
with Democrats in 1994 and 1995, but their efforts in the mid-1990s to
cut programs and shut down government over budget disputes created a
negative image for the party, and identification with the party declined.
In 2000–2002, identification with the party had increased, but by 2003,
Republican identification was once again declining, as shown in Figure 9.1. The congressional party had accepted Bush's strong leadership,

[25] Jacobson, *A Divider, Not a Uniter*, p. 140.
[26] Ibid., pp. 206–17.

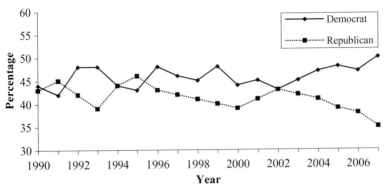

FIGURE 9.1. Party identification, 1990–2007. *Source:* Pen Foundation, see Footnote 20, this chapter.

but the public's doubts about him and his policies were dragging the party down.

By the middle of 2006, with congressional elections approaching, House and Senate members were uncertain whether to move away from Bush or remain close to him. There was no clear answer about what they should do. The trends that had put the party in power had created more districts in which Republican incumbents were running for office in districts where in which George Bush had done relatively well. There was an argument to be made that candidates running in these areas would survive, and perhaps even benefit, from sticking close to Bush. The White House political director Karl Rove made the argument that the best course of action was to defend the decision to invade Iraq and present it as an effort to transform the Middle East by establishing democracy. Rove argued that the best approach to the elections was to stress conservative positions to motivate conservative voters to turn out.[27] Furthermore, Bush was a prodigious fundraiser and he committed himself to raising large sums of money to help candidates faced with strong opponents. There were many nervous disagreements, with doubters arguing that the party needed to move away from George Bush and his policies.[28]

[27] Adam Nagourney, "Rove Lays Out Road Map for Republicans in Fall Elections," *New York Times,* January 21, 2006, p. A11.

[28] Carl Hulse, "G.O.P. Agenda in House Has Moderates Unhappy," *New York Times* (July 8, 2006), A11; Adam Nagourney and David D. Kirkpatrick, "Bad Iraq War News Worries Some in G.O.P. on '06 Vote," *New York Times,* August 18, 2005, p. A20; Adam Nagourney and Jim Rutenberg, "Rove's Word Is No Longer G.O.P. Gospel," *New York Times,* September 3, 2006.

THE 2006 ELECTIONS AND RESPONDING TO VOTER REACTIONS

The November 2006 elections were a serious setback for the Republican Party. The party lost the House and the Senate, and the exit polls indicated that negative reactions to the Iraq War and Bush largely dominated voters' decisions.[29] In 2005, Republicans controlled the House 232–203, but lost thirty seats in the 2006 elections. Democrats had a 233–202 margin in January 2007. In the Senate, Republicans lost six seats and control shifted from a Republican majority of 55–45 to a Democratic majority of 51–49. The verdict was widely interpreted as a repudiation of George W. Bush and his policies on the Iraq War.

It appeared that the party had no choice but to adapt and scale back its policies. Although others reached that conclusion, Bush himself did not. Faced with frustration about Iraq, Bush quickly moved to say he would study the situation and respond. He fended off the conclusions of the *Iraq Study Group* – a bipartisan panel appointed by Congress to assess and make recommendations regarding the war in Iraq – that suggested the United States scale back its military involvement. Instead, he defied the conventional interpretation of the election results and said that what he heard was that voters wanted to see more progress in Iraq. He proposed a "surge" in troop levels, adding thirty thousand more troops to try to reduce violence in the country. His decision surprised many, who thought the results suggested the need for another approach, and that he would have to accept that sentiment and try another approach.

Politics is filled with uncertainty and this move reflected that reality. Bush was seen as stubborn by many, and his poll ratings continued to sink. However, Bush and some political advisors had two arguments for why the U.S. effort in Iraq should be increased. First, they and their electoral base believed in the importance of persisting in Iraq if the Middle East was ever to be transformed and democracy introduced. They argued that it was imperative that change be brought about in the region and that to give up would amount to betrayal of a worthy cause. They acknowledged that the war effort had not gone well after the March 2003 invasion and felt that the solution was to accept that criticism and bolster the American military presence to reduce violence. Second, some argued that the war had severely damaged the party and that to walk away and admit

---

[29] Gary C. Jacobson, "The War, the President, and the 2006 Midterm Congressional Elections," delivered at the 2006 Midwest Political Science Association Meetings, Chicago, IL, April 2006.

TABLE 9.1. Presidential outcomes in 2004 and House winners in 2006

Presidential winner 2004	House winner 2006				
	N	Republican	N	Democrat	
Republican	193	R pres % 04: 61.1 R House % 06: 61.8	58	D pres % 04: 42.8 D House % 06: 62.5	
Democrat	9	R pres % 04: 41.2 R House % 06: 61.5	175	D pres % 04: 63.1 D House % 06: 75.4	
	202		233		

that the war was a failure would hurt the party even more. It would be admitting that Democrats were right and that American lives, resources, and credibility had been wasted. The only alternative was to try to salvage the situation with a renewed effort. The president and his party embraced the idea and began to repeatedly stress the importance of continuing the War on Terror and supporting the troops. The strategy was a clear gamble, but it fit the preferences of Bush and conservative Republicans. It also presented the possibility, if the surge was successful, that the party would have some hope for 2008.

The Democrats, taking control of Congress in 2007, had a very different view of what the 2006 elections meant. They concluded that the results clearly indicated that voters wanted out of Iraq. National polls consistently showed that approximately 60 percent thought that invading Iraq had been a mistake, and Democrats were sure that the election results plus poll results indicated they had a mandate to change the course of policy in Iraq.

The reality was that Democrats had won a majority, but that majority was not unified and not large enough to override vetoes by Bush. As Table 9.1 indicates, the additional seats that Democrats won in the House came in districts that Bush won in 2004. Of the 233 seats the party won in the 2006 elections, fifty-eight members were in districts Bush had won in 2004. The Democratic presidential candidate received an average of 42.8 in those districts in 2004, which means the House members running in these fifty-eight districts had received a percentage that was on average vote twenty points ahead of the basic partisan inclinations of their district. Such differences are unlikely to persist. Furthermore, of these fifty-eight seats, twenty-one won with 55 percent or less of the vote.

Members may be committed to working with their party, but they have to consider how their voting record will be seen within their district. If the district supported Bush in 2004, even amid a steady stream of negative news about the justification for and management of the Iraq War, then it probably reflected a moderate to conservative district. Compiling a voting record of supporting withdrawing funds for the war and being accused of not supporting the troops could result in a loss in 2008, so some Democratic members were reluctant to oppose the war completely.[30] In addition, many Democrats felt that the voting in 2006 had largely been anti-Bush and not pro-Democratic, and the party had no mandate for the policies it was advocating. Nonetheless, most Democrats opposed continuing the war while Bush and Republicans insisted on the merits of the war and emphasized supporting the troops. The result was a stalemate in which those identifying as Democrats were more and more critical of George Bush while Republicans remained very supportive. The war continued to polarize many voters.

UNCERTAINTY AND PARTY FUTURES

For Republicans, the crucial matter was that independents were also negative about Bush and the war. The events of 2007 and 2008 left Republicans very uncertain about how they would fare in the November 2008 elections. A majority of Americans still thought Iraq was a mistake, Bush had low ratings, and then the economy began to falter. Incumbent presidents are regularly blamed when economic conditions deteriorate, and developments in 2008 worried the party. For several years prior to 2008, housing prices had steadily increased. Many individuals wanted to buy homes; some to buy their first home and others to *flip* a house (buying a home, increasing its value, and selling it for a profit). Many of these individuals bought homes with an initial low interest rate that increased after two years. When the higher interest rates began, many individuals could not afford to pay their mortgages, leading to defaults on loans. Further, the speculative increases in homes began to slow and the reverse, leaving those who had bought an expensive home and betting on an increase before they sold it unable to sell their home. Many property owners began to default on their loans. Banks and financial firms were then caught with large numbers of loans that homeowners could not repay. With home values falling, homes could not be sold for enough to cover the costs of

---

[30] Carl Hulse, "Vulnerable Democrats See Fate Tied to a Clinton Run," *New York Times*, December 4, 2007, p. A1; Carl Hulse, "Gaining Seats, Democrats Find Their House Ideologically Divided," *New York Times*, May 18, 2008, p. A25.

loans. At the same time, companies began to declare large losses and lay off workers. That effect spread through the economy and unemployment increased. A declining economy was added to the woes of the Republican Party.

The party's fears begin to become reality in early 2008 as the party lost three special elections for House seats. All three seats had been held by the Republican Party for a lengthy period of time, and party leaders worried that it was a sign of what might happen in November.[31] The party struggled to decide what direction to follow. Some thought that the problem was that the party had lost its way and abandoned conservative principles. It had embraced big government, accepted the desire of George W. Bush and Dick Cheney to claim expanded spying powers, enacted an expensive, federally funded prescription drug program for seniors, and accepted large federal budget deficits. They argued that the party needed to return to the simple conservative principles of limited government, lower taxes, and support for social conservative policies.[32] The few moderates within the party argued that the party's emphasis on appealing to social conservatives was hurting the party among independents.[33] As always happens when the future is uncertain, there was no shortage of analysts offering suggestions for what direction to take.[34]

The ambiguity the party faced was even more evident in the results of the matchup of Republican nominee John McCain and Democratic nominee Barack Obama. Much to the surprise of many, McCain was running almost even with Obama in the polls in spring 2008, and also ran even with Hillary Clinton until she dropped out of the race in June. Given all the problems facing Republicans, many expected McCain to be losing to Obama by a large margin. The uncertainty was why he was doing that well. Was it because the country was so polarized that any respectable Republican candidate would get a certain percentage? Or was a large part of the country sympathetic to Republican policies and worried about national security, and the only problem the party faced was the dislike of George Bush? If the problem was the latter, then as Bush faded from the scene and voters focused on McCain than perhaps the party would

---

[31] Adam Nagourney and Carl Hulse, "Election Losses for Republicans Stir Fall Fears," *New York Times*, May 15, 2008, p. A1.

[32] Michael Gerson, "How My Party Lost Its Way," *Newsweek* (January 28, 2008): 28.

[33] Carl Hulse, "G.O.P. Agenda in House Has Moderates Unhappy," *New York Times*, July 8, 2006, p. A11.

[34] For an overview of this debate, see Benjamin Wallace-Wells, "A Case of the Blues," *New York Times Magazine* (March 30, 2008); and, George Packer, "The Fall of Conservatism," *The New Yorker* (May 26, 2008): 47–55.

do well. After all, as noted before, fifty-eight House Democrats were ru ning in districts George Bush had won. Republicans should be able to wi those seats back in 2008. Or was McCain doing well only because many Americans were not yet ready to vote for a black candidate? It was not easy to determine the answer.

Even McCain was uncertain about whether to distance himself from George W. Bush or embrace him and his conservative base. During the campaign, he embraced the endorsement of Bush,[35] but sometimes he seemed to distance himself from Bush,[36] and other times he supported Bush's policies on Iraq and tax cuts.[37]

Democrats had their own anxieties. Were they doing well only because of George W. Bush, the situation in Iraq, and the faltering economy? Did the country embrace their proposals for government-sponsored health care and repeal of tax cuts on the wealthy? Could a clearly liberal message advocating an activist federal government succeed in attracting a majority of voters, or should the party follow the more centrist Bill Clinton model that had last brought them control of the White House? The answers to these questions were not clear and remained so as the campaign came to an end.

[35] Michael Cooper and Elisabeth Bumiller, "It's Official: Party and President Back McCain," *New York Times*, March 6, 2009, p. A28.
[36] Michael Cooper, "McCain Distances Himself from Bush and Jabs Obama," *New York Times*, June 4, 2009.
[37] David Jackson, "McCain Says he Won't Run from Bush in Campaign," *USA Today*, June 6, 2008, p. 1.

10 The 2008 Election and Its Interpretation

The 2008 elections were seen as historic by many. America elected its first black president Barack Obama, a remarkable event forty years after the civil rights movement of the 1960s. Equally significant, Democrats enjoyed substantial gains in the House and the Senate for the second consecutive election. The Republicans had suffered a relatively rapid and significant setback. George W. Bush was leaving the presidency with about 30 percent approving of his performance, dragging his party down. Following the 2004 elections, Republicans held 232 of 435 House seats, their highest number since 1947. After 2008, they held 178. In 1997 and 2005, Republicans held fifty-five of the Senate seats, their highest total since 1929. After 2008, they held forty-one.[1] The party lost fifty-seven seats in the House and fifteen in the Senate over two elections. Identification with the Republican Party had dropped to 29 percent among those voting in 2008.[2] It appeared that voters had moved more Democratic.

However, as we have noted throughout this book, election results cane be seen in very different ways. Even before the final results had been tallied, the 2008 election gave way to the next struggle: how to interpret the results. The issue of what happened was crucial to the leaders of both parties. They had to decide just how enduring changes were and what policies they might pursue. Did the results signify a significant and perhaps enduring shift to Democrats, or was it a short-term setback for

---

[1] One Senate race (Minnesota) was still not decided as of April 2009. The House results reported here do not take into account any events that took place after the 2008 races were decided. In April 2009 Senator Arlen Specter, Pennsylvania, switched from Republican to Democrat, further reducing Republican fortunes.

[2] Taken from exit polls posted on CNN: http://www.cnn.com/ELECTION/2008/results/polls/#USP00p1.

Republicans? There was enough evidence for each side to make its case. The uncertainty that parties face was not dispelled.

SEEING A SHIFT TO THE DEMOCRATS

There were many reasons to see the 2006 and 2008 election results as signifying a major shift to the Democrats. Republicans in Congress had agreed to go along with President Bush on the Iraq War. As the war dragged on amid charges of mismanagement, party fortunes declined. The party was hurt even more by blame over how the federal government had responded to Hurricane Katrina. Much of the public blamed Republicans for the financial disaster that emerged in September 2008. The policy positions and governing performance of the party in power were seen as hurting its image. It was common to read sweeping judgments of an enduring shift to the Democratic Party.

> There is already a feeling of the beginning of a new era. As in 1932 and 1980, a crisis in the economy opened the way for the rejection of a reigning approach to government and the forging of a new one. Emphatically, comprehensively the public has turned against conservatism at home and neoconservatism abroad. The faith that unfettered markets and minimal taxes on the rich will solve every domestic problem, and that unilateral arrogance and American arms will solve every foreign one, is dead for a generation or more. And the electoral strategy of "cultural" resentment and fake populism has been dealt a grievous blow.[3]

Some were even more confident because they had seen trends coming, made predictions, and the trends had materialized. The party made gains in the suburbs and among professionals, as predicted.[4] Others had argued prior to the election that the Democrats did not need to fear the South because they could win without it. Furthermore, the South was no longer a monolithically conservative region. Democrats could win enough votes among professionals in some Southern urban areas to do better in the

---

[3] Hendrik Hertzberg, "Comment: Obama Wins," *The New Yorker* (November 17, 2008): 39–40. For a similar assessment, see Harold Meyerson, "A Real Realignment," *Washington Post*, November 7, 2008, p. A19.

[4] John Judis and Ruy Teixeira, *The Emerging Democratic Majority* (New York: Scribner, 2004); and John Judis, "America the Liberal: The Democratic Majority: It Emerged," *The New Republic*, http://www.tnr.com/politics/story.html?id=c261828d-7387-4af8-9ee7-8b2922ea6df0.

region and actually win a few states.[5] That had happened, with Obama having enough votes outside the South to win, but still winning Virginia, North Carolina, and Florida.[6]

There were also reasons to believe that the changes were based on demographic trends that had been developing for some time and would provide continuing support for Democrats. Immigration was continuing and many of these more recent arrivals would eventually be naturalized, register to vote, and potentially provide even more Democratic support. Latinos were particularly important here. Their numbers in America were increasing and they voted 2–1 for Obama in 2008. They were generally less well off, and a more supportive set of government policies on immigration and social welfare programs might tie Latinos to the Democratic Party for some time. For the general population, inequality was continuing to increase and the percentages without health insurance and pensions were steadily creeping up. The Democratic message about the need for government to intervene in the marketplace and provide benefits for the less affluent was perhaps once again relevant.

In addition, some argued that the Republican Party had created its own problems and found itself in a situation difficult to remedy quickly. The strategies of Republicans had come to fruition in ways the party had not expected and were damaging the arguments for why the party should be in power. First, the economic policies of the party, which had significant intuitive appeal, were not working as expected. Lowering taxes and reducing government regulations were supposed to improve economic fortunes by encouraging the growth of small businesses and more jobs. Yet median family income was growing only modestly and inequality was continuing to increase.[7] Perhaps most damaging were the perceived effects of deregulation. Beginning with President Reagan, Republicans had preached the virtues of deregulation of business. They argued that free markets would act to regulate economic behavior. Firms

---

[5] Tom Schaller, *Whistling Past Dixie: How Democrats Can Win Without the South* (New York: Simon & Schuster, 2008). Others carry the argument even further, arguing that the demographic shifts in American society and the diversity within the South are moving the South from having influence to a region that has to adapt or be left behind politically. The argument is that the conservative South must adjust to shifting national views or it will become a supportive but less influential base within the Republican Party. See Adam Nossiter, "For South, a Waning Hold on National Politics," *New York Times*, November 11, 2008, p. A1.

[6] Bob Moser, "A New, Blue Dixie," *The Nation* (December 1, 2008): 22–3.

[7] David Frum, "The Vanishing Republican Voter: Why Income Inequality is Destroying the G.O.P. Base," *New York Times Magazine* (September 1, 2008): 48–51.

operating in that context would act rationally to engage in behaviors that would improve jobs and corporate profits and ultimately the economic well-being of all Americans, or at least all Americans who were willing to work hard. As the major economic problems of 2008 unfolded, and stories emerged about finance firms engaging in risky behaviors that ultimately hurt the entire economy, it became harder for conservatives to argue for the virtues of unregulated capitalism.[8] Republicans had assured everyone that their philosophy would work and the evidence was significantly undermining their argument.

For many critics of the party, the real problem was the negative consequences of their pursuit of the "politics of resentment." Beginning in the 1960s, the party had tried to appeal to voters who disliked the government telling them who they could sell their house to or who they could employ or what sympathies they should have regarding towards minorities. They had sought to combine this empathy with expressions of support for traditional values of individual responsibility, commitment to marriage, opposition to illegitimate births, and rejection of the legitimacy of homosexuality.[9] The attempt to combine these themes had steadily attracted more religious conservatives and created more of a populist, anti"cultural elite" message. The essence of the message was that the party would represent and speak for those who felt condescendingly dismissed by cultural elites.[10]

Some saw this as a remarkably successful strategy. Thomas Frank, in analyzing why less-affluent voters in Kansas were voting Republican, argued that the party had been able to make issues like abortion salient. He argued that the less affluent and generally less educated (seen as more attached to traditional values and less tolerant of the right of individuals to have abortions) have moved more Republican because they are troubled by moral decline.[11] As Frank summarized it, Republicans were

---

[8] For a critical commentary on deregulation see, James A. Ridgeway, "It's the De-Regulation, Stupid," http://www.motherjones.com/commentary/columns/2008/03/deregulation-economic-crisis.html (March 28, 2008). Conservatives did continue to argue that deregulation was not the source of problems. See Sebastian Mallaby, "Blaming Deregulation," *Washington Post*, October 6, 2008, p. A15, http://www.washingtonpost.com/wp-dyn/content/article/2008/10/05/AR2008100501253.html; and Jim Snyder, "House Republicans Defend Deregulation," *The Hill* (October 5, 2008), http://thehill.com/leading-the-news/house-republicans-defend-deregulation-2008–10-05.html.

[9] Rick Perlstein, *Nixonland*; E. J. Dionne, *They Only Look Dead* (New York: Touchstone, 1997).

[10] Michael Kazin, *The Populist Persuasion* (New York: Basic Books, 1995).

[11] Thomas Frank, *What's the Matter with Kansas* (New York: Metropolitan Books, 2004).

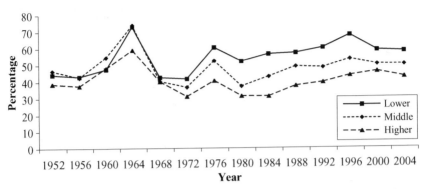

FIGURE 10.1. Democratic presidential voting by income groups, 1952–2004

wooing the less affluent, reducing their support for Democrats, and using that reduced Democratic base to enact tax cuts for the rich.

The problem with this argument was that the evidence suggested that the strategy may not have produced the expected changes in class voting and may even have produced an unexpected and undesired outcome. The first issue was whether the less affluent were moving more Republican. Figure 10.1 summarizes the results of surveys conducted from 1952 through 2004.[12] All individuals who reported voting for president are grouped by whether they are in the lower, middle, or higher third of the income distribution. The figure reports the percentage of each group that voted for the Democratic presidential candidate. As might be expected, the higher the income, the less the percentage that vote Democratic. The important matter is the trend in voting of the less affluent. They, along with everyone else, voted somewhat less Democratic in 1980 when Reagan ran for the first time. Since then, however, their support Democrats has not declined.

The 2008 exit poll results also do not indicate any change in voting by income levels.[13] Among those making less than $15,000, 73 percent voted Democratic. Among those making between $15,000 and 30,000, 60 percent voted Democratic. Among those making $30,000 and 50,000, 55 percent voted Democratic. The presumption that the less affluent have been pulled away from Democrats is not supported by the evidence.

Equally important is the unexpected change among the more affluent. When the culture wars are discussed, the focus is generally on the working class. The implicit presumption has been that Republicans have

---

[12] The data are taken from the NES cumulative file, 1948–2004. All respondents voting are included.

[13] http://www.cnn.com/ELECTION/2008/results/polls/#USP00p1.

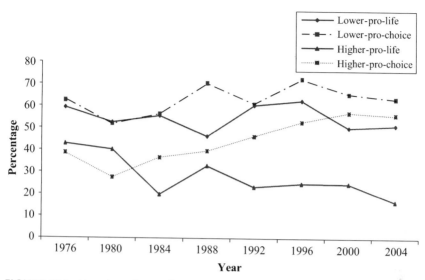

FIGURE 10.2. Abortion views, class, and Democratic presidential voting, 1976–2004

been able to retain the support of the more affluent, while accentuating cultural issues to attract the support of those Americans who are less affluent. However, something else has happened. Since the 1980s, there has been a gradual increase in the percentage of the more affluent who are voting Democratic. In the 2008 exit polls, 38 percent of voters were in the category of annual incomes between $50,000 and 100,000 and they split their vote, 49–49, between Obama and McCain. Another 26 percent made more than $100,000, and they also voted 49 percent Obama and 49 percent McCain. Democrats did much better among the more affluent in 2008 than indicated in the 2004 and 2006 exit polls.

The worry of moderates within the GOP is that the focus on cultural issues is alienating those with more education, who are more tolerant of abortion rights and equal rights for homosexuals. The evidence indicates that issues like abortion have played a role that many in the party may not have expected. Figure 10.2 presents Democratic presidential voting among lower and higher income groups, but by their position on abortion. Voters within the two income groups are also grouped by whether they are pro-life or pro-choice.[14] The trends for each of the four resulting

[14] The NES has asked respondents about their opinions on abortion since 1972. Respondents are presented with four options and asked which they endorse. Option 1 is to never allow abortion and 2 is only under unusual circumstances, such as to preserve the life of the mother or if incest occurred. They are classified as pro-life. The third option is

groups are important for assessing the impact of the rising prominence of cultural issues and the Republican Party's support for pro-life positions. The two top lines indicate the partisan voting of those in the lower income group. Those who are pro-choice *and* less affluent are most supportive of the Democratic Party. Their positions and the policies of Democrats are compatible. Those less affluent *and* pro-life represent the group that presumably is being pulled away from the Democratic Party by Republican efforts to make abortion a significant issue. There is limited evidence for that. From 1992 through 2004, their support drops from 61 to 51 percent.

The other end of the income spectrum represents the two groups that have become significant in the last several presidential elections. Those who are affluent and pro-life are in agreement with the Republican Party, and their support for Democrats has declined from 43 to 17 percent since 1976. The problem for Republicans, however, is that higher income voters are also more likely to have higher education levels and to be more pro-choice. As the issue of abortion has become more salient, they have moved steadily more Democratic.[15] Republicans probably presumed they could hold the more affluent by emphasizing lower tax rates, but they are losing at least some of these voters.

Concern about losing the more affluent and more educated increased during the 2008 campaign. The selection of Governor Sarah Palin of Alaska as the Republican vice-presidential candidate crystallized the issues of conservative social values and the party's stance regarding expertise and competence. Although she made a positive first impression, in subsequent interviews she appeared to have little knowledge about major issues facing the country and conveyed a sense that this lack of knowledge and expertise did not matter all that much. She was, however, strongly committed to conservative social values. Her candidacy prompted conservative columnist David Brooks to question the direction the party was taking.

> ...over the last few decades, the Republican Party has driven away people who live in cities, in highly educated regions, and on the coasts. The big [reason] is this: Republican political tacticians decided to mobilize their coalition with a form of social class warfare. Democrats kept nominating coastal, pointy-heads like Michael Dukakis so Republicans attacked coastal pointy-heads. The nation [became] divided between

---

to allow abortion in most circumstances and the fourth is to never prohibit it. The last two options are classified as pro-choice.

[15] Mark D. Brewer, Rebekah Liscio, and Jeffrey M. Stonecash, "The Unexpected Effect of the Cultural Wars," unpublished manuscript, 2009.

the wholesome Joe Sixpacks in the heartland and the oversophisticated, overeducated, oversecularized denizens of the coasts. Republicans developed their own leadership style. If Democratic leaders prized deliberation and self-examination, Republicans would govern from the gut. The Republicans have alienated whole professions. It has lost the educated class by sins of commission – by telling members of that class to go away.[16]

Chris Shays, the sole remaining Republican member of the House of Representatives from New England who lost in 2008, summed up the problems of the party with expertise: "I think people thought the president was competent but arrogant and after [Hurricane] Katrina they said, 'Oh my God, they're incompetent, and they're still arrogant.'"[17] As critics saw it, the issue was whether the Republican Party had dismissed experts and thoughtfulness to the point that the party had lost its credibility among the more educated for being able to handle complex situations and was alienating those with higher education.[18] The exit polls from 2008 indicated that 17 percent of voters had a postgraduate education and they voted for Obama 58–40.[19] There were reasons for Republicans to worry about the image the party had developed and whether voters thought the party could be trusted to devise solutions to problems.

In summary, many Democrats and some critics of the Republican Party saw reasons to believe that the electorate had taken a decisive swing to

---

[16] David Brooks, "The Class War Before Palin," *The New York Times* (October 10, 2008), A33.

[17] Peter Applebome, "With G.O.P Congressman's Loss, a Moderate Tradition Ends in New England," *New York Times*, November 6, 2008, p. A26.

[18] Gregory Rodriquez, "The GOP and the Perils of Populism," *Los Angeles Times*, October 13, 2008. http://www.latimes.com/news/columnists/la-oe-rodriguez13–2008oct13, 0,7551792.column. The same point was made by Charlie Cook, "Learn or Languish: The GOP's Focus on Social, Cultural, and Religious Issues Cost its Candidates Dearly Among Upscale Voters," NationalJournal.com (November 15, 2008). Not only were Republicans losing the more educated voters, but the percentage of voters who defined themselves as professional or upper-middle class was increasing: Mark Penn, "Most Affluent Voters Key to Obama Sweep," *Politico* (November 11, 2008), http://www. politico.com/news/stories/1108/15471.html; Alan Abramowitz and Ruy Teixeira, "The Decline of the White Working Class and the Rise of a Mass Upper-Middle Class, " in Ruy Teixeira (ed.), *Red, Blue and Purple America: The Future of Election Demographics* (Washington, DC: Brookings, 2008).

[19] http://www.cnn.com/ELECTION/2008/results/polls/#USP00p1. For Republicans, the important matter was that the advantage the party had enjoyed among those with higher education was gradually slipping away. NES data indicate that from 1952 through 1988, with the exception of 1964, in presidential elections Republicans had always done relatively better among those with some college, a bachelors, or higher education. In 1992–2000, Democrats won a plurality or majority of these groups. In 2004, Republicans recaptured both groups, in the 2008 election, Obama bested McCain among this group 58 to 40 percent.

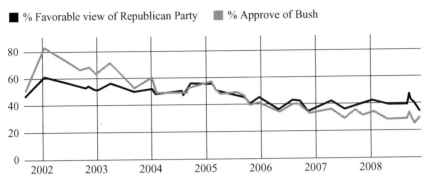

■ % Favorable view of Republican Party   ▨ % Approve of Bush

FIGURE 10.3. Republican Party's image vs. President George W. Bush's overall job approval rating, September 2001–November 2008

the Democratic Party. The electorate had rejected eight years of the policies of George W. Bush. Many felt that the Republican Party's pursuit of social conservatives and a populist theme had alienated parts of the electorate that it had to have to regain its credibility and a majority.

"WE WILL RECOVER"

Although many saw fundamental problems for the Republican Party, others saw essentially a typical short-term setback. The election had occurred in a remarkably negative political environment for the party and, in many ways, it was a miracle that things had not been worse. The war in Iraq had not gone as the party had hoped. The handling of Katrina had seriously harmed the public's perception of the competence of the Bush administration. The government was running large deficits and then the economy began to steadily decline in late 2007 before the wheels came off entirely in fall 2008. The conditions were not good for a party seen as the incumbent party, even though Democrats controlled Congress after 2006. To some, the real problem was President George W. Bush. He had become the most visible face of the party, and the public's perception of him had steadily declined since early 2002. As his ratings declined, the ratings of the party had also declined. Figure 10.3 indicates just how much his ratings and that of the Republican Party had declined.[20] Over the same time period, ratings of the Democratic Party had remained stable.

These short-term forces were dragging down the prospects for a Republican candidate. Then, probably the worst short-term event occurred in

[20] Gallup Poll, "GOP Image Takes Another Hit Post-Election," November 20, 2008, http://www.gallup.com/poll/112015/GOP-Takes-Another-Image-Hit-PostElection.aspx.

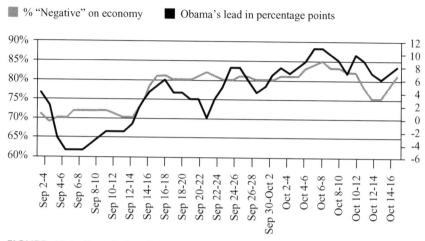

FIGURE 10.4. Correlation between Obama's lead and "negative" views of economy

September: the financial markets began to unravel and the value of the stock market dropped dramatically. As Figure 10.4 indicates, Obama's lead rose as the public came to see the economy negatively.[21] The events of prior years had made the Republican situation bad and the abrupt decline of the economy had provided Obama with the last push he needed.

In short, the Republican setback was a product of conditions that would all go away. Iraq would someday cease to be an issue. The memory of Katrina would fade. George Bush left office on January 20, 2009. The economy would eventually recover. As these conditions faded from the scene, the environment would become more neutral and there would be fewer short-term forces pushing voters away from the Republican Party.

Even with the difficult environment, some were quick to point out that John McCain had not done that badly. McCain received 46 percent of the vote, and Obama attracted only 5 percent more of the vote than John Kerry did in 2004. Republicans in the electorate had remained remarkably loyal to the party, with 89 percent of GOP identifiers voting for McCain. Surely the small percentage who voted against the Republican candidate could be coaxed back into the fold once the overall environment improved. The party had lost Senate and House seats, but there was an argument to be made that they could regain many of those seats.

---

[21] Gallup Poll, "As the Economy Goes, the Vote Goes," October 21, 2008, http://www. gallup.com/poll/111283/Economy-Goes-Goes-Vote.aspx.

TABLE 10.1. Composition of the electorate: Exit poll results, 2004–2008[22]

Category	2004	2006	2008
Age			
18–29	17	12	18
30–44	29	24	29
45–64	38	45	37
65 plus	16	19	16
Race			
White	77	79	74
African-American	11	10	13
Latino	8	8	9
Ideology			
Liberal	21	20	22
Moderate	45	47	44
Conservative	34	32	34

There were also other signs that the party had grounds for some optimism down the road. First, the composition of the electorate – despite all the media discussion of a surge of youth activism and the likely effect on the turnout of youth and minorities of a black presidential candidate – was not very different from prior years. Table 10.1 indicates the composition of voters for three important categories for 2004, 2006, and 2008. Young voters turn out more in presidential elections. That occurred in 2004 and 2008, and they constituted a greater proportion in those years. The reality, however, is that in 2008 they did not vote at levels sufficient to make themselves a significantly greater percentage of the electorate. Their percentage increased from 17 percent in 2004 to 18 percent in 2008. They did vote strongly for Obama, but the claim that the composition of the electorate was going to be reshaped by an influx of pro-Democratic young voters did not materialize. Furthermore, in 2010, an off-year election, their presence would probably be more like 2006, when they slipped to 12 percent of all voters. There were reasons for Republicans to not yet worry about young voters changing the world.

The same conclusion might be stated about the racial composition of the electorate changing. It might be that eventually Blacks and Latinos would come to comprise a much larger percentage of the electorate, but

[22] Results are from the following: http://www.cnn.com/ELECTION/2004/pages/results/states/US/P/00/epolls.0.html; http://www.cnn.com/ELECTION/2006/pages/results/states/US/H/00/epolls.0.html; http://www.cnn.com/ELECTION/2008/results/polls/#val=USP00p1.

Table 10.2. Distribution of Republican presidential support in House districts, 2004 and 2008, and how Democrats fared

Republican presidential candidate %	Bush in 2004		% House seats won by Democrats		McCain in 2008		% House seats won by Democrats
	#	% of districts	2004	2006	#	% of districts	2008
<40	92	21	100.0	100.0	141	32	97.9
40–44	46	11	95.7	100.0	50	12	86.0
45–49	42	10	64.3	83.3	57	13	50.9
50–54	56	13	28.6	44.6	68	16	36.8
55–59	75	17	20.0	28.0	50	11	22.0
60+	124	29	7.3	10.7	69	16	15.9

in 2008, even with a Black presidential candidate, the increase in their percentage of voters was very small. It was not yet the case that Republicans had to worry about a transformed electorate.

Finally, and probably most important to Republicans, the ideological composition of voters had not changed.[23] Liberals were still in a minority among voters. Those identifying themselves as conservatives still comprised 34 percent of voters and liberals were only 22 percent. Indeed, shortly after the 2008 election a Gallup Poll found that 59 percent of Republicans wanted their party and its candidates to move in a more conservative direction.[24] The conclusion was clear to many Republicans. The electorate was still much the same as when the party won majorities. The party had screwed up and short-term forces had hurt them, but they were still facing essentially the same electorate. According to this logic, all the Republicans need to do is wait for a little time to pass, and work on regaining the trust and support of an unchanged electorate.

If the GOP could reestablish its credibility among voters, it could regain high levels of support among conservatives and split support among moderates and be in good shape. If the Republicans were able to accomplish this, they would be able to regain seats in Congress that under normal circumstances should be theirs. Table 10.2 provides information on House elections organized as many Republicans would see the results. House

[23] Michael G. Franc, "Conservative Nation," *National Review Online* (November 24, 2008), http://article.nationalreview.com/?q=M2M2MjNjNDY2YjFjM2ZiMDUzYzEyMTBiYzMz N2FkOWM=.

[24] Gallup Reports, "Many Republicans Want a More Conservative GOP," November 20, 2008, http://www.gallup.com/video/112021/Many-Republicans-Want-More-Conservative-GOP.aspx.

districts are first classified according to how Republican presidential candidates did in 2004 and 2008 (George W. Bush in 2004 and John McCain in 2008). Then results for Democrats in House districts for 2004, 2006, and 2008 by Republican presidential vote percentages are shown. For example, in districts in which George W. Bush received 50 to 54 percent in 2004, Democrats won 28.6 percent of those seats in 2004. In 2006, as the electorate turned against Bush and the Republicans, Democrats did better (winning 44.6 percent of seats) in districts where Bush won 50–54 percent of the vote.

To many Republicans, the 2004 elections were close and probably reflect the division of the nation. If Bush could win 50–54 percent in a district, it seems unlikely that Democrats can continue to win 44.6 percent of seats within such districts. Once the short-term forces fade the party should be able to win back many of the seats in which Bush won a majority in 2004, but a Democrat won the House election. The same is true for districts where Bush won 55–59 percent. Their presumption is likely to be that Democrats cannot continue to win 28 percent of the seats in these districts.

The 2008 results indicate just how much the electorate shifted against the party over four years. As the right side of the table indicates, the number of districts in which the Republican presidential candidate got 60 percent or more declined from 124 in 2004 to 69 in 2008. Republicans are likely to assume that factors like Iraq and the economy will not hurt the party in 2012, so more districts may shift towards the Republicans. Further, the party should be able to improve how it does in districts where McCain did well. After the 2008 elections, Democrats were winning 36.8 percent of the sixty-eight districts where McCain got 50–54 percent. Once conditions improved for the party, they should be able to do better. From their perspective, many of the Democratic House winners in 2008 were a product of dissatisfaction with Bush and the conditions in the country. As conditions changed, many of the seats in districts that voted for McCain but for a Democratic House member could be returned to being Republican.

The central question for the Republican Party was what direction to take. As often happens, it was not entirely clear.[25] The moderates within

---

[25] David D. Kirkpatrick, "Win or Lose, Republicans Will Revisit the Party's Image," *New York Times*, October 31, 2008, p. A22; Sam Tanenhaus, "A Once-United G.O.P. Emerges, in Identity Crisis," *New York Times*, November 6, 2008, p. P1; Michael Cooper, "Among Republicans, a Debate Over the Party's Roadmap Back to Power," *New York Times*, November 17, 2008, p. A17.

the party urged that they not move to the right. They argued that a too-conservative image was costing the party seats in the Northeast, and the party could not do well if it wrote off an entire region.[26] Yet those who had brought Republicans to power did not embrace the argument. Karl Rove, the chief political advisor to George W. Bush, wrote, "Suggestions that we abandon social conservatism, including our pro-life agenda, should be ignored. These values are often more popular than the GOP itself. Republicans, in championing our values agenda, need to come across as morally serious rather than as judgmental."[27] He argued that the setback of 2008 was not as big as some concluded. Turnout did not increase that much, four million Republicans did not vote, and Democrats did not make significant gains in state legislative elections. In 2010, the party could make a comeback as short-term factors faded.[28]

DEMOCRATIC UNCERTAINTY

The election results of 2008 were clear. Barack Obama and the Democrats won control of the White House and increased their margins in the House and Senate. Republicans had moved from complete control following the 2000 election to minority status. As has happened again and again in American politics, the problem was making sense of the results. For Republicans, the sources of their considerable ambiguity were obvious. There were serious questions about whether they should moderate their views on certain issues in the hopes of attracting more moderate voters, reaffirm their conservative roots and wait for the memory of the Bush administration to pass, or simply hope Democrats would overreach, as they often had in the past.[29] Yet even with their success in the 2008 election cycle, the Democrats faced significant uncertainty as well.

For Democrats the power acquired gave them the potential to solve some problems and create long-term support within the electorate and build an enduring majority. In the early 2000s, Republicans had similar aspirations and those hopes were now dashed.[30] The uncertainties facing

[26] Carl Hulse, "3 Successful Republicans Caution Against a Move to the Right," *New York Times*, November 14, 2008, p. A33.
[27] Karl Rove, "A Way Out of the Wilderness," *Newsweek* (November 24, 2008): 43.
[28] Karl Rove, "History Favors Republicans in 2010," *Wall Street Journal*, November 13, 2008, http://online.wsj.com/article/SB122653996148523063.html.
[29] Charlie Cook, "How to Right the GOP," *National Journal* (December 2, 2008), http://www.nationaljournal.com/njonline/ot_20081201_3322.php.
[30] Joshua Green, "The Rove Presidency," *The Atlantic* (September 2007), http://www.theatlantic.com/doc/200709/karl-rove.

Table 10.3. Percentage of Democratic House Party from district types, 2008

McCain percent in 2008	House seats won by Democrats			
	#	% of districts	#	% from
<40	141	32	138	53.7
40–44	50	12	43	16.7
45–49	57	13	29	11.3
50–54	68	16	25	9.7
55–59	50	11	11	4.3
60+	69	16	11	4.3

Democrats were how to interpret the results and what electoral gains and losses might accompany various policy actions.

That uncertainty was particularly acute for many new members of the House and Senate. Democrats now had more seats in the House, and they might interpret that increase as a mandate for change. However, some argued that the only reason that Democrats were in power was because Republicans had made mistakes. Caution should be used in assuming there was support for a Democratic agenda, especially an aggressively liberal one.[31] Particularly important to many members was assessing their district electoral base. As Table 10.2 indicates, Democrats had gained many seats in districts that had been won by McCain in 2008. These new members had to decide whether they could disregard that result or regard it as meaningful. It could be that the country had moved away from the Republican Party and Democrats coming from these districts were relatively safe. Yet what if the vote reflected some underlying support for Republicans that might reemerge in 2010, particularly because voting by blacks and younger people might decline without Obama on the ticket?

This latter concern was important to a large part of the House majority in the 111th Congress. Table 10.3 presents House results the way a House leader might have to assess matters. It indicates the kind of districts House members in 2009 come from. Districts are grouped by how well McCain did in 2008.

The 2008 results indicate the problems the party faced in uniting against Republican positions After 2008, 18.3 percent of all Democratic House members came from districts in which McCain won more than

[31] John Harwood, "Democrats Have G.O.P. to Thank, at Least in Part," *New York Times*, November 10, 2008, p. A19.

50 percent of the votes. These forty-seven party members had to interpret the 2008 results and decide what 2010 might hold. They provided the party's majority and many would not go along with a liberal agenda. There were also many Democrats in districts in which McCain got 45–49 percent who were surely worried that the "normal" Republican support within the district might be higher than was shown in 2008. The same party issue existed in the Senate. Although Democrats had at least fifty-eight seats, thirteen of the Democratic senators came from states that McCain won in 2008. They were also unlikely to be enthusiastic about a liberal agenda.

The bottom line is that uncertainty reigned among both parties in the aftermath of the 2008 election cycle, and it was not likely to go away for some time. Charting a party path and responding to the electorate is never a simple matter, and both Democrats and Republicans were debating how they should interpret the 2008 results and what they should do in light of their interpretations. As we have seen a number of times throughout American history, each party saw opportunities for future success, but these opportunities were all accompanied by risks.

11 Parties and the Pursuit of Majorities

CHANGE AND UNCERTAINTY

Political parties must continually assess their situations and determine if they need to adjust in order to achieve their goals. When a party is in the majority, there are concerns about what must be done to maintain the majority. Is there a coherent coalition in place, or does the party have to worry about balancing competing and potentially conflicting needs that could result in the fracturing of the party's coalition? During the era of the New Deal coalition, Democrats consistently faced this latter scenario with a Northern, urban contingent that wanted more government programs, and over time, greater action on civil rights. The Southern delegation was much less receptive to more government programs and was vehement in opposition to any civil rights legislation. Republicans in the early 2000s had a coalition of antigovernment economic conservatives and social conservatives that wanted to use government to encourage particular personal behaviors. In both cases, maintaining a coalition to keep a majority involved satisfying competing and potentially conflicting needs and desires. With Democrats, the coalition eventually ruptured. With Republicans, the balancing act is ongoing.

Parties in the minority face a different challenge. They must assess who they are currently attracting, determine which groups they might be able to add, and try to figure out whether existing supporters and potential supporters could be cobbled together to form a winning coalition. Democrats in the 1880s and 1890s were only occasionally in power, and some thought their best bet was to add Northern urban workers to their existing base of Southern and Western agrarian interests to create a grand coalition of the have-nots. This plan failed in 1896 but to a large extent succeeded in 1932 and especially 1936. Republicans in the 1950s and

1960s thought that ideological conservatives opposed to an activist federal government could become the mainstay of the party. Then in the 1970s and 1980s, Republicans made a transition to trying to attract working-class whites with an antigovernment/populist/antispecial treatment for minorities appeal. By the 1980s and 1990s, they added messages aimed at attracting social conservatives troubled by trends in Americans' personal behavior. Republicans were continually adjusting to seek a larger and lasting electoral base connected by different variants of conservatism, and by the early 2000s the party was largely successful in achieving this goal.

The decisions to shift emphases to attract new voters are fraught with ambiguity and uncertainty. Sometimes appeals are made on the basis of careful analysis and a conviction that the right appeal will work. During the early 1900s, Democrats viewed the pro-capitalism positions of the Republican Party, and decided that it should be possible to pull Northern urban workers into the Democratic Party by sponsoring labor legislation. In the 1970s and 1980s, Republicans conducted polls and listened to the rising concern of social conservatives about moral decay and thought that it should be possible to bring them into the Republican Party and expand the party base. In each case, the logic seemed clear.

Other times, instinct and ambition play a greater role in determining positions and appeals. By all accounts, Lyndon Johnson pushed civil rights legislation because of building political pressures to address racial inequities, but also because he thought it was the moral thing to do. His ambition to be seen as a major figure in American history was no small part of the decision.[1] Several years later, Richard Nixon made his appeal to disgruntled white voters based on his sense that it would win him needed votes, but also because he personally shared the anger of white, working-class men at protesting presumably well-off college students.[2]

Regardless of whether careful analysis or instinct guides political choices, the implications of the strategies parties pursue are never clear when the decisions are made. As we study the history of political parties, the sequence of events is often presented as logical and the result of a series of well-informed decisions that lead to a particular shift. To those involved in making these decisions, however, the future impact is never

---

[1] Robert Caro, *The Years of Lyndon Johnson*, 3 vols. (New York: Alfred A. Knopf, 1982); William E. Leuchtenburg, *The White House Looks South: Franklin D. Roosevelt, Harry S. Truman, and Lyndon B. Johnson* (Baton Rouge: Louisiana State University Press, 2005).

[2] Rick Perlstein, *Nixonland: The Rise of a President and the Fracturing of America* (New York: Scribner, 2008).

quite so clear. At any juncture, parties are filled with those who argue for
and against particular directions. When Democrats became more responsive to the concerns of blacks in the 1960s, there were those who argued
that the group could constitute the next big voting bloc to add to the party
and create a dominant majority. There were also those who argued that
being seen as too tied to that bloc could cost the party white votes. When
Republicans began their push in the 1980s to attract social conservatives,
many of them in the South, there were many who argued that Southern fundamentalists were unlikely to identify with a party filled with the
affluent from Eastern urban centers. There were others who worried that
bringing in religious right leaders could drive away the older base of the
party.

The debates within a party about consequences of strategies are often
intense and emotional. What often looks in retrospect to be a reasonable political decision to change a party coalition is in reality an act of
uncertainty and risk at the time that it is made. Will a group respond to
a message? Will the group turn into a reliable source of support? Will
bringing in that group alienate existing parts of the coalition? More often
than not, the answers to these questions are unclear, and party leaders
are left to contemplate what amounts to a leap of faith in an atmosphere
of ambiguity. As we have seen throughout this book, sometimes these
leaps pay off, and sometimes they do not.

SEEKING FEEDBACK AND INTERPRETING CHANGE

Once a strategy is adopted, parties and candidates are continually seeking
evidence of whether their strategy is working. That assessment process is
also filled with uncertainty, and often considerable patience is required.
Sometimes a political plan is adopted, changes occur gradually and consistently, and there is a sense that the appeal is working. Republicans
thought they could make inroads into the South, and beginning in the
1950s with Eisenhower's success in presidential elections, there was a
steady increase in Republican success in that region. Yet even then the
change was gradual and those urging a Southern strategy had to argue
for patience as they waited for incumbent Southern Democrats to retire
so they could replace them with Republicans. With the South growing
rapidly in population in the 1960s and 1970s and the Northeast experiencing little population growth, Republicans assumed they were gaining
votes where they wanted and that this area would become a source of
more votes in the future. However, there was uncertainty about how

much of the Northeast might be lost. There was also uncertainty about whether the influx of Latino immigrants would make the Sunbelt less Republican than expected.

There are other times when change is abrupt and perhaps unexpected. In 1912, Democrats won because the Republican vote was split between Progressives and conservatives within the party. In 1932 and 1936, Democrats expected to benefit from frustration with Republicans, but the magnitudes of the changes were probably greater than most expected. In 1964, Democrats picked up an enormous number of congressional seats and in 1994, Republicans likewise gained. The gains in 1964 and 1994 were beyond what had been expected. In 2006, Democrats gained enough seats to reverse twelve years of Republican control of the House.

In all of these cases, party leaders faced the issue of what the surge of votes meant and if the party could hold the seats gained. Party officials have to go through election results and determine if the votes reflect a logical and consistent movement toward the party. Did the party gain in election districts populated by voters the party was appealing to, or did the party gain in areas dominated by voters generally not supportive of the party and not sought by the party? If the former occurred, the party can have confidence that the vote is connected to their appeal; they can assume that they can pursue policies reflecting the concerns articulated. If it is the latter, then the party may have to be very careful in what policies they presume they can pursue.

There is also the issue of consistency of results. Is there evidence that the areas voting for the party in, say, House elections, are also voting that way in presidential and Senate elections? In 1912, Democrats knew that the party had won House seats in many districts that had been traditionally Republican. The party could try to hold these seats by giving those elected considerable freedom to "localize" their appeal and downplay party ties, but the party knew it would be a challenge to hold on to those seats. In 1964, Democrats won in many House districts that had not been voting for the party. While many saw the results as an indication that the country was moving in a more liberal direction, there were grounds for assuming the party might not be able to hold those seats. The same was true in the 1974 elections. In 2006, it was difficult for Democrats to see the results as reflecting support for their policies rather than as opposition to George W. Bush and the Iraq War.

In 1932, circumstances were different. Democrats won House seats in many Northern urban districts that from 1900 to 1920 had no history of electing Democrats. However, during the 1920s and noticeably when

Governor Al Smith of New York ran as the party's candidate in 1928, the urban areas appeared to be moving toward the Democratic Party.[3] In the analyses following the election, the party realized that after years of trying to build a connection with voters in these areas, they had finally succeeded. The party concluded that there was a possibility of retaining these seats and they focused on passing legislation favoring labor and social programs that would be more beneficial to those in urban areas.

In 1994, Republicans could also see the results as reflecting consistent support for their party. Most Republican gains in the House came in districts that had supported Republican presidential candidates. Many were in the South where the party had been making steady gains over the last several decades. The results were seen as confirmation of the value of the party's message of lower taxes, less government, more support for policies reflecting a traditional view of morality, and the culmination of more than thirty years of Republican efforts to reconfigure their coalition. The party's voting gains in areas containing the groups targeted and the consistency of results across different offices reinforced the sense that the appeal was not just for individual candidates but for the party itself and its policies.

The interpretation of results is also affected by a powerful desire to see what one wants to see. Party members who want to expand their party base work for years in pursuit of that goal. They review results, develop arguments, devise plans, and try to persuade others to believe in their ideas. They become committed to their interpretation. When election results move in their direction, they may be inclined to believe that the results are a response to their efforts.

Prior to 1964, many Northern Democrats had worked for years to build support for a liberal agenda. The results of that year's election cycle were embraced by liberals as evidence that the country finally supported them. In the years prior to 1994, conservative Republicans had worked to build a conservative movement. They issued a conservative "Contract with America" prior to the election and won. It was easy for them to believe that a majority of voters supported their vision. In both cases, however, they saw more of a mandate than there was. After the 2004 election,

---

[3] Jerome M. Clubb and Howard W. Allen, "Cities and the Election of 1928: Partisan Realignment?" *American Historical Review* 74 (April 1969): 1205–20; Carl N. Degler, "American Political Parties and the Rise of the Cities: A Historical Interpretation," *Journal of American History* 51 (June 1964): 41–59; Samuel J. Eldersveld, "The Influence of Metropolitan Party Pluralities in Presidential Elections since 1920: A Study of Twelve Key Cities," *American Political Science Review* 43 (December 1949): 1189–1206.

George W. Bush said he had a mandate and set out to change Social Security. He did not have a mandate and his support was eroding as conditions in Iraq worsened. It is not easy to be objective about election results when one is heavily invested in their meaning and interpretation.

The interpretation of change is further complicated by the reality that some election results are simply erratic and hard to explain. In some years, election results will favor a party and there will be numerous analyses concluding that some set of voters is moving toward a party, only to discover after the next election that the so-called trend did not persist. Results moved back to where they had been and the conclusion is that the election was a deviating one, or one in which some unusual and non-repeating conditions or events pushed the results in one way. Once those circumstances disappear, the results return to where they were before their appearance.[4]

Anticipating the intrusions of short-term factors is never easy. As the 2008 elections approached, many expected the election to be about the policies of George W. Bush and the Iraq War. Then, in the early part of the year, the economy began to decline and candidates found themselves spending a considerable amount of time talking about their economic policies rather than Iraq. By mid-summer, casualties of American soldiers in Iraq were down and economic trends were dominating the news. The presidential candidates were struggling to decide how much to emphasize their policies on foreign affairs versus economic matters. Discerning what will be important by Election Day is a continual challenge for political candidates and their advisors. Indeed, few would have predicted on January 1, 2008, that 63 percent of respondents would tell exit pollsters on November 4, 2008, that the economy was the most important issue facing the nation, whereas only 10 percent would choose Iraq.

THE UNCERTAINTY OF VOTERS

As parties struggle with the questions of which strategies and voters to pursue, they have to always remember that most of the electorate does not follow politics. Only somewhat more than 50 percent of the eligible electorate votes in a presidential election, and the percentages drop for years of congressional-only elections. For local elections, it is not uncommon to have a voter turnout of 20 to 40 percent. Much of the electorate is

---

[4] Angus Campbell, Philip E. Converse, Warren E. Miller, and Donald E. Stokes, *Elections and the Political Order* (New York: John Wiley and Sons, 1966).

tuned out to the grand strategies of parties.[5] It is never possible for party leaders to assume that their message has gotten to its intended audience. It is also risky to assume that if it is received, it will prompt the desired reaction of activating someone to vote for the party.

Among those interested enough to vote, there are enormous variations in the amount of information they have.[6] Those voters who are highly informed are often the most settled in their partisan choices. The challenge is to get messages to voters with less information. These voters have a rough process of sorting through various cues to come up with choices reasonably approximating their preferences.[7] Achieving the goal of getting information to voters is not easy. Over the years, the press has provided less simple reporting of the positions of parties and candidates and now focuses more on the strategies and motives of candidates.[8] Many more people rely on television than newspapers for their news, and television news has significantly less depth than print news. While this trend has been occurring, there has been a proliferation of cable and Internet sources of information. Although many thought this would increase voter information, it appears that many voters are increasingly choosing news sources that fit their political dispositions. Those not interested in politics, presented with a wealth of entertainment channels, are opting to avoid political news.[9]

The result is that it becomes harder for political parties to be sure that their message is getting to those it is intended for. Some in the electorate follow political news only sporadically, so candidates and the parties must endlessly repeat their message. They must engage in broad, relatively simple images of their positions in the hope that those with marginal interest in politics come across their message and can quickly sense a position. Even then, it is difficult to assume that voters get a sense of the subtle differences between candidates.[10] The process of getting messages to voters

---

[5] Carroll J. Glynn, et al., "Public Opinion and Democratic Competence," in Carroll J. Glynn, et al., *Public Opinion*, second edition (Boulder, CO: Westview Press, 2004), 283–346.

[6] John R. Zaller, *The Nature and Origins of Mass Opinion* (New York: Cambridge University Press, 1992).

[7] Samuel L. Popkin, *The Reasoning Voter* (Chicago: University of Chicago Press, 1994).

[8] Thomas E. Patterson, *Out of Order* (New York: Alfred A. Knopf, 1993).

[9] Markus Prior, *Post-Broadcast Democracy* (New York: Cambridge University Press, 2007).

[10] While it is only one example, in June 2004 one author was attending a high school reunion. One individual, upon hearing that I taught American politics courses, announced that he had checked out of politics. After being asked why, he said, "Oh come on, here we have an election between two guys who both went to Yale, both were members of the secret Skull and Bones Society, and both are rich. This thing is fixed." Although academics were discussing polarization, this voter saw no real difference between the candidates.

requires lots of money for radio, television ads, mail, constant repetition, and considerable patience. The messages may eventually get to substantial percentages of voters, but it takes time. That means that any strategy intended to move voters from one party to another takes time. The process is slow, but over time significant portions of the American electorate have discerned changes in party positions and have moved from one party to another in response.

PARTIES AND DEMOCRACY

We began this book with a discussion of the role of parties in a democracy. There are vast differences in opinions and interests in our society. Somehow we need to get those views represented and considered when policies are being debated. Somehow we need to simplify these diverse interests so we can have a reasonably coherent debate about what directions to pursue as a nation. Parties play a crucial role in all this. They are collections of activists and other less engaged supporters which we hope contribute to making democracy work. Sometimes parties find and organize voters with interests compatible with the party. Other times they respond to groups that are concerned about issues and take the initiative to seek a party that will advocate for their cause. There is an ongoing dynamic or interaction between parties and groups that leads to a sorting out of voters. The process of sorting out concerns is slow. Often, new issues emerge to disrupt the slow process of realignment, or sorting, that is occurring.

The process of searching for a majority is not a search without principle. Much of the public thinks that politicians are inclined to say and support whatever is necessary to get elected. There is always a percentage of such politicians within either party, but they are not a substantial number. Most politicians have clear convictions and principles they are committed to.[11] They advocate for the principles they believe in. They know they have to compromise as they try to forge a majority to pass legislation, but they still have convictions and do not change their views just to please voters.[12] They pursue a majority but with the strong desire that the members of the coalition be compatible with their goals.

When the search and sorting process creates reasonably coherent parties, then we can presume that they play some of the roles we expect.

---

[11] Grant Reeher, *Narratives of Justice* (Ann Arbor: University of Michigan Press, 1996).

[12] Lawrence R. Jacobs and Robert Y. Shapiro, *Politicians Don't Pander* (Chicago: University of Chicago Press, 2000).

They will present different interpretations of problems in the nation and advocate different priorities. They will propose different regulations and policies. Among students of political parties, this *conditional party government* is comprised of party voters representing a fairly coherent set of concerns. When parties meet the stated conditions, they will propose different policies and enact different policies when they are in power.[13]

Over the last forty years, we have witnessed a slow but steady realignment that has sorted out the electorate to a degree not seen since the early part of the last century. We have major differences of opinion in our society about whether we have problems of equality of opportunity and the distribution of income. The parties represent those differences. We have major differences of opinion about whether individuals should be allowed to pursue their own notions of morality and lifestyles in privacy. We differ about whether we should accept homosexuals and abortion rights or whether we should adhere to a universal and enduring moral code (which homosexuality and abortion violate), and whether government should adopt policies to encourage moral behavior. Democrats and Republicans differ about these matters. We have major differences of opinion about whether the United States should act unilaterally and use military force to try and affect the world, with Democrats less supportive of this approach and Republicans believing we must to protect our way of life.

The differences about these issues are significant and, for the moment at least, it appears they will endure for awhile. Parties are now playing out the role often outlined as an ideal in textbooks about parties – organizing and arguing for broad differences in public policy. The divisions between Democrats and Republicans in Congress are so persistent and emotional that now the concern of many is that the divisions are too sharp, making it difficult for government to function.[14] Although once we worried

---

[13] This argument that parties take on meaningful roles in organizing policy debates and enacting different policies has been made in numerous works. For a sampling of these ideas, see John Aldrich, *Why Parties?* (Chicago: University of Chicago Press, 1995); V. O. Key, Jr., *Southern Politics* (New York: Alfred A. Knopf, 1949); David W. Rohde, *Parties and Leaders in the Post-Reform House* (Chicago: University of Chicago Press, 1991).

[14] Ronald Brownstein, *The Second Civil War: How Extreme Partisanship Has Paralyzed Washington and Polarized America* (New York: Penguin Press, 2007; Morris P. Fiorina, with Samuel J. Adams and Jeremy C. Pope, *Culture War? The Myth of a Polarized America*, second edition (New York: Pearson Longman, 2006); John Harwood and Gerald F. Seib, *Pennsylvania Avenue: Profiles in Backroom Power* (New York: Random House, 2008); Nicol C. Rae, "Be Careful What You Wish For: The Rise of Responsible Parties in American National Politics," *Annual Review of Political Science* 10 (2007): 169–91.

that parties did not stand for anything, now we worry that they are too divided.

The conflicts trouble many, but there is no doubt that parties are playing out the central role that we expect of them within a democracy. They do stand for real differences, and they do give voters meaningful choices. Those voters who think government is too big and taxes too much, are conservative on cultural issues, desire a return to more traditional standards and definitions of morality and acceptable behavior, and support the Iraq War specifically and a more aggressive foreign policy generally gradually figured out that the party to vote for was Republican. Those who want more social programs to address economic and racial inequality, want government to ensure the right to an abortion and equal treatment for homosexuals, and want to end the Iraq War and be more cautious and multilateral in foreign affairs figured out that they should vote Democratic. The process of getting to this point has been gradual and lengthy, but the endless search by political parties for a majority coalition has worked to help voters and politicians sort out their allegiances. It is a process that will continue as new issues emerge, new groups appear in the electorate, and new divisions form.

Political parties' never-ending quests for a winning coalition that will control the mechanisms of government power are crucial for representative democracy. Parties stand for things; they have policy agendas and broad, programmatic goals about what they want to accomplish. To achieve these goals they must win elections, and in order to win elections, parties must appeal to voters and their interests. Without this dynamic, the representative element of America's representative democracy would be significantly diminished.

Bibliography

Abramowitz, Alan I. 1994. "Issue Evolution Reconsidered: Racial Attitudes and Partisanship in the U.S. Electorate." *American Journal of Political Science* 1 (February): 1–24.

Abramowitz, Alan I., and Kyle L. Saunders. 1998. "Ideological Realignments in the U.S. Electorate." *Journal of Politics* 60 (August): 634–52.

Abramowitz, Alan I., and Kyle L. Saunders. September 2004. "Rational Hearts and Minds: Social Identity, Ideology, and Party Identification in the American Electorate." Presented at the 2004 American Political Science Association Meetings, Chicago, IL.

Abramowitz, Alan I., and Kyle L. Saunders. 2005. "Why Can't We All Just Get Along? The Reality of a Polarized America." *The Forum* Vol. 3, Issue 2, http://www.bepress.com/forum/vol3/iss2/art1/.

Abramson, Paul R., John H. Aldrich, and David W. Rohde. 1995. *Change and Continuity in the 1992 Elections*. Washington, DC: CQ Press.

Adams, Greg D. 1997. "Abortion: Evidence of an Issue Evolution." *American Journal of Political Science* 41 (July): 718–37.

Adler, David Gray. 2004. "George Bush, the War Power, and the Imperial Presidency." Presented at the Annual Meeting of the American Political Science Association, Chicago, IL.

Aldrich, John. 1995. *Why Parties?* Chicago: University of Chicago Press.

Aldrich, John. 2003. "Electoral Democracy during Politics as Usual – and Unusual," in Michael B. MacKuen and George Rabinowitz (eds.), *Electoral Democracy*. Ann Arbor: University of Michigan Press, 279–310.

Alford, Robert R. 1963. *Party and Society: The Anglo-American Democracies*. Westport, CT: Greenwood Press.

Allswang, John M. 1971. *A House for All Peoples: Ethnic Politics in Chicago, 1890–1936*. Lexington: University Press of Kentucky.

Allswang, John M. 1978. *The New Deal and American Politics: A Study in Political Change*. New York: John Wiley & Sons.

Anbinder, Tyler. 1992. *Nativism and Slavery: The Northern Know-Nothings and the Politics of the 1850s*. New York: Oxford University Press.

Andersen, Kristi. 1979. *The Creation of a Democratic Majority 1928–1936*. Chicago: University of Chicago Press.

Ansolabehere, Stephen, Jonathan Rodden, and James M. Snyder, Jr. 2008. "The Strength of Issues: Using Multiple Measures to Gauge Preference Stability, Ideological Constraint, and Issue Voting." *American Political Science Review* 102 (May): 215–32.

Aron-Dine, Aviva. March 27, 2008. "New Data Show Income Concentration Rose Again in 2006." Center on Budget and Policy Priorities. Available at: https://www.policyarchive.org/handle/10207/7406.

Baer, Kenneth S. 2000. *Reinventing Democrats: The Politics of Liberalism from Reagan to Clinton*. Lawrence: University Press of Kansas.

Baker, Wayne. 2005. *America's Crisis of Values: Reality and Perception*. Princeton, NJ: Princeton University Press.

Balz, Daniel J., and Ronald Brownstein. 1996. *Storming the Gates: Protest Politics and the Republican Revival*. Boston: Little, Brown, and Company.

Barnes, James. 1990. "The Democrats' 'Vision Thing.'" *The American Enterprise* (March/April): 92–94.

Bartels, Larry M. 2000. "Partisanship and Voting Behavior, 1952–1996." *American Journal of Political Science* 44 (January): 35–49.

Beck. Paul Allen. 1977. "Partisan Dealignment in the Postwar South." *American Political Science Review* 71 (June): 477–96.

Beck. Paul Allen. 1979. "The Electoral Cycle and Patterns of American Politics." *British Journal of Political Science* 9 (April): 129–56.

Bell, Daniel. 1962. *The End of Ideology*. New York: Collier Books.

Bell, Daniel. 1973. *The Coming of Post-Industrial Society*. New York: Basic Books.

Bensel, Richard F. 2000. *The Political Economy of American Industrialism, 1877–1900*. New York: Cambridge University Press.

Berlet, Chip, and Matthew N. Lyons. 2000. *Right-Wing Populism in America: Too Close for Comfort*. New York: Guilford Press.

Bibby, John F., and Brian F. Schaffner. 2008. *Politics, Parties, and Elections in America*, 6th ed. Boston: Thomson-Wadsworth.

Billington, Ray Allen. 1938. *The Protestant Crusade 1800–1860: A Study of the Origins of American Nativism*. New York: Macmillan.

Bishop. Bill. 2008. *The Big Sort: Why Clustering of Like-Minded Americans is Tearing Us Apart*. New York: Houghton-Mifflin.

Bjerre-Poulsen, Niels. 2002. *Right Face: Organizing the American Conservative Movement, 1945–1965*. Copenhagen: Museum Tusculanum Press.

Black, Earl, and Merle Black. 1987. *Politics and Society in the South*. Cambridge, MA: Harvard University Press.

Black, Earl, and Merle Black. 1992. *The Vital South*. Cambridge, MA: Harvard University Press.

Black, Earl, and Merle Black. 2002. *The Rise of Southern Republicans*. Cambridge, MA: Harvard University Press.

Black, Earl, and Merle Black. 2007. *Divided America: The Ferocious Power Struggle in American Politics*. New York: Simon & Schuster.

Blakely, Edward J., and Mary Gail Snyder. 1997. *Fortress America: Gated Communities in the United States*. Washington, DC: Brookings Institution Press.

Blum, John Morton. 1956. *Woodrow Wilson and the Politics of Morality*. Boston: Little, Brown, and Company.

Blum, John Morton. 1980. *The Progressive Presidents: Roosevelt, Wilson, Roosevelt, Johnson*. New York: W.W. Norton.

Bonafede, Dom. 1981. "For the Democratic Party, It's a Time for Rebuilding and Seeking New Ideas." *National Journal* (February 21): 317–20.

Bond, Jon R., and Richard Fleisher (eds.). 2000. *Polarized Politics: Congress and the President in a Partisan Era*. Washington, DC: Congressional Quarterly Press.

Brady, David W., John F. Cogan, Brian J. Gaines, and Douglas Rivers. 1996. "The Perils of Presidential Support: How Republicans Took the House in the 1994 Midterm Elections." *Political Behavior* 18 (December): 345–67.

Brewer, Mark D. 2003. *Relevant No More? The Catholic/Protestant Divide in American Electoral Politics*. Lanham, MD: Lexington Books.

Brewer, Mark D. 2005. "The Rise of Partisanship and the Expansion of Partisan Conflict within the American Electorate." *Political Research Quarterly* 58 (June): 219–29.

Brewer, Mark D. 2009. *Party Images in the American Electorate*. New York: Routledge.

Brewer, Mark D., and Jeffrey M. Stonecash. 2001. "Class, Race Issues, Declining White Support for the Democratic Party in the South." *Political Behavior* 23 (June): 131–55.

Brewer, Mark D., and Jeffrey M. Stonecash. 2007. *Split: Class and Cultural Divides in American Politics*. Washington, DC: CQ Press.

Brewer, Mark D., and and Jeffrey M. Stonecash, "Changing the Political Dialogue and Political Alignments: George Wallace and his 1968 Presidential Campaign," Presented at the 2009 Midwest Political Science Association Meetings, Chicago, Illinois, April 2009.

Broder, David. 1972. *The Party's Over: The Failure of Politics in America*. New York: Harper & Row.

Brown, Peter. 1991. *Minority Party: Why the Democrats Face Defeat in 1992 and Beyond*. Washington, DC: Regenry Gateway.

Brownstein, Ronald. 2007. *The Second Civil War: How Extreme Partisanship Has Paralyzed Washington and Polarized America*. New York: Penguin Press.

Bryan, William Jennings. July 9, 1896. "Cross of Gold." Delivered at the Democratic National Convention, Chicago, IL.

Buckley, Mary, and Robert Singh. 2006. *The Bush Doctrine and the War on Terrorism: Global Reactions, Global Consequences*. New York: Routledge.

Bullock, Charles S. III, Donna R. Hoffman, and Ronald Keith Gaddie. 2006. "Regional Variations in the Realignment of American Politics, 1944–2004." *Social Science Quarterly* 87 (September): 494–518.

Burner, David. 1968. *The Politics of Provincialism: The Democratic Party in Transition, 1918–1932*. New York: Alfred A. Knopf.

Burnham, Walter Dean. 1965. "The Changing Shape of the American Political Universe." *American Political Science Review* 59 (March): 7–28.

Burnham, Walter Dean. 1970. *Critical Elections and the Mainsprings of American Politics*. New York: W.W. Norton.

Burnham, Walter Dean. 1975. "Insulation and Responsiveness in Congressional Elections." *Political Science Quarterly* 90 (Fall): 411–35.

Busch, Andrew E. 2005. *Reagan's Victory: The Presidential Election of 1980 and the Rise of the Right*. Lawrence: University Press of Kansas.

Campaign Finance Institute. 2002. Located at: http://www.cfinst.org/studies/vital/commentary.html#noninc.

Campbell, Angus, Philip E. Converse, Warren E. Miller, and Donald E. Stokes. 1960. *The American Voter*. New York: John Wiley & Sons.

Campbell, Angus. 1966. *Elections and the Political Order*. New York: John Wiley & Sons.

Campbell, James E. 2006. "Party Systems and Realignments in the United States, 1868–2004." *Social Science History* 30 (Fall): 359–86.

Carlson, Peter. March 4, 2008. "The Ballot Brawl of 1924." *Washington Post*, C01.

Carmines, Edward G., and Geoffrey C. Layman. 1997. "Issue Evolution in Postwar American Politics: Old Certainties and Fresh Tensions," in Byron E. Shafer (ed.), *Present Discontents: American Politics in the Very Late Twentieth Century*. Chatham, NJ: Chatham House Publishers, 89–134.

Carmines, Edward G., and James A. Stimson. 1989. *Issue Evolution: Race and the Transformation of American Politics*. Princeton, NJ: Princeton University Press.

Caro, Robert. 1982. *The Years of Lyndon Johnson*. 3 vols. New York: Alfred A. Knopf.

Carsey, Thomas M., and Geoffrey C. Layman. 2006. "Changing Sides or Changing Minds? Party Identification and Policy Preferences in the American Electorate." *American Journal of Political Science* 50 (April): 464–77.

Carter, Dan T. 1995. *The Politics of Rage: George Wallace, the Origins of the New Conservatism, and the Transformation of American Politics*. New York: Simon & Schuster.

Carter, Dan T. 1996. *From George Wallace to Newt Gingrich: Race in the Conservative Counterrevolution*. Baton Rouge: Louisiana State University Press.

Citrin, Jack, and David O. Sears. 1982. *Tax Revolt: Something for Nothing in California*. Cambridge, MA: Harvard University Press.

Clubb, Jerome M., and Howard W. Allen. 1969. "The Cities and the Election of 1928: Partisan Realignment?" *American Historical Review* 74 (April): 1205–20.

Clubb, Jerome M., William H. Flanigan, and Nancy H. Zingale. 1980. *Partisan Realignment: Voters, Parties, and Government in American History*. Beverly Hills, CA: Sage Publications.

Coleman, James A. 1966. *Equality of Educational Opportunity*. Washington, DC: U.S. Department of Health, Education, and Welfare, Office of Education.

Collins, Robert M. 2007. *Transforming America: Politics and Culture in the Reagan Years*. New York: Columbia University Press.

Congressional Quarterly. 1957. "How Big is the North-South Democratic Split?" *Congressional Quarterly Almanac*. Washington, DC: Congressional Quarterly Inc., 813–17.

Congressional Quarterly. 1958. "Basic Democratic Divisions Examined." *Congressional Quarterly Almanac*. Washington, DC: Congressional Quarterly Inc., 764–9.

Congressional Quarterly. 1959. "Extent of North-South Democratic Split Analyzed." *Congressional Quarterly Almanac*. Washington, DC: Congressional Quarterly Inc., 135–46.

Congressional Quarterly. 1960. "Extent of North-South Democratic Split Analyzed." Congressional Quarterly Almanac. Washington, DC: Congressional Quarterly Inc: 117–30.

Congressional Quarterly. 1961. "Extent of North-South Democratic Split Analyzed." *Congressional Quarterly Almanac*. Washington, DC: Congressional Quarterly Inc.: 642–57.

Congressional Quarterly. 1962. "Extent of North-South Democratic Split Analyzed." *Congressional Quarterly Almanac*. Washington, DC: Congressional Quarterly Inc.: 723–35.

Congressional Quarterly. 1963. "Extent of North-South Democratic Split Analyzed." *Congressional Quarterly Almanac*. Washington, DC: Congressional Quarterly Inc.: 740–54.

Congressional Quarterly. 1964. "Democrats from North and South Split on 24% of Votes." *Congressional Quarterly Almanac*. Washington, DC: Congressional Quarterly Inc.: 745–60.

Congressional Quarterly. 1965. "Democrats Regional Divisions Remain Great in 1965." *Congressional Quarterly Almanac*. Washington, DC: Congressional Quarterly Inc.: 1083–98.

Conniff, Richard. 1994. "Federal Lands." *National Geographic* 185 (February): 2–39.

Cook, Charlie. December 2, 2008. "How to Right the GOP." *National Journal*. Located at: http://www.nationaljournal.com/njonline/ot_20081201_3322.php.

Cooper, Michael. June 4, 2008. "McCain Distances Himself from Bush and Jabs Obama." *New York Times*, A21.

Cooper, Michael, and Elisabeth Bumiller. March 6, 2008. "It's Official: Party and President Back McCain." *New York Times*, A28.

Cooperman, Alan, and Thomas B. Edsall. November 8, 2004. "Evangelicals Say They Led Charge For the GOP." *Washington Post*, A01.

Cosman, Bernard. 1966. *Five States for Goldwater: Continuity and Change in Southern Presidential Voting Patterns*. University: University of Alabama Press.

Critchlow, Donald. 2007. *The Conservative Ascendancy*. Cambridge, MA: Harvard University Press.

Dallek, Robert. 1998. *Flawed Giant: Lyndon Johnson and His Times, 1961–1973*. New York: Oxford University Press.

Danziger, Sheldon, and Peter Gottschalk. 1995. *American Unequal*. Cambridge, MA: Harvard University Press.

Degler, Carl N. 1964. "American Political Parties and the Rise of the City: An Interpretation." *Journal of American History* 51 (June): 41–59.

Dionne, E. J., Jr. 1997. *They Only Look Dead*. New York: Touchstone.

Divine, Robert A. 1981. *The Johnson Years, Volume One: Foreign Policy, the Great Society, and the White House*. Lawrence: University Press of Kansas.

Dolan, Jay P. 1992. *The American Catholic Experience: A History from Colonial Times to the Present*. Notre Dame, IN: University of Notre Dame Press.

Domke, David. 2004. *God Willing? Political Fundamentalism in the White House, 'The War on Terror,' and the Echoing Press*. London: Pluto Press.

Draper, Robert. 2007. *Dead Certain: The Presidency of George W. Bush*. New York: The Free Press.

Dubin, Michael J. 1998. *United States Congressional Elections, 1788–1997*. Jefferson, NC: McFarland and Company, Inc.

Edsall, Thomas Byrne, and Mary D. Edsall. 1991. *Chain Reaction: The Impact of Race, Rights, and Taxes on American Politics*. New York: W.W. Norton.

Edsall, Thomas B. 2006. *Building Red America: The Conservative Coalition and the Drive for Permanent Power*. New York: Basic Books.

Eldersveld, Samuel J. 1949. "The Influence of Metropolitan Party Pluralities in Presidential Elections Since 1920: A Study of Twelve Key Cities." *American Political Science Review* 43 (December): 1189–1206.

Erikson, Robert S., and Gerald C. Wright. 2001. "Voters, Candidates, and Issues in Congressional Elections," in Lawrence C. Dodd and Bruce I. Oppenheimer (eds.), *Congress Reconsidered*, 7th ed. Washington, DC: Congressional Quarterly Press, 67–95.

Erikson, Robert S., Michael B. MacKuen, and James A. Stimson. 2002. *The Macro Polity*. New York: Cambridge University Press.

Fauntroy, Michael K. 2007. *Republicans and the Black Vote*. Boulder, CO: Lynne Rienner.

Ferguson, Thomas, and Joel Rogers. 1986. "The Myth of America's Turn to the Right." *Atlantic Monthly* (May): 43–53.

Fiorina, Morris P. 1981. *Retrospective Voting in American National Elections*. New Haven, CT: Yale University Press.

Fiorina, Morris P., with Samuel J. Abrams and Jeremy C. Pope. 2006. *Culture War? The Myth of a Polarized America*, second ed. New York: Pearson/Longman.

Fischer, Hannah, Kim Klarman, and Mari-Jana Oboroceanu. 2007. "American War and Military Operation Casualties: Lists and Statistics." Washington, DC: Congressional Research Service.

Fleisher, Richard, and Jon R. Bond. 2000. "Congress and the President in a Partisan Era," in Jon R. Bond and Richard Fleisher (eds.), *Polarized Politics: Congress and the President in a Partisan Era*. Washington, DC: Congressional Quarterly Press, 1–8.

Fleisher, Richard, and Jon R. Bond. 2000. "Partisanship and the President's Quest for Votes on the Floor of Congress," in Jon R. Bond and Richard Fleisher (eds.), *Polarized Politics: Congress and the President in a Partisan Era*. Washington, DC: Congressional Quarterly Press, 154–85.

Foner, Eric. 1988. *Reconstruction: America's Unfinished Revolution: 1863–1877*. New York: Cambridge University Press.

Foner, Eric. 1998. *The Story of American Freedom*. New York: W.W. Norton.

Fordham, Benjamin O. 2007. "The Evolution of Republican and Democratic Positions on Cold War Military Spending: A Historical Puzzle." *Social Science History* 31 (Winter): 603–36.

Frank, Thomas. 2004. *What's the Matter with Kansas? How Conservatives Won the Heart of America*. New York: Metropolitan Books.

Franklin, Charles F. 1992. "Measurement and the Dynamics of Party Identification." *Political Behavior* 14 (September): 297–309.

Frederickson, Kari. 2001. *The Dixiecrat Revolt and the End of the Solid South, 1932–1968*. Chapel Hill: University of North Carolina Press.

Galbraith, John Kenneth. 1958. *The Affluent Society*. Boston: Houghton-Mifflin.

Gale, Dennis E. 1996. *Understanding Urban Unrest: From Reverend King to Rodney King*. Thousand Oaks, CA: Sage Publications.

Galston, William. 1985. "The Future of the Democratic Party." *The Brookings Review* (Winter): 16–24.

Galston, William, and Elaine C. Kamarck. 1989. "The Politics of Evasion: Democrats and the Presidency." Washington, DC: The Progressive Policy Institute.

Gardner, Michael. 2003. *Harry Truman and Civil Rights: Moral Courage and Political Risks*. Carbondale: Southern Illinois University Press.

Gerring, John. 1998. *Party Ideologies in America, 1828–1996*. New York: Cambridge University Press.

Gerson, Michael. 2008. "How My Party Lost Its Way." *Newsweek*, January 28, 28.

Gienapp, William E. 1985. "Nativism and the Creation of a Republican Majority in the North before the Civil War." *Journal of American History* 72 (December): 529–59.

Gilens, Martin. 1999. *Why Americans Hate Welfare: Race, Media, and the Politics of Anti-Poverty Policy*. Chicago: University of Chicago Press.

Gillon, Steven M. 1992. "The Trail of the Democrats: Search for a New Majority," in Peter B. Kovler (ed.), *Democrats and the American Idea*. Washington, DC: Center for the National Policy Press, 288–9.

Glassman, Ronald M. 1989. *Democracy and Equality*. New York: Praeger.

Glenn, Norval D. 1972. "Class and Party Support in the United States: Recent and Emerging Trends." *Public Opinion Quarterly* 37 (Spring): 31–47.

Goldman, Ralph M. *Search for Consensus: The Story of the Democratic Party*. Philadelphia: Temple University Press.

Goldwater, Barry. 1960. *The Conscience of a Conservative*. New York: Hillman Books.

Golebiowska, Ewa A. 1995. "Individual Value Priorities, Education, and Political Tolerance." *Political Behavior* 17 (March): 23–48.

Goodwyn, Lawrence. 1978. *The Populist Moment: A Short History of the Agrarian Revolt in America*. New York: Oxford University Press.

Gordon, Michael R., and Bernard E. Trainor. 2006. *Cobra II: The Inside Story of the Invasion and Occupation of Iraq*. New York: Pantheon.

Gould, Lewis L. 1974. "The Republicans Under Roosevelt and Taft," in Lewis L. Gould (ed.), *The Progressive Era*. Syracuse, NY: Syracuse University Press, 55–82.

Green, Donald P., Bradley Palmquist, and Eric Shickler. 2002. *Partisan Hearts and Minds: Political Parties and the Social Identities of Voters*. New Haven, CT: Yale University Press.

Green, John C., Lyman A. Kellstedt, Corwin E. Smidt, and James L. Guth. 1998. "The Soul of the South: Religion and the New Electoral Order," in Charles S. Bullock III and Mark J. Rozell (eds.), *The New Politics of the Old South*. Boulder, CO: Rowman and Littlefield, 26 –76.

Green, Joshua. 2007. "The Rove Presidency." *Atlantic Monthly* (September): http://www.theatlantic.com/doc/200709/karl-rove.

Greenberg, Stanley B. 1996. *Middle-Class Dreams: Politics and Power of the New American Majority*. New Haven, CT: Yale University Press.

Guth, James L., John C. Green, Lyman A. Kellstedt, and Corwin E. Smidt. 2003. "Faith and Foreign Policy: A View from the Pews." *Review of Faith and International Affairs* 3 (Fall): 3–9.

Hacker, Jacob. S. 2006. *The Great Risk Shift: The Assault on American Jobs, Families, Health Care, and Retirement, and How You Can Fight Back*. New York: Oxford University Press.

Hale, Jon F. 1995. "The Making of the New Democrats." *Political Science Quarterly* 110 (Summer): 207–32.

Handlin, Oscar. 1958. *Al Smith and His America*. Boston: Little, Brown, and Company.

Harrington, Michael. 1962. *The Other America*. New York: Macmillan.

Hartz, Louis. 1955. *The Liberal Tradition in America*. New York: Harcourt Brace.

Harwood, John, and Gerald F. Seib. 2008. *Pennsylvania Avenue: Profiles in Backroom Power*. New York: Random House.

Haskings, Ron. 2006. *Work Over Welfare: The Inside Story of the 1996 Welfare Reform Law*. Washington, DC: Brookings Institution Press.

Hayek, Friedrich A. von. 1944. *The Road to Serfdom*. Chicago: University of Chicago Press.

Hays, Samuel P. 1964. "The Politics of Reform in Municipal Government." *Pacific Northwest Quarterly* 55 (October): 157–69.

Hershey, Marjorie Randon. 2009. *Party Politics in America*, 13th ed. New York: Pearson/Longman.

Hetherington, Marc J. 2001. "Resurgent Mass Partisanship: The Role of Elite Polarization?" *American Political Science Review* 95 (September): 619–32.

Hetherington, Marc J., and William J. Keefe. 2007. *Parties, Politics, and Public Policy in America*, 10th ed. Washington, DC: CQ Press.

Hetherington, Marc J., and Michael Nelson. 2003. "Anatomy of a Rally Effect: George W. Bush and the War on Terrorism." *PS: Political Science and Politics* 36 (January): 37–42.

Hetherington, Marc J., and Jonathan Weiler. 2009. Authoritarianism and Polarization in American Politics. New York: Cambridge University Press.

Hicks, John D. 1931. *The Populist Revolt*. Minneapolis: University of Minnesota Press.

Hicks, John D. 1960. *Normalcy and Reaction 1921–1933: An Age of Disillusionment.* Washington, DC: Service Center for Teachers of History.

Hicks, John D. 1960. *Republican Ascendancy, 1921–1933*. New York: Harper and Row.

Higham, John. 1959. "The Cult of the 'American Consensus': Homogenizing Our History." *Commentary* 27: 94–5.

Hoffmann, Charles. 1956. "The Depression of the Nineties." *Journal of Economic History* 16 (June): 137–64.

Hofstader, Richard. 1948. *The American Political Tradition and the Men Who Made It.* New York: Alfred A. Knopf.

Hofstader, Richard. 1960. *The Age of Reform: From Bryan to F.D.R.* New York: Vintage Books.

Hoover, Herbert. 1934. *The Challenge to Liberty*. New York: Charles Scribner's Sons.

Hough, Jerry F. 2006. *Changing Party Coalitions: The Mystery of the Red State–Blue State Alignment*. New York: Agathon Press.

Hulse, Carl. July 18, 2006. "G.O.P. Agenda in House Has Moderates Unhappy." *New York Times*, A11.

Hulse, Carl. December 4, 2007. "Vulnerable Democrats See Fate Tied to a Clinton Run." *New York Times*, A1.

Hulse, Carl. May 18, 2008. "Gaining Seats, Democrats Find Their House Ideologically Divided." *New York Times*, A25.

Hunter, James Davison. 1991. *Culture Wars: The Struggle to Define America*. New York: Basic Books.

Huntington, Samuel P. 1974. "Postindustrial Politics: How Benign Will it Be?" *Comparative Politics* 6 (January): 163–91.

Inglehart, Ronald. 1971. "The Silent Revolution in Europe." *American Political Science Review* 65 (December): 991–1017.

Inglehart, Ronald. 1977. *Silent Revolution*. Princeton, NJ: Princeton University Press.

Inglehart, Ronald. 1997. *Modernization and Postmodernization*. Princeton, NJ: Princeton University Press.

Isikoff, Michael, and David Corn. 2006. *Hubris: The Inside Story of Spin, Scandal, and the Selling of the War in Iraq*. New York: Crown.

Jackson, Kenneth T. 1985. *Crabgrass Frontier: The Suburbanization of the United States*. New York: Oxford University Press.

Jacobson, Gary C. 2000. "Party Polarization in National Politics: The Electoral Connection," in Jon R. Bond and Richard Fleisher (eds.), *Polarized Politics: Congress and the President in a Partisan Era*. Washington, DC: Congressional Quarterly Press, 9–30.

Jacobson, Gary C. 2001. *The Politics of Congressional Elections*, 5th ed. New York: Addison Wesley Longman.

Jacobson, Gary C. 2003. "Party Polarization in Presidential Support: The Electoral Connection." *Congress and the Presidency* 30 (Spring): 1–36.

Jacobson, Gary C. 2003. "Reconsidering 'Reconsidering the Trend in Incumbent Vote Percentages in House Elections': A Comment." *American Review of Politics* 24: 241–4.

Jacobson, Gary C. April 2004. "Explaining the Ideological Polarization of the Congressional Parties since the 1970s." Presented at the Midwest Political Science Association Meetings, Chicago, Illinois.

Jacobson, Gary C. April 2005. "The Public, the President, and the War in Iraq." Presented at the Annual Meeting of the Midwest Political Science Association, Chicago, IL.

Jacobson, Gary C. April 2006. "The War, the President, and the 2006 Midterm Congressional Elections." Presented at the Annual Meeting of the Midwest Political Science Association, Chicago, IL.

Jacobson, Gary C. 2007. *A Divider, Not a Uniter: George W. Bush and the American People*. New York: Pearson/Longman.

Jacobs, Lawrence R., and Robert Y. Shapiro. 2000. *Politicians Don't Pander*. Chicago: University of Chicago Press.

Jacoway, Elizabeth. 2007. *Turn Away Thy Son: Little Rock, the Crisis that Shocked the Nation*. New York: The Free Press.

James, Scott C. 2000. *Presidents, Parties, and the State: A Party System Perspective on Democratic Regulatory Choice, 1884–1936*. New York: Cambridge University Press.

Jensen, Richard. 1971. *The Winning of the Midwest*. Chicago: University of Chicago Press,

Jones, Maldwyn Allen. 1992. *American Immigration*, 2nd ed. Chicago: University of Chicago Press.

Josephson, Matthew, and Hannah Josephson. 1969. *Al Smith: Hero of the Cities*. Boston: Houghton-Mifflin.

Judd, Dennis R., and Todd Swanstrom. 2008. *City Politics: The Political Economy of Urban America*, 6th ed. New York: Pearson/Longman.

Judis, John B., and Ruy Teixeira. 2002. *The Emerging Democratic Majority*. New York: Scribner.

Kaplan, Marshall, and Peggy L. Cuciti, eds. 1986. *The Great Society and Its Legacy: Twenty Years of U.S. Social Policy*. Durham, NC: Duke University Press.

Kazin, Michael. 1995. *The Populist Persuasion*. New York: Basic Books.

Kazin, Michael. October 19, 1995. "The Worker's Party?" *New York Times*, A25.

Keith, Bruce E., David B. Magleby, Candice J. Nelson, Eliazbeth Orr, Mark C. Westlye, and Raymond Wolfinger. 1992. *The Myth of the Independent Voter*. Berkeley: University of California Press.

Key, V. O., Jr. 1949. *Southern Politics in State and Nation*. New York: Knopf.

Key, V. O., Jr. 1955. "A Theory of Critical Elections." *Journal of Politics* 17 (February): 3–18.

Key, V. O., Jr. 1959. "Secular Realignment and the Party System." 1959. *Journal of Politics* 21 (May): 198–210.

Key, V. O., Jr. 1966. *The Responsible Electorate*. Cambridge, MA: Harvard University Press.

Kinzer, Donald L. 1964. *An Episode in Anti-Catholicism: The American Protective Association*. Seattle: University of Washington Press.

Kirk, Russell. 1953. *The Conservative Mind*. Chicago: Henry Regnery Company.

Kleppner, Paul. 1970. *The Cross of Culture: A Social Analysis of Midwestern Politics, 1850–1900*. New York: The Free Press.

Kleppner, Paul. 1979. *The Third Electoral System, 1853–1892*. Chapel Hill: University of North Carolina Press.

Kleppner, Paul. 1981. "Partisanship and Ethnoreligious Conflict: The Third Electoral System, 1853–1892," in Paul Kleppner (ed.), *The Evolution of American Electoral Systems*. Westport, CT: Greenwood Press, 114–46.

Kleppner, Paul. 1987. *Continuity and Change in Electoral Politics, 1893–1928*. Westport, CT: Greenwood Press.

Knapp, Daniel, and Kenneth Polk. 1971. *Scouting the War on Poverty: Social Reform Politics in the Kennedy Administration*. Lexington, MA: Heath Lexington Books.

Kousser, J. Morgan. 1974. *The Shaping of Southern Politics: Suffrage Restriction and the Establishment of the One-Party South, 1880–1910*. New Haven, CT: Yale University Press.

Krugman, Paul R. 2007. *The Conscience of a Liberal*. New York: W.W. Norton.

Kuhn, David Paul. 2007. *The Neglected Voter: White Men and the Democratic Dilemma*. New York: Palgrave Macmillan.

Kusch, Frank. 2004. *Battleground Chicago: The Police and the 1968 Democratic National Convention*. Westport, CT: Praeger.

Kuttner, Robert. 1987. *The Life of the Party: Democratic Prospects in 1988 and Beyond*. New York: Penguin Books.

Ladd, Everett Carll, Jr. 1970. *American Political Parties: Social Change and Political Response*. New York: W.W. Norton.

Ladd, Everett Carll, Jr. 1976–7. "Liberalism Turned Upside Down." *Political Science Quarterly* 91 (Winter): 577–600.

Ladd, Everett Carll, Jr. 1984. "Is Election '84 Really a Class Struggle?" *Public Opinion* (April/May): 41–51.

Ladd, Everett Carll, Jr. 1997. "1996 Vote: The 'No Majority' Realignment Continues." *Political Science Quarterly* 112 (Spring): 1–28.

Ladd, Everett Carll, Jr., and Charles Hadley. 1975. *Transformations of the American Party System*. New York: W.W. Norton.

Ladd, Everett Carll, Jr., Charles Hadley, and Lauriston King. 1971. "A New Political Realignment?" *Public Interest* 23 (Spring): 46–63.

Lang, Robert E., and Jennifer B. LeFurgy. 2007. *Boomburbs: The Rise of America's Accidental Cities*. Washington, DC: Brookings Institution Press.

Lassiter, Matthew D. 2007. *The Silent Majority: Suburban Politics in the Sunbelt South*. Princeton, NJ: Princeton University Press.

Lawrence, David G. 1991. "The Collapse of the Democratic Majority: Economics and Vote Choice Since 1952." *Western Political Quarterly* 44 (December): 797–820.

Lawrence, David G. 1996. *The Collapse of the Democratic Presidential Majority*. Boulder, CO: Westview Press.

Lawrence, W. H. September 20, 1957. "Eisenhower 'Deeply Disappointed' in Impasse at Little Rock." *New York Times*, A1.

Lawrence, W. H. February 1, 1959. "Study of Voting Shows G.O.P. Faces Difficult Task Next Year." *New York Times*, A1.

Layman, Geoffrey C. 1999. "'Cultural Wars' in the American Party System." *American Politics Quarterly* 27 (January): 89–121.

Layman, Geoffrey C. 2001. *The Great Divide: Religious and Cultural Conflict in American Party Politics*. New York: Columbia University Press.

Layman, Geoffrey C., and Thomas M. Carsey. 2002. "Party Polarization and Party Structuring of Policy Attitudes: A Comparison of Three NES Panel Studies." *Political Behavior* 24 (September): 199–236.

Layman, Geoffrey C., and Thomas M. 2002. "Party Polarization and "Conflict Extension" in the American Electorate." *American Journal of Political Science* 46 (October): 786–802.

Layman, Geoffrey C., Thomas M. Carsey, and Juliana Menasce Horowitz. 2006. "Party Polarization in American Politics: Characteristics, Causes, and Consequences." *Annual Review of Political Science* 9: 83–110.

Leege, David C., Kenneth D. Wald, Brian S. Krueger, and Paul D. Mueller. 2002. *The Politics of Cultural Differences*. Princeton, NJ: Princeton University Press.

Lemann Nicholas. 1991. *The Promised Land*. New York: Knopf.

Leogrande, William M., and Alana S. Jeydel. 1997. "Using Presidential Election Returns to Measure Constituency Ideology: A Research Note." *American Politics Quarterly* 25 (January): 3–18.

Leuchtenburg, William E. 1958. *The Perils of Prosperity, 1914–1932*. Chicago: University of Chicago Press.

Leuchtenburg, William E. 1963. *Franklin D. Roosevelt and the New Deal, 1932–1940*. New York: Harper and Row.

Leuchtenburg, William E. 2005. *The White House Looks South: Franklin D. Roosevelt, Harry S. Truman, and Lyndon B. Johnson*. Baton Rouge: Louisiana State University Press.

Link, Arthur S. 1954. *Woodrow Wilson and the Progressive Era, 1910–1917*. New York: Harper and Brothers.

Lipset, Seymour Martin. 1981. *Political Man*, exp. ed. Baltimore: Johns Hopkins University Press.

Lubell, Samuel. 1956. *The Future of American Politics*, 2nd ed., rev. Garden City, NY: Doubleday Anchor Books.

Lublin, David. 2004. *The Republican South: Democratization and Partisan Change*. Princeton, NJ: Princeton University Press.

MacInnes, Gordon. 1996. *Wrong, for all the Right Reasons: How White Liberals Have Been Undone by Race*. New York: New York University Press.

Mackenzie, G. Calvin, and Robert Weisbrot. 2008. *The Liberal Hour: Washington and the Politics of Change in the 1960s*. New York: Penguin Press.

MacKeun, Michael B., Robert S. Erikson, and James A. Stimson. 1989. "Macropartisanship." *American Political Science Review* 83 (December): 1125–42.

Magnet, Myron. 1993. *The Dream and the Nightmare: The Sixties Legacy to the Underclass.* New York: William Morrow.

Maisel, L. Sandy, and Mark D. Brewer. 2008. *Parties and Elections in America,* 5th ed. Lanham, MD: Rowman and Littlefield.

Mann, James. 2004. *The Rise of the Vulcans: The History of Bush's War Cabinet.* New York: Viking Adult.

Maraniss, David, and Michael Weisskopf. 1996. *Tell Newt to Shut Up.* New York: Simon & Schuster.

Mayhew, David R. 1974. *The Electoral Connection.* New Haven, CT: Yale University Press.

Mayhew, David R. 1974. "Congressional Elections: The Case of the Vanishing Marginals." *Polity* 6 (Spring): 295–317.

Mayhew, David R. 1991. *Divided We Govern: Party Control, Lawmaking, and Investigations, 1946–1990.* New Haven, CT: Yale University Press.

Mayhew, David R. 2003. *Electoral Realignments: A Critique of an American Genre.* New Haven, CT: Yale University Press.

McClellan, Scott. 2008. *What Happened: Inside the Bush White House and Washington's Culture of Deception.* New York: Public Affairs.

McClosky, Herbert. 1964. "Consensus and Ideology in American Politics." *American Political Science Review* 58 (June): 361–82.

McCormick, Richard L. 1986. *The Party Period and Public Policy: American Politics from the Age of Jackson to the Progressive Era.* New York: Oxford University Press.

McGerr, Michael E. 1986. *The Decline of Popular Politics.* New York: Oxford University Press.

McGirr, Lisa. 2002. *Suburban Warriors: The Origins of the New American Right.* Princeton, NJ: Princeton University Press.

Meyerson, Harold. 1996. "Wither the Democrats?" *American Prospect* (March/April): 79–88.

Micklethwait, John, and Adrian Wooldridge. 2004. *The Right Nation: Conservative Power in America.* New York: Penguin Press.

Milkis, Sidney M. 1993. *The President and the Parties: The Transformation of the American Party System Since the New Deal.* New York: Oxford University Press.

Milkis, Sidney M. 2006. "Lyndon Johnson, the Great Society, and the Modern Presidency," in Sidney M. Milkis and Jerome M. Mileur (eds.), *The Great Society and the High Tide of Liberalism.* Amherst: University of Massachusetts Press, 1–49.

Miller, S. M., and Karen Marie Ferroggiaro. 1995. "Class Dismissed?" *American Prospect* 21 (Spring): 100–4.

Mitchell, Alison. August 20, 1996. "Democrats Again Face Voter Doubt Over Values." *New York Times,* A18.

Mitchell, Alison. May 4, 1999. "Two Parties Seek to Exploit a Relentless Suburban Boom." *New York Times,* A1.

Moen, Matthew C. 1989. *The Christian Right and Congress*. Tuscaloosa: University of Alabama Press.

Moley, Raymond. 1939. *After Seven Years*. New York: Harper and Brothers.

Moley, Raymond. 1949 [1979]. *27 Masters of Politics*. Westport, CT: Greenwood Press.

Moore, James, and Wayne Slater. 2006. *The Architect: Karl Rove and the Master Plan for Absolute Power*. New York: Crown Publishers.

Moore, John Robert. 1967. "The Conservative Coalition in the United States Senate, 1942–45." *Journal of Southern History* 33 (August): 369–76.

Morris, John D. September 28, 1961. "First Kennedy Congress Responds Coolly to the Call of the New Frontier." *New York Times*, 32.

Mueller, John E. 1970. "Presidential Popularity from Truman to Johnson." *American Political Science Review* 64 (March): 18–34.

Mueller, John E. 1973. *War, Presidents, and Public Opinion*. New York: John Wiley & Sons.

Muirhead, Russell. 2006. "A Defense of Party Spirit." *Perspectives on Politics* 4 (December): 713–27.

Munton, Don, and David A. Welch. 2007. *The Cuban Missile Crisis: A Concise History*. New York: Oxford University Press.

Nagourney, Adam. January 21, 2006. "Rove Lays Out Road Map for Republicans in Fall Elections." *New York Times*, A11.

Nagourney, Adam, and Carl Hulse. May 15, 2008. "Election Losses for Republicans Stir Fall Fears." *New York Times*, A1.

Nagourney, Adam, and David D. Kirkpatrick. August 18, 2005. "Bad Iraq War News Worries Some in G.O.P. on '06 Vote." *New York Times*, A20.

Nagourney, Adam, and Jim Rutenberg. September 3, 2006. "Rove's Word is No Longer G.O.P. Gospel." *New York Times*, A1.

Nash, George H. 1976. *The Conservative Intellectual Movement in America*. New York: Basic Books.

National Advisory Commission on Civil Disorders. 1968. *Report of the National Advisory Commission on Civil Disorders*. New York: Bantam Books.

Nevins, Alan. 1932. *Grover Cleveland: A Study in Courage*. New York: Dodd, Mead, and Company.

Nichols, David A. 2007. *A Matter of Justice: Eisenhower and the Beginning of the Civil Rights Revolution*. New York: Simon & Schuster.

Nie, Norman, Sidney Verba, and John Petrocik. 1976. *The Changing American Voter* Cambridge, MA: Harvard University Press.

Nisbet, Robert A. 1959. "The Decline and Fall of Social Class." *Pacific Sociological Review* 2 (Spring): 11–17.

Nivola, Pietro S., and David W. Brady, eds. 2006. *Red and Blue Nation?* Vol. 1. Washington, DC: Brookings Institution Press.

Olasky, Marvin. 1992. *The Tragedy of American Compassion*. Washington, DC: Regnery Publishing.

Olasky, Marvin. 2000. *Compassionate Conservatism: What It Is, What It Does, and How It Can Transform America*. New York: Free Press.

Oldfield, Duane M. 1996. *The Right and the Righteous: The Christian Right Confronts the Republican Party*. Lanham, MD: Rowman and Littlefield.

Oldfield, Duane M. May 26, 2008. "The Fall of Conservatism." *The New Yorker*, 47–55.

Packer, George. 2005. *The Assassins' Gate: America in Iraq*. New York: Farrar, Straus, and Giroux.

Page, Benjamin I., and Robert Y. Shapiro. 1992. *The Rational Public: Fifty Years of Trends in Americans' Policy Preferences*. Chicago: University of Chicago Press.

Palmer, John L., and Isabel V. Sawhill (eds.). 1982. *The Reagan Experiment*. Washington, DC: The Urban Institute Press.

Palmer, John L., and Isabel V. Sawhill. 1984. *The Reagan Record*. Cambridge, MA: Ballinger Publishing.

Patterson, James T. 1966. "A Conservative Coalition Forms in Congress, 1933–1939." *Journal of American History* 52 (March): 757–72.

Palmer, John L., and Isabel V. Sawhill. 1967. *Congressional Conservatism and the New Deal: The Growth of the Conservative Coalition in Congress, 1933–1939*. Lexington: University of Kentucky Press.

Palmer, John L., and Isabel V. Sawhill. 2003. *Restless Giant: The United States from Watergate to Bush v. Gore*. New York: Oxford University Press.

Patterson, Thomas E. 1993. *Out of Order*. New York: Alfred A. Knopf.

Paulson, Arthur C. 2000. *Realignment and Party Revival: Understanding American Electoral Politics at the Turn of the Twenty-First Century*. Westport, CT: Praeger.

Paulson, Arthur C. 2007. *Electoral Realignment and the Outlook for American Democracy*. Boston: Northeastern University Press.

Penn, Mark J. 1998. "The New Democratic Electorate." *The New Democrat* (January/February): 6–9.

Perlstein, Rick. 2001. *Before the Storm*. New York: Hill and Wang.

Perlstein, Rick. 2008. *Nixonland: The Rise of a President and the Fracturing of America*. New York: Scribner.

Petrocik, John R. 1981. *Party Coalitions: Realignments and the Decline of the New Deal Party System*. Chicago: University of Chicago Press.

Pew Research Center for the People and the Press. March 22, 2007. "Trends in Political Values and Core Attitudes, 1987–2007: Political Landscape More Favorable to Democrats." http://people-press.org/report/?reportid=312.

Pierce, Neal R., and Jerry Hagstrom. November 8, 1980. "The Voters Send Carter a Message: Time for a Change–to Reagan." *National Journal*. 1876–8.

Piven, Frances Fox, and Richard A. Cloward. 1971. *Regulating the Poor: The Functions of Public Welfare*. New York: Pantheon.

Piven, Frances Fox, and Richard A. Cloward. 2006. "The Politics of the Great Society," in Sidney M. Milkis and Jerome M. Mileur (eds.), *The Great Society and the High Tide of Liberalism*. Amherst: University of Massachusetts Press.

Plotke, David. 1996. *Building a Democratic Political Order: Reshaping American Liberalism in the 1930s and 1940s*. New York: Cambridge University Press.

Phillips, Kevin P. 1969. *The Emerging Republican Majority*. New Rochelle, NY: Arlington House.

Polmar, Norman, and John D. Gresham. 2006. *DEFCON-2: Standing on the Brink of Nuclear War during the Cuban Missile Crisis.* New York: John Wiley and Sons.

Polsby, Nelson. 1983. *Consequences of Party Reform.* New York: Oxford University Press.

Polsby, Nelson. 2004. *How Congress Evolves: Social Bases of Institutional Change.* New York: Oxford University Press.

Pomper, Gerald M. 1972. "From Confusion to Clarity: Issues and American Voters, 1956–1968." *American Political Science Review* 66 (June): 415–28.

Poole, Keith T., and Howard Rosenthal. 1984. "The Polarization of American Politics." *Journal of Politics* 46 (November): 1061–79.

Poole, Keith T., and Howard Rosenthal. 1985. "A Spatial Model for Legislative Roll Call Analysis." *American Journal of Political Science* 29 (May): 357–84.

Poole, Keith T., and Howard Rosenthal. 1991. "Patterns of Congressional Voting." *American Journal of Political Science* 35 (February): 228–78.

Poole, Keith T., and Howard Rosenthal. 1997. *Congress: A Political-Economic History of Roll Call Voting.* New York: Oxford University Press.

Popkin, Samuel L. 1994. *The Reasoning Voter: Communication and Persuasion in Presidential Elections.* Chicago: University of Chicago Press.

Prior, Markus. 2007. *Post-Broadcast Democracy.* New York: Cambridge University Press.

Prothro, James W., and Charles W. Griggs. 1960. "Fundamental Principles of Democracy: Bases of Agreement and Disagreement." *Journal of Politics* 22 (February): 276–94.

Radosh, Ronald. 1996. *Divided They Fell: The Demise of the Democratic Party, 1964–1996.* New York: The Free Press.

Rae, Nicol C. 1989. *The Decline and Fall of the Liberal Republicans from 1952 to the Present.* New York: Oxford University Press.

Rae, Nicol C. 1992. "Class and Culture: American Political Cleavages in the Twentieth Century." *Western Political Quarterly* 45 (September): 629–50.

Rae, Nicol C. 2007. "Be Careful What You Wish For: The Rise of Responsible Parties in American National Politics." *Annual Review of Political Science* 10: 169–91.

Rand, Ayn. 1943. *The Fountainhead.* Indianapolis, IN: Bobbs-Merrill.

Rand, Ayn. 1957. *Atlas Shrugged.* New York: Random House.

Reeher, Grant. 1996. *Narratives of Justice.* Ann Arbor: University of Michigan Press.

Reiter, Howard L. 2001. "The Building of a Bifactional Structure: The Democrats in the 1940s." *Political Science Quarterly* 116 (Spring): 107–29.

Reiter, Howard L. November 15–18, 2007. "Counter-Realignment: Electoral Trends in the Northeast, 1900–2004." Paper presented at the Social Science History Meetings, Chicago, IL.

Ribuffo, Leo P. 2006. "Family Policy Past as Prologue: Jimmy Carter, the White House Conference on Families, and the Mobilization of the New Christian Right." *Review of Policy Research* 23 (March): 311–37.

Ricks, Thomas E. 2006. *Fiasco: The American Military Adventure in Iraq.* New York: Penguin Press.

Rieder, Jonathon. 1989. "The Rise of the 'Silent Majority,'" in Steve Fraser and Gary Gerstle (eds.), *The Rise and Fall of the New Deal Order*. Princeton, NJ: Princeton University Press, 248–58.

Ritter, Gretchen. 1997. *Goldbugs and Greenbacks: The Antimonopoly Tradition and the Politics of Finance in America, 1865–1896*. New York: Cambridge University Press.

Rohde, David W. 1991. *Parties and Leaders in the Postreform House*. Chicago: University of Chicago Press.

Rosenof, Theodore. 2003. *Realignment: The Theory that Changed the Way We Think About American Politics*. Lanham, MD: Rowman and Littlefield.

Rusher, William A. February 12, 1963. "Crossroads for the GOP." *National Review*, 109–112.

Rusher, William A. 1984. *The Rise of the Right*. New York: William Morrow and Company, Inc.

Rusk, Jerrold G. 2001. *A Statistical History of the American Electorate*. Washington, DC: CQ Press.

Samuelson, Robert J. August 23, 1980. "A Schizophrenic Party." *National Journal*, 1408.

Sanders, Arthur. 1992. *Victory*. Armonk, NY: M. E. Sharpe.

Sanders, Elizabeth. 1999. *Roots of Reform: Farmers, Workers, and the American State*. Chicago: University of Chicago Press.

Scammon, Richard M., and Ben J. Wattenberg. 1970. *The Real Majority*. New York: Conrad-McCann.

Schattschneider, E. E. 1942. *Party Government*. New York: Holt, Rinehart, and Winston.

Schattschneider, E. E. 1960. *The Semisovereign People: A Realist's View of Democracy in America*. New York: Holt, Rinehart, and Winston.

Schlesinger, Arthur M., Jr. 1957. *Crisis of the Old Order*. Boston: Houghton-Mifflin.

Schlesinger, Arthur M., Jr. 1959. *The Coming of the New Deal*. Boston: Houghton-Mifflin.

Schlesinger, Arthur M., Jr. 1960. *The Politics of Upheaval*. Boston: Houghton-Mifflin.

Schlesinger, Arthur M., Jr. 1966. *The Bitter Heritage: Vietnam and American Democracy*. Boston: Houghton-Mifflin.

Schneider, William. 1988. "An Insider's View of the Election." *Atlantic Monthly* (July): 29–57.

Schreiber, E. M. 1971. "'Where the Ducks Are: Southern Strategy Versus Fourth Party." *Public Opinion Quarterly* 35 (Summer): 157–67.

Shafer, Byron E (ed.). 1991. *The End of Realignment? Interpreting American Electoral Eras*. Madison: University of Wisconsin Press.

Shafer, Byron E., and Richard Johnston. 2006. *The End of Southern Exceptionalism: Class, Race, and Partisan Change in the Postwar South*. Cambridge, MA: Harvard University Press.

Shefter, Martin. 1994. *Political Parties and the State: The American Historical Experience*. Princeton, NJ: Princeton University Press.

Shelley, Mack C., II. 1983. *The Permanent Majority: The Conservative Coalition in the United States Congress.* University of Alabama Press.

Silbey, Joel H. 1967. *The Transformation of American Politics, 1840–1860.* Englewood Cliffs, NJ: Prentice Hall.

Silbey, Joel H. 1991. *The American Political Nation, 1838–1893.* Stanford, CA: Stanford University Press.

Skocpol, Theda. 1997. *Boomerang: Health Care Reform and the Turn Against Government.* New York: W.W. Norton.

Skowronek, Stephen. 1982. *Building a New American State: The Expansion of National Administrative Capacities, 1877–1920.* New York: Cambridge University Press.

Smith, Christian, with Michael Emerson, Sally Gallagher, Paul Kennedy, and David Sikkink. 1998. *American Evangelicalism: Embattled and Thriving.* Chicago: University of Chicago Press.

Smith, Mark A. 2007. *Right Talk.* Princeton, NJ: Princeton University Press.

Speel, Robert W. 1998. *Changing Patterns of Voting in the Northern United States: Electoral Realignment, 1952–1996.* University Park: Pennsylvania State University Press.

Stanley, Harold W., and Richard G. Niemi. 2001. *Vital Statistics on American Politics, 2001–2002.* Washington, DC: CQ Press.

Stimson, James A. 1999. *Public Opinion in America: Moods, Cycles, and Swings,* 2nd ed. Boulder, CO: Westview Press.

Stimson, James A. 2004. *Tides of Consent: How Public Opinion Shapes American Politics.* New York: Cambridge University Press.

Stonecash, Jeffrey M. 2000. *Class and Party in American Politics.* Boulder, CO: Westview Press.

Stonecash, Jeffrey M. 2003. "Reconsidering the Trend in Incumbent Vote Percentages in House Elections." *American Review of Politics* 24 (Fall): 225–39.

Stonecash, Jeffrey M. 2003. "Response to Jacobson's Comments." *American Review of Politics* 24 (Fall): 245–8.

Stonecash, Jeffrey M. 2007. "The Rise of the Right: More Conservatives or More Concentrated Conservatism," in John C. Green and Daniel J. Coffey (eds.), *The State of the Parties,* 5th ed. Lanham, MD: Rowman and Littlefield, 317–30.

Stonecash, Jeffrey M. 2008. *Reassessing the Incumbency Effect.* New York: Cambridge University Press.

Stonecash, Jeffrey M., Mark D. Brewer, and Mack D. Mariani. 2002. "Northern Democrats and Polarization in the U.S. House." *Legislative Studies Quarterly* 27 (August): 423–44.

Stonecash, Jeffrey M., Mark D. Brewer, and Mack D. Mariani. 2003. *Diverging Parties: Social Change, Realignment, and Party Polarization.* Boulder, CO: Westview Press.

Stonecash, Jeffrey M., and Mack D. Mariani. 2000. "Republican Gains in the House in the 1994 Elections: Class Polarization in American Politics." *Political Science Quarterly* 115 (Spring): 93–113.

Stonecash, Jeffrey M., and Everita Silina. 2005. "Reassessing the 1896 Realignment." *American Political Research* 33 (January): 3–32.

Stouffer, Samuel. 1955. *Communism, Conformity, and Civil Liberties*. New York: Doubleday.

Summers, Mark Wahlgren. 2000. *Rum, Romanism, and Rebellion: The Making of a President, 1884*. Chapel Hill: University of North Carolina Press.

Summers, Mark Wahlgren. 2004. *Party Games: Getting, Keeping, and Using Power in Gilded Age Politics*. Chapel Hill: University of North Carolina Press.

Sundquist, James L. 1968. *Politics and Policy: The Eisenhower, Kennedy, and Johnson Years*. Washington, DC: Brookings Institution Press.

Sundquist, James L. 1983. *Dynamics of the Party System: Alignment and Realignment of Political Parties in the United States*, rev. ed. Washington, DC: Brookings Institution.

Taylor, Paul, and Richard C. Fry. December 6, 2007. "Hispanics and the 2008 Election: A Swing Vote." The Pew Hispanic Center. http://pewhispanic.org/reports/report.php?ReportID=83.

Teixeira, Ruy A., and Joel Rogers. 2000. *America's Forgotten Majority: Why the White Working Class Still Matters*. New York: Basic Books.

Thomas, Evan, Eleanor Clift, Jonathan Darman, Kevin Peraino, and Peter Goldman. 2004. *Election 2004: How Bush Won and What You Can Expect in the Future*. New York: Public Affairs.

Trilling, Lionel. 1950. *The Liberal Imagination*. New York: Harcourt, Brace, Jovanovich.

Trilling, Richard J. 1976. *Party Image and Electoral Behavior*. New York: John Wiley and Sons.

Tugwell, Rexford G. 1957. *The Democratic Roosevelt: A Biography of Franklin D. Roosevelt*. Garden City, NY: Doubleday and Company.

Tugwell, Rexford G. 1967. *FDR: Architect of an Era*. New York: Macmillan.

Tugwell, Rexford G. 1968. *The Brains Trust*. New York: Viking.

Tugwell, Rexford G. 1968. *Grover Cleveland*. New York: Macmillan.

Tugwell, Rexford G. 1972. *In Search of Roosevelt*. Cambridge, MA: Harvard University Press.

Tugwell, Rexford G. 1977. *Roosevelt's Revolution*. New York: Macmillan.

Turner, Julius, and Edward V. Schneier. 1970. *Party and Constituency: Pressures on Congress*, revised ed. Baltimore: Johns Hopkins Press.

Unger, Irwin. 1996. *The Best of Intentions: The Triumphs and Failures of the Great Society under Kennedy, Johnson, and Nixon*. New York: Doubleday.

U.S. Bureau of the Census. 1998. *Measuring 50 Years of Economic Change Using the March Current Population Survey*. Current Population Reports, P6–203. Washington, DC: U.S. Government Printing Office.

Vogt, W. Paul. 1997. *Tolerance and Education: Learning to Live with Diversity and Difference*. Thousand Oaks, CA: Sage Publications.

Wald, Kenneth D., and Allison Calhoun Brown. 2007. *Religion and Politics in the United States*, 5th ed. Lanham, MD: Rowman and Littlefield.

Walker, Daniel. 1968. *Rights in Conflict: Chicago's 7 Brutal Days*. New York: Grosset and Dunlap.

Wallace-Wells, Benjamin. March 30, 2008. "A Case of the Blues." *New York Times Magazine*, 44.?

Ware, Alan. 2002. *The American Direct Primary: Party Institutionalization and Transformation in the North*. New York: Cambridge University Press.

Ware, Alan. 2006. *The Democratic Party Heads North, 1877–1962*. New York: Cambridge University Press.

Wattenberg, Martin P. 1990. *The Decline of American Political Parties, 1952–1988*. Cambridge, MA: Harvard University Press.

Wattenberg, Martin P. 1991. *The Rise of Candidate-Centered Politics*. Cambridge, MA: Harvard University Press.

Wattenberg, Martin P. 1998. *The Decline of American Political Parties, 1952–1996*. Cambridge, MA: Harvard University Press.

Welch, Robert E., Jr. 1988. *The Presidencies of Grover Cleveland*. Lawrence: University Press of Kansas.

Weisberg, Jacob. 2008. *The Bush Tragedy*. New York: Random House.

White, John K. 2003. *The Values Divide: American Politics and Culture in Transition*. New York: Chatham House Publishers.

Wiebe, Robert H. 1967. *The Search for Order, 1877–1920*. New York: Hill and Wang.

Wilensky, Harold L. 1966. "Class, Class Consciousness, and American Workers," in William Haber (ed.), *Labor in a Changing America*. New York: Basic Books, 12–28.

Wills, Garry. 1988. *Reagan's America*. New York: Penguin Books.

Woodward, C. Vann. 1951. *Origins of the New South, 1877–1913*. Baton Rouge: Louisiana State University Press.

Woodward, C. Vann. 1951. *Reunion and Reaction: The Compromise of 1877 and the End of Reconstruction*. Boston: Little, Brown, and Company.

Wuthnow, Robert. 1988. *The Restructuring of American Religion: Society and Faith since World War II*. Princeton, NJ: Princeton University Press.

Zaller, John R. 1992. *The Nature and Origins of Mass Opinion*. New York: Cambridge University Press.

Zelizer, Julian E. 2004. *On Capitol Hill: The Struggle to Reform Congress and Its Consequences, 1948–2000*. New York: Cambridge University Press.

DATA ON CONGRESSIONAL DISTRICTS

Cook, Rhodes, Alice V. McGillivray, and Richard M. Scammon. 2007. *America Votes 27*. Washington, DC: CQ Press.

Congressional Quarterly Service, Inc. 1966. *Representation and Apportionment*. Washington, DC: Congressional Quarterly Press.

Congressional Quarterly. 1964. *Congressional Quarterly's Guide to U.S. Elections*, 3rd ed. Washington, DC: Congressional Quarterly Press.

Congressional Quarterly. 2001. *Congressional Quarterly's Guide to U.S. Elections*, 4th ed. Washington, DC: Congressional Quarterly Press.

Dubin, Michael J. 1998. *United States Congressional Elections, 1788–1997.* Jefferson, NC: McFarland and Company, Inc.

Martis, Kenneth C. 1982. *The Historical Atlas of U.S. Congressional Districts, 1789–1983.* New York: The Free Press.

Scammon, Richard M., Alice V. McGillivray, and Rhodes Cook. 2000. *America Votes 24.* Washington, DC: CQ Press.

Scammon, Richard M., Alice V. McGillivray, and Rhodes Cook. 2003. *America Votes 25.* Washington, DC: CQ Press.

Scammon, Richard M., Alice V. McGillivray, and Rhodes Cook. 2006. *America Votes 26.* Washington, DC: CQ Press

Turner, Julius. 1949. "Voting Behavior in the House of Representatives: A Study of Representative Government and Political Pressure." Doctoral dissertation, Johns Hopkins University.

Turner, Julius. 1951. "Party and Constituency: Pressures on Congress. The Johns Hopkins University Studies in Historical and Political Science," Series LXIX, No. 1. Baltimore: The Johns Hopkins Press.

U.S. Department of Commerce, U.S. Bureau of the Census. 1945. "Population of the United States by Congressional Districts." Population – Special Reports. Series p-45, No. 6. July 3. Washington, DC: U.S. Government Printing Office. 1–2.

U.S. Department of Commerce, U.S. Bureau of the Census. County and City Data Book 1956. "Appendix G: Selected Data for Congressional Districts." Washington, DC: U.S. Government Printing Office, 495–512.

U.S. Bureau of the Census. 1961. Congressional District Data Book (Districts of the 87th Congress) – A Statistical Abstract Supplement. Washington, DC: U.S. Government Printing Office.

U.S. Bureau of the Census. 1963. Congressional District Data Book (Districts of the 88th Congress) – A Statistical Abstract Supplement. Washington, DC: U.S. Government Printing Office.

U.S. Department of Commerce, Bureau of the Census. 1983. Congressional District Profiles, 98th Congress: Supplementary Report PC80-S1–11, September. Washington, DC: U.S. Government Printing Office.

Index

Made in the USA
Middletown, DE
28 August 2017